FAIRWAY TO HEAVEN

Fairway to Heaven

Victors and Victims of Golf's Choking Game

Tim Glover and Peter Higgs

MAINSTREAM
PUBLISHING

EDINBURGH AND LONDON

First published in Great Britain in 1999 by
MAINSTREAM PUBLISHING COMPANY (EDINBURGH) LTD
7 Albany Street
Edinburgh EH1 3UG

ISBN 1 84018 146 X

A catalogue record for this book is available from the British Library

Typeset in Bembo
Printed and bound in Great Britain by Butler & Tanner Ltd

Contents

THE US PGA

Preface

When it comes to the ultimate climax in golf, the players need no extra stimulus, no Viagra, to supplement what is already a surge of adrenaline of Niagara proportions.

Nowhere is it more abundant than at the closing stages of a major championship. The crowd, absorbed in every shot, convey the tension to the players, who are also involved in another contest – the mind game.

Before missing the most notorious putt in the history of the Open Championship, Doug Sanders was already thinking about which side of the gallery he would turn to first to acknowledge the applause. When he missed from three feet, a putt that would have won him the old silver claret jug, there was no applause. Instead people reacted as if they had just witnessed a terrible accident – which, in a sporting context, they had.

It was Jack Nicklaus, rather than Sanders, who went for the jugular and, in the process, took possession of the jug. The line between victor and victim can be measured not only in millions of dollars but also in fractions of inches. 'One minute you're on cloud nine,' Sam Snead remarked, 'the next you can't scratch a whale's belly.'

When Nick Faldo won the Open at Muirfield in 1992, he broke down in tears. It had felt more like 15 heavyweight rounds than 18 holes of golf and the gut-wrenching intensity of it reduced the ice man to meltdown. 'I went to the edge of seeing what real failure was,' said Faldo. 'If it had gone wrong it would have been a tough one to live with. I've been lucky in avoiding the major scars in this game.'

Some are scarred for life. The greater the prize, the greater the pressure, and putts that a professional golfer could make with his eyes closed are suddenly missable when a place in history beckons. In the choking atmosphere at Muirfield, Faldo survived; John Cook, who missed a putt at the 17th that was even shorter than the one Sanders missed at St Andrews, did not.

Years later, Sanders said of The Putt, 'It doesn't bother me. Sometimes I go five minutes without it crossing my mind.'

When a golfer misses a tiddler there is, of course, no one else involved, but if there is an analogy with football it is the player who misses a penalty when the stakes are at their highest.

The manifestation of pressure is at its most obvious on the greens but its effects are felt in other areas too. A player stands on the 18th tee for the last time and all he needs to secure a place in history is a par four. A good drive is important. So is the approach shot. Then the nervous system has to withstand a serious onslaught of mental pressure to give the putter a chance. You might be able to recover from a poor drive but you can't recover from the long, sharp shock of missing a sitter.

Of the four major championships, only the Masters has a permanent home. However, familiarity with Augusta National tends to breed respect rather than contempt. When Greg Norman is in contention playing the 18th and he hits his second shot into the crowd rather than onto the green, it's almost as shocking as the little one that got away.

Then, of course, there's the unique condition of asphyxiation by water. The presence of H_2O on a golf course has almost the same effect as the wreckers who lured vessels onto the rocks and a watery grave. There's no lighthouse at Augusta. Look at Ray Floyd at the 11th, or Tom Weiskopf at the 12th, or Curtis Strange at the 13th, or Seve Ballesteros at the 15th, or Norman at the 16th. There have been huge improvements in courses, equipment and golf balls, but nobody has yet found a way of playing out of a pond. It is the penultimate stymie. The ultimate is what lies not from tee to green but between a player's ears.

So this is what it usually comes down to on Sunday, bloody Sunday, the fallout from a slow-burning four-day fuse. And that is what this book is about. Not the commanding victories, however impressive, but those memorable major championships which went to the bitter end. The most dramatic finishes in golf's colourful history are chronicled in the following pages. We hope you enjoy them.

The Open

Cursed be the hand that made these fatal holes!

– Richard III

Hard Times and Heroes

Beneath the calm exterior of the Royal and Ancient game lie passions which are usually kept admirably under control. But not always. There have been walk-outs, a walk-over, allegations of match-fixing, putts being taken from the wrong place, players being misled by spectators, caddies deliberately giving their bosses wrong information and rudeness displayed to the winners. And then, of course, there are the countless heart-breaking tales of failure within sight of victory.

During the 1950s the British won only a single major championship and would go until 1969 before they won another. They were lean years compared to the harvest of the '80s. Yet some of the best players from these islands missed their chance to, at least, finish equal first in the Open because they could not par the final hole. Welshman Dai Rees, Scot Eric Brown and Christy O'Connor from Ireland all suffered that fate. It happened to Jack Nicklaus, too, but while the three mentioned above never won a major championship, the Golden Bear was to more than atone for his lapse.

Throughout the history of the Open there have been last-hole dramas, many of them tainted by dispute and controversy. Back in 1876 the title was won by Bob Martin, a bearded, mournful-looking Scot, after his scheduled opponent Davie Strath refused to take part in the play-off. Martin, 28, had merely to walk over the Old Course at St Andrews to be declared the champion. Strath, a native of the town, had reached the last two holes of the championship needing to complete them in ten strokes to win but had been involved in an incident at the Road Hole (17th). Thinking he could not reach the green, he had played into the group ahead, where his ball hit someone (either a player or a spectator) to stop it going onto the road. Unaware of what had happened, Strath putted out for a five believing that he required a similar score at the last to win the Open for the first time. Not only did he take a six to finish level with Martin but he learned that demands were being made for his disqualification for the 17th-hole incident. When the R and A ruled the play-off should go ahead while the protest was reviewed, Strath refused to be part of it and received a great deal of sympathetic support. Three years later he died of consumption at the age of 39.

Ill health and premature death among leading players were an accepted part of history during the hard times of the nineteenth century.

The 1891 Open champion Hugh Kirkcaldy was to die from influenza, aged only 31, five years after he was crowned champion. The circumstances of his victory led to rumour-mongering that his more famous brother Andrew allowed Hugh to win because of his poor health. Andrew, or Andra, as he was known, needed two fours at St Andrews to take the trophy but finished with a five and a six. When questioned about his form, the player regarded as the best of his era never to win the Open admitted he had played badly but insisted he had tried his hardest.

Willie Park Jnr kept a family tradition alive when he followed his father to the title in 1887 and 1889. Yet he knew the misery of last-green failure when he committed a disastrous three-putt to lose the 1898 championship to Harry Vardon. Needing a par three at Prestwick's 18th to draw level, Park found the green, putted up to three feet and, as the crowd jostled round so that Vardon could not see, missed the little putt.

Around that time the Great Triumvirate of Vardon, James Braid and J.H. Taylor dominated the championship, winning a total of 16 times in the 20 years from 1894 to 1914. Yet even these men of outstanding talent and indomitable competitive spirit suffered occasions when Lucifer tapped them on the shoulder and said, 'Not today, laddie.'

At Hoylake in 1902, victory went to another St Andrews native, Sandy Herd, who made two significant contributions to the sport. Even though he was renowned as a fast player, Herd was famous for 'the waggle' as he addressed the ball, a habit that was to be adopted by legions of players down the years.

It was not this idiosyncrasy, however, but his use of a revolutionary ball which gave him a distinct advantage over his rivals. Since 1848 the standard ball had been a guttie, made of solid rubber from the latex of a Malaysian tree and painted white. But in 1898 a wealthy American amateur, Coburn Haskell, created a new variety by winding lengths of rubber around a solid core. The Haskell not only flew longer through the air and bounced further, it also performed better even when mis-hit. In 1901 Walter J. Travis won the US amateur championship using the new rubber-wound ball and the following year – when the ball was still in short supply in Britain – Herd was persuaded to try it before the Open. The Huddersfield-based professional was an instant convert and was the only man not to use the guttie in the tournament. His subsequent victory not only led to the Haskell being adopted throughout the game but also created a surge in the sport's popularity.

Yet he nearly didn't win. For Vardon came to the last two holes needing a pair of fours to share the lead. The great man from Jersey achieved the first of them comfortably and hit a fine drive at the last. A play-off looked certain but Vardon duffed his second shot, knocked his third six feet past the pin and missed the return. Herd and the Haskell had triumphed. Fate had played a crucial hand and left some hypothetical questions unanswered. How quickly would the new ball have been accepted had not Vardon uncharacteristically mis-hit his second shot? And how might golf history have been changed but for that final-hole blunder?

Two years later the other two members of the triumvirate, Braid and Taylor, were central figures in a fascinating saga at Sandwich. Yet neither of them was destined to win as communication suffered a failure which hopefully would not be repeated today. In those times there were no scoreboards around the course informing players and spectators of the leading positions. The participants relied on word of mouth. So when Braid was told by a spectator that Jack White, the Sunningdale professional, had taken 70 in the final round to lead the event, he, naturally enough, believed him. Braid assessed that by playing the last three holes in level fours he would go into a play-off, in which he would be confident of victory. But he had been misinformed. White had taken 69 and as Braid achieved his objective of three fours he received the news that he had lost by a shot. Not surprisingly, he was a little upset.

At that point reporters filed their stories that White's record-breaking score of 296 (the first time that 300 had been bettered) had made him the champion. The players still out on the course were considered to be too far behind to matter. But Taylor was in the process of producing the best round yet seen in the Open. Needing a 67 to tie, the former Somerset greenkeeper came to the last capable of making the evening papers, which were reaching the streets with the result, look slightly ridiculous. But he failed by a shot and several nervous newspapermen were spared acute embarrassment – and possibly their jobs.

It would be tempting to claim that journalism today has advanced to prevent such risks being taken were it not for the fact that a few years ago one of the most esteemed tennis correspondents presumed that Jimmy Connors would be knocked out of Wimbledon when he trailed 6–1, 6–1, 4–1 and informed his readers of the 'fact'. The American left-hander fought back to win, leaving the readers confused and the writer somewhat shame-faced.

Drama and embarrassment were evident in large measure at the Open Championship of 1921, when the trophy went across the sea to America for the first time. A young British amateur, Roger Wethered, should have won but made two elementary errors. In the third round he walked ahead to study the line of his shot and returned to tread on his ball for a one-shot penalty.

Then, on the last hole at St Andrews, a par four would have been enough, but after striking a good drive Wethered pitched short of the green and took three more from the Valley of Sin. When Jock Hutchison, a former St Andrews resident who had emigrated to the United States, matched his 296 total with a last-round 70, Wethered astonished officials by expressing doubts about whether he could stay for the 36-hole play-off because . . . he had promised to turn out for his village cricket team!

He was persuaded that the villagers would understand his desire to keep the Open trophy in Britain but was subsequently routed 159–150. It was reported afterwards that the chairman of the Green Committee took the departure of the cup to America so badly that he was ungracious to the winner. The *St Andrews Citizen* said, 'The chairman of the Green Committee was such a poor loser that he practically threw the cup at Hutchison, did not call for cheers for the new champion – instead he at once called for "Three cheers for Roger Wethered".'

The British were soon to learn that their grip on the event had been broken as Americans won every year in the '20s except one (1923, when Arthur Havers beat Walter Hagen by two shots). Hagen proved to be an outspoken revolutionary, sweeping away the pompous prejudices of the past and leading professional golfers towards the status and wealth they enjoy today. He was scathing in his criticism of attitudes he discovered in Britain and was not afraid to expose them. When professionals were refused permission to change or eat in the clubhouse at Royal St George's for the 1922 Open, he hired a Daimler limousine for changing and eating – and parked it right in front of the clubhouse. Hagen duly went ahead and won the Open for the first time and declared the first prize of £75 so derisory that he promptly handed the cheque to his caddie.

What is less well-remembered – because everyone forgets who came second – is that the highly rated Scot George Duncan could have prevented Hagen's win and immediately turned back the tide of American influence. The 39-year-old professional at Hangar Hill had won the Open at Deal in 1920 and was noted not only as one of the best British players of that time but also for the speed of his play. The author of *Golf at the Gallop* came racing up the 18th needing a four for a 68 to tie with Hagen. But after his approach missed the green he hit a quick pitch which left him a testing putt. Barely pausing to check the line, he knocked it past the hole. Duncan might have looked nervous but he always played that way, often very effectively.

A year later, when Havers held off Hagen to win by a stroke, officials at Troon relented and allowed the colourful New Yorker into the clubhouse for the presentation. Hagen refused, invited spectators along to the local pub for a drink and considerably reduced the attendance at the official ceremony.

He was a difficult man to keep out of the limelight. Even when Bobby Jones won for the first time at Lytham in 1926, causing the revered John Henry Taylor to shed tears at the prize-giving and proclaim Jones 'the greatest golfer who ever lived', Hagen provided the excitement on the last hole. Although faced with an apparently hopeless task, 'The Haig' kept a gathering of illustrious players in the clubhouse in a state of agitated apprehension as he refused to settle for second place and tried to hole a full-iron shot on the 18th to finish level with Jones. Even Hagen could not manage that.

Between them the two great Americans won seven Opens in nine years from 1922 to 1930 as they vied for the distinction of being the dominant player of the age. Invariably their talent brought victory by a sufficiently wide margin to avoid any alarms on the home green. The next American citizen to triumph, Tommy Armour, was not so fortunate. He was to go through a traumatic experience he would never forget in front of the clubhouse at Carnoustie.

The Silver Scot had emigrated from Edinburgh in the '20s and built an enviable reputation in winning the 1927 US Open and the 1930 US PGA Championship. Back in Scotland in 1931, he set up the chance of claiming the title he wanted above all others with a flawless final round. Flawless, that is, until he reached the 71st green, where, within sight of victory, he missed a short putt.

So Armour came down the last knowing that he could not afford a similar lapse. Remarkably, he presented himself with an almost identical problem to the one which had proved beyond him on the previous hole. A dreaded short putt. This is how he described what happened: 'I took a new grip, holding the club as tightly as I could with stiff wrists. From the moment the club left the ball on the backswing I was blind and unconscious.' He holed for a 71 and a total of 296 and then waited anxiously to discover whether his score would be good enough. The Argentinian Jose Jurado could have won with a par finish of four, five. But at the 17th he topped a four-iron into the burn in front of him, took six and was then wrongly advised that a five at the last would give him a tie for the lead. He played the hole conservatively and lost by a stroke. Like Braid 27 years earlier, he was a victim of poor communication.

The 1933 success of Densmore Shute at St Andrews was a victory for romantics. A few weeks prior to the event the American had cost his country the Ryder Cup when he three-putted the final green at Southport to lose his match to Syd Easterbrook. This time he beat Easterbrook by a single stroke to finish tied with his compatriot Craig Wood before going on to win the play-off by five shots (149 to 154).

The most memorable shot that year was a yipped putt at the last by Leo Diegel. Renowned for his nerves on the green, the man from

Detroit had a tiny putt to reach the play-off but jerked it a foot wide. Wood's play-off defeat was the first of four he would suffer in each of the majors during the '30s.

British pride was restored with a first victory for 11 years when Henry Cotton won by five strokes at Sandwich in 1934 to inspire a run of six successive victories by golfers from the United Kingdom. The second of his three triumphs, at Carnoustie in 1937, was not as emphatic but was nonetheless welcome in the year that Britain lost the Ryder Cup on home soil for the first time, prompting Leonard Crawley, later to become golf correspondent of the *Daily Telegraph*, to miss the Open in the firm belief that a home win was unlikely in the face of the transatlantic strength.

Cotton played what he considered to be one of the best rounds of his career in miserable conditions of heavy rain and sodden greens on the final afternoon. At the last he eschewed the safe route of playing short of a burn across the fairway and launched a massive drive as far from the out of bounds on the left as possible. A two-iron found the right-hand greenside bunker, he splashed out of the muddy sand and took two putts for a par five, a round of 71, a two-stroke victory over Reg Whitcombe – and a telegram from Crawley admitting his misjudgement.

The resurgence of the British game during the '30s culminated in a long-awaited triumph at St Andrews in 1939. For the first time in 29 years a resident of the UK took the championship at the home of golf. The honour went to Dick Burton, a tall, fair-haired Lancastrian, and he won in the grand manner. Burton, possibly the longest driver in the field, came to the 18th at St Andrews needing a par to beat the American Johnny Bulla. He promptly cracked his tee-shot 300 yards down the rails on the right, lofted a nine-iron to 15 feet and holed the putt for a birdie to win by two – just as Seve Ballesteros would do to the delight of millions of television viewers 45 years later.

Burton's victory, although witnessed by far fewer people, brought pleasure to a country in the grip of poverty and depression. He would make very little from his glory. Within a matter of weeks, Britain had fallen under the shadow of war.

★ ★ ★

Rarely does a single shot change a golfer's popularity with the public. Once he has established an image, good or bad, he usually has to perform out of character over a period of time in order to shift opinions. Yet Frank Stranahan was transformed in the eyes of thousands from villain to hero by one of the most extraordinary strokes ever witnessed in the Open Championship. Ultimately the shot failed. Yet it was such a glorious failure that it won its executor an army of fans.

Stranahan was a rich American amateur with a boorish manner. His arrogance was resented by opponents and spectators alike. Caddies took a particular dislike to him when he refused to take any notice of their advice, acquired from years of experience. On one occasion a bagman gained sweet revenge when sent ahead to give Stranahan the line for a blind shot to the green. Instead of pointing towards the flag, he directed the player into a thick gorse bush. When Stranahan's ball duly landed in the bush, the caddie said to him gleefully, 'Well, sir, if you think you know so much about it, let's see you get out of that' . . . and promptly walked off the course.

When he arrived at the Open at Hoylake in 1947, the tall, fair-haired American known as 'Muscles' (because he used weight training to build up his physique) was given a cool reception. Earlier in the season he had sullied his reputation by his petulant behaviour towards an English opponent at the British amateur championship. Matters worsened at a pre-tournament interview. Asked whether Henry Cotton, the British hero, would win, Stranahan replied, 'No, I can beat Cotton.'

He turned out to be right. By the start of the fourth round, four players shared the lead: Fred Daly, from Northern Ireland, the Britons Arthur Lees and Cotton, and Norman von Nida of Australia. Stranahan was a shot behind. But over the closing holes, as the others dropped out of contention, Daly and Stranahan were left to contest the prize. The crowd's support was strongly behind Daly, a typically genial Irishman, who returned a 72 to set a target of 293. The 25-year-old American could force a tie if he finished four, three at two relatively straight-forward par fours. All hope seemed to disappear, though, when Stranahan, trying too hard for a birdie, three-putted the 17th from 35 feet.

Yet if the spectators thought the championship had been decided, one brash young man certainly did not. Stranahan sent his drive at the 395-yard 18th straight down the middle, leaving him 150 yards downwind to the flag. He immediately set about the task of trying to hole the shot.

He walked forward to the green, studied the precise line and returned to his ball. Then he walked forward again, while the spectators waited, not really caring what happened, such was their hostility towards the frosty foreigner.

Finally Stranahan took his nine-iron and swung. The shot was almost perfect. The ball never left the flagstick, pitched on the green and rolled up towards the hole right on line. Surely it could not go in, could it? Well, no, not quite. The ball stopped eight inches short . . . and Fred Daly had won the Open.

Yet such was the audacity, the expertise, the brilliance of Stranahan's attempt that the spectators were overwhelmed. They hoisted the

American high and carried him towards the green. With one stroke he had lost the Open but won their hearts. 'That shot changed my whole life in England,' he would say later. 'From then on I was welcomed there.'

★ ★ ★

Harry Bradshaw will always be associated with 'The Shot in the Bottle'. At the fifth hole in the second round of the 1949 Open at Sandwich, the Irishman found his ball wedged up against a broken beer bottle. Although he thought he was entitled to a free drop (which he was), he was not sure. So he played the ball as it lay, smashing it forward only 15 yards and being hit in the eye by a flying piece of glass.

The incident was to have a crucial bearing on the championship. For Bradshaw took a six instead of a probable four and ended up on the final green tied with Bobby Locke for the lead. He lost the play-off by 12 shots. Bradshaw could never look at a beer bottle in the same light again.

If Locke could count himself slightly fortunate on that occasion, he had even more reason to thank his lucky stars when he won at St Andrews in 1957. Before he putted out on the final green, holding a comfortable three-shot lead, the portly South African moved his ball a couple of putterheads' distance from his line to allow another competitor, Bruce Crampton, to hole out. Locke then putted from the wrong place. Nothing untoward was noticed at the time, until the error was spotted on a newsreel film. R and A officials met to decide whether the champion should be disqualified in retrospect and the title given to runner-up Peter Thomson. They ruled that no benefit had been gained and the result stood. But Locke never wore his trademark plus fours again as a reminder of his good fortune and the R and A's compassion.

Around that period, Britain's attempts to regain the trophy were doomed to failure. From the time Max Faulkner won at Portrush in 1951 until Tony Jacklin's victory at Lytham in 1969, the country's players came so near and yet so far.

In 1954 Dai Rees arrived at the last hole at Royal Birkdale needing a par four to tie with Peter Thomson. He hit a solid four-iron to the green but the ball ran through the back and Rees failed to get down in two. The Welshman, once labelled 'the best British player never to win the Open', had let his finest chance slip.

The odds on a home victory in 1958 appeared excellent when three players – Dave Thomas of Wales, Eric Brown of Scotland and Christy O'Connor of Ireland – were all on the leaderboard in the closing stages. Thomas was poised for victory when he faced a routine seven-iron to Lytham's 17th green. But he hit the shot 'fat', it fell short and he bogeyed the hole. All three men could finish tied for first place if they parred the 18th. O'Connor failed and so did Brown when he drove into a bunker from the tee. Thomas successfully negotiated the problem to finish level with Peter Thomson, but subsequently lost the play-off (139 to 143) as the Australian claimed the fourth of his five titles. The big Welshman, rated the longest straight driver in the world at the time, would have been champion if only he had not erred at the 17th. 'If only' ... those two little words.

The men who slipped 'twixt cup and lip could find some consolation in the fact that even the mightiest have fallen at the most unexpected times. On the same final hole where the three Britons' fate was settled, a young American named Jack Nicklaus stood five years later. He was 23 years of age and, although he had already won the US Open and the Masters, golf's rising star had yet to add the oldest of all the majors to his collection. At Lytham came his chance. A par four at the last would have given him a share of first place and a play-off against Phil Rodgers of America and the eventual winner Bob Charles of New Zealand. But Nicklaus, wrongly calculating that a bogey would be good enough, hooked his drive into a steep bunker and finished one stroke behind.

Some men might have dwelt on the error, allowing it to dominate their memories of the event. For Nicklaus, that uncharacteristic failure was a mere blip along the way. The next time he was in a similar situation, the Golfer of the Century would show exactly why he deserved such an accolade. Nicklaus came to the 427-yard 18th at Muirfield in 1966 needing a par four to beat Doug Sanders and Dave Thomas by a stroke. He took a one-iron to avoid the knee-high rough and found the centre of the fairway, 208 yards from the flag. After hesitating over a four-iron, Nicklaus plumped for the three-iron and described what happened as follows: 'The impact felt magical, as solid a strike as I've ever made. The wonderful feeling continued as I watched the ball start left, then soar up and hold its line perfectly against the wind, dropping like a butterfly, hole-high and about 25 feet right of the flag.' Two putts later Nicklaus had won his first Open and gone into history as one of only four men to complete the Grand Slam of all four majors.

His ability to play the closing holes so well under the utmost pressure made him such a dangerous opponent even when behind. The following year Nicklaus birdied both the 16th and the 18th of the final round at Hoylake to threaten Roberto de Vicenzo's lead. The Argentinian had to prove himself a worthy winner and did so with a huge straight drive down the final fairway. The triumph at 44 years and 93 days of the oldest champion of modern times was warmly received throughout the country. He, like Nicklaus, had provided the perfect response to what is needed at the knee-knocking, gut-wrenching final hole.

In closing this chapter, it is appropriate to draw attention to one other splendid example of how the demons can be pushed aside to produce a glorious finale. The year was 1969. Once again the setting was Lytham, where the man going through a maelstrom of emotions was a 25-year-old from Lincolnshire called Tony Jacklin. Anticipation was high throughout the land that here was a young golfer capable of lifting British golf out of the trough into which it had sunk. Here was a player to take on the world.

The driver's son from Scunthorpe was a man of the people and he did not let them down. He led the field by two shots after three days and was five ahead at the fourth hole of the final round. By the time he reached the last, Jacklin was two ahead of his playing partner Bob Charles and fully aware of the dangers that lay in wait at the 389-yard bunker-infested final hole. Lesser men might have opted for a careful one-iron or three-wood. Not Jacklin. He pulled out the driver. 'I remembered how many good players had lost the championship by making a six,' he would recall later. 'But I decided I would not be cautious.'

Jacklin drove his tee-shot over the left bunkers and slid it back into the wind to find the middle of the fairway 260 yards away. It was a brave, bold, brilliant strike. From there he surely could not fail. A controlled half-shot with the seven-iron from 130 yards deposited the ball 12 feet from the pin. When the birdie putt stopped on the lip, Jacklin became a national hero with one of the shortest putts ever to win the Open.

The final hole had summed up his style and courage. Things would never be the same again. In the next 20 years this man would have a massive influence on the changing world of golf. One shot, one drive, did not make him. But it showed what he was made of.

The Miss of All Time

'Maybe I wasn't destined to win that dude.'

With those words Doug Sanders was able to console himself more than 20 years after one of sport's most famous misses. It took place on the 18th green at St Andrews, the home of golf, in the final round of the 1970 Open Championship.

Sanders, clad in signature purple, stood over a three-foot putt for a victory that would have climaxed a colourful and successful career. He was 36 years old, had won 19 tournaments on the US Tour and had come close to winning three previous major championships. In 1959 he'd been runner-up to Bob Rosburg in the US PGA Championship. In 1961 he was second to Gene Littler in the US Open, and in 1966 he was runner-up to Jack Nicklaus in the Open at Muirfield. Now came his best chance. He had merely to hole this little putt to beat Nicklaus, the best player the game had ever seen, and take his place in history.

As any student of golf lore knows, Sanders dribbled the putt wide on the low – or amateur – side and went into history for a totally different reason. It was a moment of sporting failure that is still replayed at every suitable opportunity. Whenever the name of Doug Sanders is mentioned, particularly in Britain, The Putt is always brought to mind.

Yet the man himself firmly believes that his error has gained him a permanent place in the hearts of the British public. 'As far as the people of Britain are concerned I won the Open,' he said recently. 'If it hadn't been for the fact that Jack Nicklaus was the one to take advantage of my mistake, I don't think anyone would have remembered who did win. It will always be the tournament that Doug lost rather than Jack won.'

Sanders is one of those people who, in his own words, 'things happen to. They just seem to find me.' His story is a fascinating one, and the drama at St Andrews fits neatly into the script.

He was born and raised in Cedartown, a poor farming community in the north-west corner of Georgia, close to the Alabama and Tennessee borders. As a cotton-picking schoolboy he was caught fiddling the weight of cotton he was checking in and put on a punitive rate. 'I worked from sunup to sundown for two dollars every 100 lbs,' he said. 'I couldn't pick 100 lbs in two weeks!'

So he discovered caddying, at the town's single, nine-hole course, as an alternative income. At 12 years old he learned the ways of the world when the other caddies 'robbed' him of his wages in a putting competition. Sanders took to practising in secret and gained his revenge by winning a caddies' tournament at 13, his first victory.

When he was 17, ten local businessmen forked out ten dollars each to send him to the national junior finals in North Carolina. The journey cost him 27 dollars but on arrival the rest of the money was stolen. He borrowed ten dollars, entered a poker game and not only won enough cash to finance the week but went on to win the championship as well.

An illustrious career was born. They made a film of the tournament entitled *The Boy Next Door*. Back in Cedartown, a Doug Sanders Day parade was held. On the strength of his junior title, the teenager was awarded a scholarship to the University of Florida. When still an amateur he won on the US Tour, the Canadian Open of 1956, and he soon turned professional.

Throughout the '60s Sanders was a prominent player in America, finishing in the top 23 every year between 1958 and 1967, and appearing in the 1967 Ryder Cup. Nothing in his build-up to the 1970 Open, though, indicated a major breakthrough. He had slipped down on the US money list and had to pre-qualify. Then on the first hole of the Old Course he drove into the Swilcan Burn to begin with a double-bogey six. Not an auspicious start.

But in a memorable tournament Sanders soon made up ground. Britain's Neil Coles led on 65 at the end of the first round, with Nicklaus and Sanders in a group on 68 which also included Arnold Palmer and Peter Thomson. The big news of the first day was a sensational outward half of 29 by the holder Tony Jacklin, who was then delayed by torrential rain immediately after he had pushed his second shot into a gorse bush on the 14th. When he returned to complete his round the following day the magic had gone and he laboured to a 67. Although the English hero put up a worthy defence, he was to fall out of contention on the last afternoon.

Sanders, meanwhile, was playing consistently well. He was three shots behind the halfway leader Lee Trevino and had reduced the gap to two going into the final round. As the Mexican uncharacteristically slumped to a last-round 77, two men were left to battle out the championship: Nicklaus and Sanders.

They had started the round level but Nicklaus was in determined mood. He had finished second to Tony Lema the last time the Open was held at St Andrews in 1964 and was desperate to crown his phenomenal career with victory at the most prestigious of venues. The Golden Bear led by a stroke at the turn, which he reached in 35. But he bogeyed the par-three 11th to allow his rival to draw level, and when another shot slipped away at the 16th, Sanders took the lead ... with just two holes left.

The player with one of the shortest swings in golf was displaying exemplary control in the blustery winds while all around him the fancied names were being blown away. On the treacherous Road Hole Sanders played like a true champion. After his second landed in the cavernous Road Bunker – from where Tommy Nakajima took a nine in the 1978 Open – he played a spectacular recovery to three feet and holed the putt for par to keep his lead.

'That would have gone down as one of the great bunker shots in history,' said Sanders. 'It would have been the shot that won the British Open and they would have played it time after time. But it kinda got lost because of what happened at the 18th. I used a pitching wedge instead of a sand wedge to cut through the sand and I played a hell of a shot.'

Sanders was just one simple hole away from glory. Compared to some treacherous major championship finishing holes, the 18th at St Andrews is relatively innocuous. Named Tom Morris, it measures only 354 yards and has a very wide fairway and large green. Trouble lies in the Valley of Sin in front of the green or – as Sanders was to discover – in being too far at the back, leaving a difficult downhill putt.

None of these pitfalls was in Sanders' mind on the tee. 'I had all the confidence in the world. As I was walking from the 17th, one of the caddies came up to me and said, "Here's a tee peg with Tony Lema's name on it. Hit it for Tony." ['Champagne' Tony Lema, the previous St Andrews Open champion, had been killed in a plane crash in 1966.]

'I never use a white tee because of a superstition I have. It represents a five to me. But on this occasion I didn't think about it. I put the ball down and just knocked it down there.

'The biggest mistake I made was that when I reached the ball I then walked all the way to the green to pace out the distance. It was 76 yards. I had some new clubs and I knew that I hit my sand wedge 80 yards. But I played it by yardage instead of by feel . . . and I carried the ball too far.

'In Scotland it doesn't matter how far you are from the green. You can be 100 yards away and you have to hit a four-iron. Or you can be 300 yards away and you still hit a four-iron. It all depends on the weather.

'I was at the peak of my game and one of the reasons I played so well was that I was always a good shot-maker. I could play a lot of different shots and manoeuvre the ball. The pitch was the right shot to play rather than the bump and run because I had room to stop the ball. But I hit it too long. I should have played it by feel instead of by yardage. That was my biggest mistake.'

Sanders was left with a downhill putt of about 12 yards from the back of the green. Pace was the problem. He rolled it on line but the ball pulled up about three feet short of the hole. 'When I hit that putt I thought it was going in and I would have been the only player to break par for all four days,' said Sanders.

Nicklaus could do no better than a par four and so the moment of truth arrived. Around the green thousands looked on, not suspecting that they were about to witness one of sport's most memorable moments. Millions of TV viewers, some enjoying colour for the first time, were given the perfect view of the purple-clad figure as he lined up the left-to-right curling putt. 'Here's Sanders,' intoned commentator Henry Longhurst. 'The supreme moment.'

Then an extraordinary thing happened. Sanders spotted a brown speck on the line of his putt and bent forward to pick it up. He did not move his feet and took the putter back only a few inches from the ball, leaning on it to take his weight. Ben Hogan, watching the drama on TV, shouted at the screen, 'Back away, back away, back away!'

But remarkably Sanders did not do so. He stood up, put the blade back behind the putter and prepared to putt. 'I don't know why I didn't back off,' said Sanders. 'I didn't want to take a lot more time. I was more concerned with other things and I still didn't think I was going to miss it. I was thinking about which side of the gallery I'd turn to when I'd holed it. But I never really got set on that thing.'

As he struck the putt, Sanders knew immediately that he'd missed and stretched out in an involuntary motion with his putter as if he was going to give the moving ball a tap into the hole. 'I just went ahead and hit the thing, hit it in the neck, and zap, off it went, and it was history,' said Sanders.

As the ball veered right of the hole, Longhurst told viewers, 'Missed it . . . Yes, a certainty. That's the side you're bound to miss it . . . There it is . . . and there but for the grace of God . . .'

That evening the normally cheerful extrovert appreciated the importance of his blunder, even though he had the chance to atone for it in the next day's play-off. 'I was very down,' said Sanders. 'Mark McCormack came out to see me. I'd rented this old farmhouse and I went out to feed the cows. My thoughts were miles away. I was trying to give them sugar until my wife told me that cows eat salt.'

For the first time in Open Championship history the play-off was over 18 holes rather than 36 and when it arrived Sanders acquitted himself well. There was no self-pitying capitulation. Again the contest was close. And again it went to the final hole.

'I really lost the tournament at the 11th,' said Sanders. 'I left the ball in the bunker. It took two shots to get out and I made a bogey.'

Four behind with only five holes to play, Sanders staged a storming comeback. He holed a long putt at the 14th, birdied the 15th, and moved within a shot of the Bear when, for the second successive day, Nicklaus bogeyed the 16th.

As in the final round, both men splendidly parred the Road Hole, where disaster lurks at every swing. And so they came to the last with the roles reversed. This time Nicklaus held a one-shot lead. Sanders, with the honour, hit a huge drive which drifted slightly to the right and stopped less than ten yards from the green. Realising that his opponent had a chance to make a birdie and draw level, Nicklaus decided to go for broke. He would try for the green. Spectators watched in amazement as the great man peeled off his sweater, wound himself up and belted a massive, wind-assisted drive towards the clubhouse. 'I crushed it,' Nicklaus would later say of his astonishing shot.

The ball bounded on, ran through the green and stopped on some heavy grass on a slope at the back, only a few feet from the out-of-bounds. It had travelled more than 360 yards.

Unlike at his previous visit to the green, Sanders did not have to play across the Valley of Sin. He could use the pitch and run, at which he was so adept, and promptly coaxed the ball to within five feet of the flag. All the pressure was now on Nicklaus, who chose the moment to play what he described as one of his most memorable shots in the majors. 'I needed to get down in two to avoid sudden death,' he recalled. 'But I'm looking at a severe downhill lie to a slick, down-sloping green, with the Valley of Sin an eager receptacle if I'm a hair too strong. The only good part is that the long grass nestled around the ball slants towards the green, reducing my chance of snagging the club.'

He chose his 'maximum-confidence club' for that situation, the sand wedge, and took several practice swings, working on the positioning of feet and hands plus the weight of the shot. 'I told myself to "stay still" a couple of times and then swung,' said Nicklaus. 'The ball popped out perfectly and rolled down to stop eight feet short of the cup.'

Nicklaus was still further from the hole than Sanders but with a good chance of a birdie. Even then the gods might have rescued Sanders. But Nicklaus had that vital element of good fortune when his well-struck putt caught the right lip and spun left but dropped into the hole. In his delight the champion hurled his putter high into the air and saw it drop perilously close to Sanders. One day he misses a vital putt, the next he's nearly brained. Such is life.

After shaking hands with his conqueror, Sanders gave the occasion a further ironic twist by holing his birdie putt from a longer distance than he had missed from on Saturday. In a thrilling finale, both men had birdied St Andrews' final hole. 'Quite something, wasn't it?' said Sanders. 'But I'd rather have had a little ol' four the day before and we wouldn't have had to worry about it.'

The result was an ambition realised for Nicklaus. He said on his arrival, 'If you want to be a player who is remembered, you have to win at St Andrews. All the famous players have won at St Andrews.' And now he was one of them.

Sanders was still an outsider, and one who had made a costly error. 'I believe that missing out on the Open cost me at least $10 million,' he said. 'I would have made more out of it than Tony Jacklin, and he made millions. My stage was set. I was one of the first that walked up to the gallery and laughed with them, said "Good morning" and signed autographs. The way I did it, the flair I had – I would have made a fortune.

'Some of them cannot do it. Charles Coody won the Masters, George Archer won the Masters, Tommy Aaron won the Masters, and they all made nothing out of it. Their stage wasn't set. Gene Littler beat me by a stroke to win the US Open and after he played an exhibition for $500 he said he felt like a cheat. You have to have something else to go with it. You have to set that stage.'

Sanders did the next best thing. He cashed in on his miss. The tour is full, he says, of 'plain vanilla' professionals who don't have the combination of 'chocolate and strawberry, peach and banana all messed up together'. Sanders did. You only had to look at his clothing. His extrovert character and colourful attire won him friends and endorsements. He lived a full life off the course, enjoying the company of both sexes. His friends included showbusiness stars Frank Sinatra, Clint Eastwood, Dean Martin, Andy Williams and Willie Nelson. He once boasted, 'Sinatra told me there are very few who did it their way – you, me and Errol Flynn.'

Known as Doug 'Keep the Change' Sanders, he also claimed there would never be a world recession with more people like him around. 'I've made more millions than you could chuck a stick at – but I've spent millions, too,' he said. 'I just keep the money moving around.'

Wherever he went, people wanted to talk to him about The Putt. Sanders played it mostly for laughs. 'It's not so bad now,' he said a few years back. 'Some days I can go for five minutes without thinking about it.'

Whereas some players could have been badly affected, Sanders retained a healthy perspective. 'It's never bothered me one way or another,' he said. 'I wish I had won the tournament but it didn't have an adverse effect on me. Missing that putt was like losing out on 30 pretty girls in a week. But there are other weeks and a lot more pretty girls. My life has been wonderful. If I died and was given the chance to come back as anyone, I'd come back as Doug Sanders.'

He would make just one change. 'I'd rather be remembered as Doug Sanders, the British Open champion,' he said, 'than Doug Sanders, the guy who missed that little putt.'

The Duel in the Sun

On a Saturday evening in July 1977 in a hotel room high above the Ayrshire coast, Tom Watson and his wife Linda were drinking champagne when they both began to cry. The haunting tune of a lone Scottish piper playing on the terrace below had so disturbed their emotions that neither of them could stop the flow of tears.

This for Watson was the end of a perfect day. It was the day he took part in the most memorable final in the 117 years of the Open Championship. Yet he had done more than merely take part. He had won. He had beaten the greatest player the game had ever seen playing close to his best. In claiming his second title, Watson, the freckle-faced professional from Kansas City, had truly arrived at the peak of the game. Only in later years would it become completely clear just what a great golfer he was. Yet on this day he dropped a pretty big clue.

It was an occasion all those who crammed onto Turnberry's dusty links would never forget. Neither, inevitably, would Tom and Linda. The time sport can truly be said to reach its highest level is when outstanding competitors play the game to the extent of their ability. Nobody relents and in the end somebody has to reach that extra level to win. There is no collapse, no dropping of standards under pressure. Nobody throws it away, but a champion triumphs through excellence. The clash between Watson and Jack Nicklaus at Turnberry in 1977 was one such occasion. In golf it has never been bettered.

At the time Nicklaus was 37, his rival ten years younger. This was the classic match of the king against the pretender to the throne. Minnesota Fats v. Fast Eddie, Sonny Liston v. Cassius Clay . . . or even Arnold Palmer v. Jack Nicklaus 15 years earlier.

Since the chubby ex-college player from Columbus had overcome the 'Fat Boy' taunts of Arnie's Army to capture a string of titles, his reputation had grown and grown. The list of successes had stretched to include 14 major championships (two Opens, five Masters, three US Opens and four US PGA Championships). He had won four of the previous five US PGA Player of the Year awards. His position at the pinnacle of golf was beyond dispute. The Golden Bear was king of the jungle.

Although champions such as Gary Player, Lee Trevino and Johnny

Miller had briefly threatened his reign, nobody had stormed the ramparts and taken up permanent residence in the throne room. Here at last, though, was a warrior charging at the gates who had to be treated seriously. And Nicklaus had been looking a little vulnerable of late. He had failed to win any of the previous six major championships, the most recent setback coming three months earlier at the Masters, where he was tied for the lead with four holes to play but lost by two shots. The man who beat him was Tom Watson.

In his early career, the insurance broker's son had been labelled a 'choker', as he let slip tournaments which were his for the winning. At the 1974 US Open at Winged Foot he led at halfway but had a 79 in the final round to finish five strokes behind the winner, Hale Irwin. A year later, at Medinah, he opened with rounds of 67 and 68 but faded out of the picture as he returned scores of 78 and 77.

He was clearly a talented golfer in need of help. The necessary guidance was provided by Byron Nelson, a legendary champion of the '40s. Nelson approached Watson after his disaster at Winged Foot and suggested they might work together. Although the partnership was not immediately successful (as could be seen at Medinah), it was to bear rich fruit in subsequent years. Before the final round of the Open at Carnoustie in 1975, Nelson advised Watson how he should react to the inevitable problems of wind and rain. The essence of his words was 'Don't worry'. Watson would hit bad shots but so would others in these conditions. He should just play the best he could.

Watson followed the advice to the letter. He three-putted three successive greens (the 10th, 11th and 12th) as howling winds swept across the course. But he did not give up. On the 72nd hole he hit a 300-yard drive downwind, a 148-yard nine-iron and a 20-foot putt to birdie the hole, tie with Australian Jack Newton and go on to win the next day's 18-hole play-off by a stroke (71–72) for his first major title. Not bad for a 'choker'.

There were, however, critics, especially in America, still ready to pin the label on him. And the accusation arose again during the early months of 1977 when Watson lost two successive tournaments after leading by three shots. So when he shared the lead with Ben Crenshaw after three rounds of the Masters, speculation was rife over whether Watson would 'blow up' under pressure. That same evening, Nelson telephoned to say that he had been watching on TV and thought that his friend was driving the ball well and that his tempo was fine. That was all Watson needed to hear.

He was ready to handle anything. Even when a three-putt blunder on Augusta's 14th allowed the fast-charging Nicklaus, three behind at the start of play, to draw level, he did not wilt. Under the gun, Watson held his nerve and played the golf, going ahead on the 17th by holing a 16-foot downhill putt with a four-foot right-to-left break. Nicklaus was in the middle of the 18th fairway, thinking a par would earn him a play-off, when the putt dropped. Forced to change his strategy and go for a birdie, the Bear made a rare error, dumped his six-iron into the front bunker and took a bogey five, enabling Watson to win his first Green Jacket by two shots.

The victory effectively removed the slur against Watson's name – and it was never to be raised again after the finish at Turnberry. The showdown – for a showdown it certainly was – was set up perfectly. Neither man had played the Ailsa course before that week. Never before had they been paired together in the final round of a major championship. Two heavyweights were meeting head-to-head on a neutral venue.

Unlike the following year, when Nicklaus would regain the Open partly because of his knowledge of St Andrews, he had to figure out the mysteries of Turnberry just as Watson did. This most coastal of the seven courses on the Open rota has a splendour of its own. The former Second World War airbase, with its monument overlooking the 12th green and its lighthouse dominating the skyline, can be a brutal test when the wind blows in from the Firth of Clyde. Yet during the week of the 106th Open Championship (Turnberry's major championship début), the weather was so kind that some spectators cast off their garments like Florida sun-worshippers, some young males stripping to the waist in their enthusiasm to take advantage of the welcome rays.

Let it not be said, though, that Watson and Nicklaus had it easy. The third-placed player, Hubert Green, finished the tournament at one under par, ten shots behind the mighty twosome. They were simply in a league of their own.

The battle was joined on the Friday with the spectators given little inkling of what was to come. Watson and Nicklaus had returned identical scores of 68 and 70 over the first two rounds to be a shot behind the halfway leader, Roger Maltbie. Perhaps it was the fact that they were paired together that inspired them. Maybe they would have done it anyway. Who knows? The point was they took control of the tournament from that moment onwards and no other player mattered.

The contest followed an unmistakable pattern. Nicklaus would pull away and Watson would fight back. In the third round the older man led by two after eight holes and held the advantage to the 14th, but then Watson drew level by the 16th and that's the way it stayed until the end. Both men were round in 65 (Nicklaus 31, 34, Watson 33, 32) and could still not be separated. They were three ahead of Crenshaw, and if the public, at this stage, was still reluctant to recognise a duel taking place, there was no escaping the reality in the final round.

As the drama built up, the spectators could hardly contain their excitement, rushing from one vantage point to the next, anxious not to miss a moment of this history in the making. At one stage, around the ninth, the players called for a delay so that the stewards could calm the agitated masses.

The British public, of course, knew Nicklaus. They recognised him as a great champion, whose many triumphs had twice included the Open. Watson they were less sure about. Although he had won the Open two years before, he remained a private, distant figure yet to build an army of supporters on this side of the Atlantic. Only in later years would the public be captivated not merely by his wonderful talent but by his charm, warmth and integrity. He wasn't a Lee Trevino but the quiet American had a reserved touch of class which is characteristic among the best of British. He would become well liked, but back in 1977 few appreciated his qualities. Nicklaus was the gallery favourite, and he drew the louder cheers.

The Golden Bear's fans had plenty to shout about as he swept into the lead on the last day. A ten-foot birdie putt at the second hole, where Watson bogeyed, put the senior partner into a two-stroke lead. And when he holed a 20-footer for another birdie at the fourth, the prospect of a runaway win loomed large. All the extra experience and hardened competitiveness of Nicklaus looked set to bring him yet another title.

But Watson believed he would win. And over the next four holes he showed why. At the fifth he struck a five-iron to 16 feet and rolled the ball in. His fightback was bunkered at the sixth, where he faced a crucial up-and-down from the sand. He made it, holing from six feet for par to stay two behind.

The gap narrowed to one on the seventh thanks to a shot that mere mortals can only dream about. On the 528-yard, par-five hole Nicklaus comfortably outdrove his opponent to leave a three-iron to the green. Realising he was in danger of falling further behind, 'Huckleberry Dillinger' (the nickname given to Watson by his high-school coaches) took a driver from the fairway and smashed the ball onto the distant green. He walked off with a birdie which Nicklaus, from the better position, could not match.

The pair were level at the eighth when Watson rattled in a 20-footer for a birdie. He later confessed he was 'lucky' because he had struck the putt too hard. But he had made a brilliant recovery to keep the match alive. In four holes he'd scored three birdies and saved par from a bunker.

But then, right on cue, the unmistakable pattern emerged once more. Nicklaus pulled ahead again. After his inspired fightback, Watson faltered with a bogey at the ninth to drop one behind. In the shadow of the monument, Nicklaus rolled in a 20-footer to birdie the 12th and extend his lead. The great moments were coming thick and fast. The quality of play was exhilarating.

Six holes to go and Watson was two behind. He had to do something, and quickly. Straightaway the reigning Masters champion holed a 12-footer for a birdie at the 13th. The gap was back to one. In the context of the occasion it was a shock when Watson missed a seven-footer for a birdie at the 14th. But he would make up for it in spades at the next.

The 15th is a 209-yard par three with bunkers on the left and a bank falling away to the right. Watson went for the left side of the green but saw his ball drift away between two sand traps. Nicklaus, with the chance of grabbing a potentially winning lead, went for the flag and left himself a makeable uphill putt. Watson would do well to save par.

He did better than that. From 60 feet he took his putter, rapped the ball towards the hole – too hard – and leaped in the air in delight as the dimpled spheroid dived out of sight. Talk about a rat up a drainpipe. Nicklaus, in the act of replacing his ball, was stunned. He missed the birdie putt and, once again, these golfing gods were level, with just three holes left to play.

The 16th, halved in pars, was a chance to draw breath. Then, at the penultimate hole, the mighty Nicklaus stumbled. Turnberry's easiest hole, the 500-yard, par-five 17th, had yielded 29 eagles and 251 birdies during the four days. Its stroke average of 4.38 was lower than the second, fifth, eighth and ninth – all of which are par fours. Anything less than a birdie in this context would be deemed a failure.

Both men hit good drives, Watson dead centre, Nicklaus slightly right. Watson then drilled a three-iron to within 17 feet of the pin and watched in surprise as his opponent messed up his four-iron approach, leaving it out to the right and 50 feet short of the green. Nicklaus was in trouble but he certainly wasn't out of it and from a fluffy lie he played a good chip which stopped five feet from the pin. His ball was very close to Watson's line and he looked on intently as his rival's eagle putt stopped close to the hole before the ball was tapped in for a birdie.

In these situations Nicklaus was renowned for escaping. But he noticed that Watson's ball had curled slightly to the left as it neared the hole and mistakenly allowed for a right-left borrow. He stroked a good putt to the right of the hole – but it stayed right and missed. 'I should have followed my own instincts,' Nicklaus would say later.

For the first time in the entire tournament Watson was ahead ... with just one hole to play. It had been a sensational exhibition of the Royal and Ancient art by these two masterful players and now they provided a sensational finish. As Watson walked to the tee of the 431-yard 18th, his caddie Alfie Fyles uttered his famous remark: 'Go for the jugular!' It is doubtful whether the player needed such basic instruction, but he acted upon it nonetheless. Taking a one-iron to avoid trouble on the dog-leg par four, Watson smote the ideal shot, slightly to the left but avoiding the bunkers that lurk on that side.

Nicklaus is a man who instinctively responds to danger. But not always successfully. Just as he had gone for the flag on the 18th at Augusta three months earlier with unfortunate results, so now he took his driver on this tee for the first time all week. He wanted to boom the ball past Watson, pile on the pressure and set up a good chance of a birdie. Sadly for Nicklaus, he came off the shot slightly and pushed the drive out to the right, where it came to rest under a gorse bush.

The jugular was now exposed and Watson really did go for it, like a starving dog. Although he could normally only carry 165 yards with a six-iron, his adrenaline was so high that he plumped for a seven-iron to travel 178 yards. The full-blooded shot was perfectly struck. The ball stopped three feet from the pin. 'Elementary, my dear Watson,' said Peter Alliss from the TV booth, matching the shot with his eloquence.

The game was surely up for Nicklaus, but in the next few minutes he was to add to his immense stature in the game. While he has played many great shots to win championships, he has never played two better to lose one. Although his backswing was impeded by a branch from the gorse bush, he summoned up all his reserves of concentration and resolve, crashed an eight-iron into the ground, taking a huge divot, and launched the ball forward. Against all the odds it came to rest on the right-hand side of the putting surface, 32 feet from the pin.

As he marched off towards the green, fans broke from behind the ropes and threw coins into the divot mark his remarkable shot had made. In the desperate scramble for the green, the one sad incident of this glorious day took place. Fyles, the faithful caddie, was knocked flying by the rushing throng and strained his left wrist as he fell. A reasonable amateur golfer, he was never to play the game again as a result of this injury.

When he reached his ball, Nicklaus still had plenty of work to do. The putt went right to left, down a dip and up again. Impossible. Surely he couldn't hole it. But he did. Down in two from under a gorse bush 160 yards from the green on the last hole of the Open. Turning water into wine would be nothing after that.

What Nicklaus had achieved was twofold. He had enhanced his reputation and ensured a dramatic finish. He hadn't necessarily saved himself from defeat. But now if Tom Watson was to become champion he had to *win*. The old claret jug would not drop into his lap.

Something told the watching hordes that Watson would hole his putt. Such a magnificent match could not be settled by the disaster of a missed three-footer. Nicklaus had been let off by Doug Sanders from a similar range in 1970. For all his heroics, he could not expect to be so fortunate again. And he wasn't. Watson's putt was not perfect. But it was good enough, the ball creeping into the right half of the hole to end probably the greatest golf contest ever played.

What happened next merely enhanced the occasion. Nicklaus is not only a wonderful golfer but a fine sportsman. He knows how to behave in defeat as well as in victory. After Fyles had rushed to embrace his boss, the runner-up came to offer his congratulations. And they were neither brief nor insincere. Nicklaus looked Watson in the eye, offered his hand and wrapped an arm warmly around his shoulders. 'I'm tired of giving it my best and it not being good enough,' he said, and then led the champion slowly off the green.

Afterwards it was suggested that Watson had had a premonition about Nicklaus's birdie putt. That he *knew* that Jack was going to hole it. And that *he* would have to hole his three-footer. Fourteen years later, Watson doesn't remember it that way. He simply prepared himself for the possibility of Nicklaus holing out.

'As I walked up to the green I said to Alfie Fyles, "We have to expect Jack to make this putt. We can't rest on our laurels,"' he recounted. 'I had to do that from a competitive standpoint. I had to. It was like match-play and I had to think that I would have to make that three-foot putt to win. I had to keep thinking that.

'Jack holed his 40-footer and I was still in the frame of mind to make mine. The reason I kept that attitude was that I wanted to have no let-down whatsoever. That's the way a competitor has to react.

'Mine was a straight putt. I was nervous over it but I stroked it right into the right centre of the cup – and the championship was mine.'

The victory heralded the start of the Watson Years. He won the US PGA Player of the Year award four times in succession at the end of the '70s and in six of the next eight years. He topped the US money list in five of those years and won five more major championships. His love affair with the Open and its Scottish courses dominated the event. By 1983 he had been champion five times – four of the victories coming north of the border – to be only one short of Harry Vardon's record.

The defeat did not finish Nicklaus either. He regained the Open title a year later and added three more major championships to take his total to an unprecedented 18. Great players, both of them, who enjoyed many great days. But never quite like that Saturday in July 1977. A day for champagne and tears.

Tilting the Balance

The '80s were wonderful for European golf. It was the decade when the players on this side of the Atlantic regained their self-respect. Not only did the Ryder Cup team, under Tony Jacklin, hold the trophy for six years, but individuals triumphed at the highest level. In total nine major championships were won by European players, compared to a paltry two during the '70s. From being little more than no-hopers, golfers from different countries with different native tongues found a common bond within a continent to discover pride and inspire each other.

They were led by a Spaniard, Seve Ballesteros, who had pointed the way with victory at the 1979 Open Championship at Lytham – at the age of 22. When he turned that solitary win into a habit during the '80s, others followed. Bernhard Langer from Germany, Sandy Lyle from Scotland and Nick Faldo from England all gained the most coveted of prizes. Into the '90s and a Welshman, Ian Woosnam, was to add to the list.

Those glory days were restricted to two championships, the Masters and the Open, as one by one the new champions emerged to fight off the common foe – the Americans.

When the decade began, the United States – and one American in particular – held sway. Tom Watson, having claimed the title twice during the '70s, dominated the first four years, winning three more times. Even the year he missed out, 1981, a comparatively unknown American, Bill Rogers, gained a commanding victory at Royal St George's. The most notable 18th-hole drama came when a policeman stopped Rogers among the stampeding fans, refusing to let him advance to the green until convinced that he was, in fact, a player. Yes, Rogers was that well known.

Watson had walked away with the Open at Muirfield in 1980 after a third-round 64 gave him a four-shot lead, and at Troon in 1982 he backed into victory when the other contenders collapsed on the last nine. Nick Price from Zimbabwe led by two with four holes left, double bogeyed the 15th (after trouble in a bunker) and then needed to par the last three holes for a tie. But he missed a seven-footer at the 17th and had to birdie the 18th to force a play-off.

'My swing had got a little quick and one thing led to another,' recalled Price. 'My iron shots were okay but I kept hooking the ball off the tee. I'd had to use a spare driver because my old faithful that I'd had for 11 years had been repaired and they hadn't done the job properly. If I'd had my old faithful those last five holes, I'd have had a bit more confidence and things might have been different.'

Once again Price hooked the ball off the tee. Although he made a good recovery to reach the green, from 35 feet he could do no better than par. Watson, with a last-round 70, won by a shot.

Lucky Tom? Probably. A year later, though, it was Super Tom. He played one of the most memorable last-hole shots ever to triumph again at Royal Birkdale, his only win outside Scotland. When Watson reached the final hole he was a shot ahead of compatriot Andy Bean, needing a par to retain the championship. The 18th, a 472-yard par four with a slight left-to-right bend, can be a daunting prospect, particularly into the wind, which was blowing on this occasion.

'I had been hitting the ball pretty well all week,' he said. 'My plan on the tee was to hit a good solid fade and I did. The thing that was disconcerting about that final hole was that I had to wait so long to hit my second shot.

'I was playing with Craig Stadler and Craig was off on the right and the players ahead were taking a long time to finish out. Then it took a long time to get the crowd out of the way so that we could hit. I had a lot of time to think about that last shot.

'Sometimes that's good. I think it was good for me because I concentrated on hitting a good shot. I had a two-iron and it was about 210 yards into a wind of about 10 to 15 miles per hour. I never really had any doubt. I knew that was the shot.

'I made a good swing and hit it flush in the face. The ball started out with a slight draw and the wind straightened it out. It ended up just covering the flag. The unfortunate thing was that I never saw the ball land because of the crowd. As soon as I hit it they all rushed in front of me and formed a wall of people, so I never saw where the ball came down.

'All I knew was that the people clapped and gave a pretty good cheer up at the green so I knew it was pretty close. That was the best two-iron I ever hit. It was most enjoyable and I'll take it with me to my grave.

'After I'd hit the shot I couldn't feel good because I didn't know where the ball had ended up. But when I broke through the crowd and saw the ball so close to the hole I said to myself, "The championship is mine."'

★ ★ ★

By a twist of irony which typifies the wondrous absurdity of golf, Tom Watson hit another two-iron a year later that was to have a traumatic effect on his life and career. Unlike the immaculate strike of Royal Birkdale, it brought him disaster and cost him a third successive Open Championship.

In terms of drama, the 1984 Open at St Andrews is hard to surpass. Yet the excitement occurred not on the last hole alone but also on the 17th. On the Sunday afternoon of July 22nd, the half-mile of land that stretches from the clubhouse down across the Swilcan Burn and past the former site of the railway sheds to the 17th tee became a vast theatre in which sporting history was enacted. The two principal players were Seve Ballesteros and Watson. Unlike at the wonderful contest at Turnberry in 1977, the two combatants were not playing side by side in the same group. And the quality of golf was not quite as high. But the excitement was hardly any less.

When the final day of the 113th Open dawned, Watson shared the lead with Australian Ian Baker-Finch, surprise packet of the tournament, who was to fade out of the picture with a 79. Ballesteros was two strokes behind, playing in the match ahead of Watson. By the time the charismatic Spaniard entered 'The Stage' of the 17th tee, he had drawn level. He knew the Road Hole would be crucial. Before the round began, Ballesteros had sworn to make par there, after three bogey fives, 'even if I have to come back on Monday'.

His drive was pulled to the left into thin, wispy rough. Although the narrow green of the 461-yard hole was still reachable, the angle of approach was difficult, close to the notorious Road Bunker with the tarmac road lying in wait for the shot hit too far. There was also a danger of getting a 'flyer' out of the grass.

Seve took a six-iron and launched into the swing that he would later describe as 'the key shot of the entire Open'. The ball pitched right of the bunker and ran up to finish on the top layer of the green. Having been denied a birdie at the 16th by only an inch, Ballesteros hit another accurate long putt which stopped less than a foot from the hole. He tapped in for his par, which felt like a birdie.

Watson, meantime, had entered 'The Stage' and struck the ideal drive over the old railway sheds to land in Position A on the right side of the 17th fairway. He had taken such a tight line to the right that he was not sure whether the ball had drifted out of bounds and he stood on the tee with arms spread wide, asking for confirmation. He was relieved to know that he wouldn't have to play a second drive.

When Watson reached his ball he was in a quandary. Should he take a two-iron or a three-iron? The crucial decision may have been affected by a yardage error, Watson believing the distance to the green to be 210 yards when, in fact, it was nearer 190 yards. He fatally decided on a two-iron but before he could play the shot was distracted by the reception being given to Ballesteros as he walked up the 18th fairway. Watson backed away. Then he settled to play a shot he intended to draw round towards the pin. Instead he pushed it and watched in horror as the ball flew over the green, bounded on across the road and bounced off the stone boundary wall, coming to rest only two feet away.

Ballesteros did not know that the championship had swung dramatically his way. Perhaps it was just as well he didn't. Having played a solid drive down 18, he carefully pitched towards the green, walked away to his right to avoid the cloud of dust the shot had created and heard the applause from the green. He was 15 feet from the hole.

As he walked towards the final green to a rising crescendo of noise, Watson was reaching his ball by the wall. He needed to play a miraculous up-and-down to deny Ballesteros now. But his next shot was merely very good. After much deliberation and six practice swings, Watson jabbed the ball up the bank to stop 30 feet past the flag. Before he could attempt this make-or-break putt, Ballesteros would make his birdie attempt on 18. The Spaniard, clad since the 15th in a dark-blue sweater which was his familiar attire for the last round of a major, struck a putt of exact weight just to the right of its target. The line was not perfect but on the last roll the ball hung left and dropped into the back of the hole.

Ballesteros was ecstatic. He pumped his right arm in a war dance of celebration which finished with three triumphant thrusts into the air. 'I thought probably that's it,' he would say later in a masterpiece of understatement.

The significance of Watson's putt changed from important to decisive. If he missed, the championship was as good as over. He missed. A bogey five meant that to match the four, three finish of Ballesteros, the reigning champion had to score an eagle two at the last. He prolonged the drama by pacing out the 93-yard pitch he needed to hole if he was to force a play-off. It was a forlorn gesture, as the pitch flew over the pin and he finished with a par four to tie Bernhard Langer for second place, two shots behind the new champion. In the end Ballesteros won the title as much as Watson lost it. His birdie at the last had the effect of twisting a knife into his rival's self-inflicted wound.

In later years the championship would be regarded as a watershed in the game. It marked the end of Watson's dominance, the end of him as a major championship force. Maybe that errant two-iron destroyed him. But maybe, after seven years at the top, his time was due anyway.

For Ballesteros, victory at the home of golf was one of the highlights of his colourful career. But although he dethroned the King, the Spaniard did not inherit the crown. He was probably the best player in the game over the next few years. Yet he did not dominate in the way that Watson had done and Nicklaus before him. It was another 15 major championships before Ballesteros would win again. In that time there were 14 different major winners. The game was up for grabs.

★ ★ ★

The odd man out among the list of 14 was Sandy Lyle. He was the only player to win twice between Seve's St Andrews triumph and his next success at Lytham in 1988. In doing so the amiable Scot displayed the contrasting ways of becoming a champion. He proved that it's possible to win not only by playing the final hole brilliantly — but also by completely messing it up.

Lyle's victory at the 1988 Masters featured arguably the finest long bunker shot ever played to close out a major. But when he won the Open at Royal St George's in 1985, it was in bizarre, almost embarrassing circumstances. The 114th Open was the championship that no one seemed to want to win. No one reached out and grabbed it by the scruff of the neck. It just drifted along to a conclusion and somebody took fewer shots than the others. That somebody was Sandy Lyle.

Yet the drama there was on the final hole featured the leading contenders, crumbling under pressure. Arguably the most decisive act on the 72nd green was Peter Jacobsen's tackle to end the cavorting of a male streaker! The day had started with Australian David Graham and West Germany's Bernhard Langer three shots ahead, but both scored bogey fives at the first hole. Lyle also dropped a shot there. It was that kind of championship. St George's is a tough course, especially when the wind is blowing, as it was this day. But surely not that difficult.

Tom Kite played the front nine impressively in three under par to move to the top of the leaderboard. At the tenth he performed like a high handicapper, duffing a chip and thinning a bunker shot to take a double-bogey six and fade out of the picture.

So Lyle, after two good holes, the 14th and the 15th, where he picked up successive birdies, found himself in the lead. A par at the last would clinch Britain's first Open for 16 years. Lyle hit a good drive and then slightly pulled his six-iron approach so that it ran across the green and down into Duncan's Hollow. He faced a 35-foot chip up the bank from thick grass. He took a sand wedge and played the ball too gently. It crept up the slope, failed to reach the top and gently rolled back down again. The 20,000-plus crowd packed around the last green was then treated to the extraordinary sight of Lyle on both knees, bending head forward in the grass, banging his club on the ground in frustration. This, remember, was the eventual winner!

He found a sympathetic friend in TV commentator Peter Alliss, who remembered his own trauma on the 18th in the 1953 Ryder Cup, when he took a bogey six to deny Great Britain at least a tie. 'He played the wrong club there,' Alliss told viewers. 'He needed a straighter-faced club. I know so well because that's the sort of thing I did at Wentworth all those years ago when I needed a flat runner. Now he's got to keep his nerve and get down in two.'

Lyle did precisely that, rolling his 25-footer 18 inches past the hole and knocking in the return. But would it be enough? 'He thought he'd blown it, I know,' recalled Lyle's caddie Dave Musgrove. But, unlike Alliss, there was to be a reprieve for the likeable quiet man. While he was dropping a shot at the 18th, Graham and Langer – the two players who could stop him – were doing the same at the short 16th. Both went into the bunker on the right and failed to get up and down. Now one of them had to play the last two holes in one under par to force a play-off. Neither looked remotely like getting the birdie he needed. At the 17th both second shots were more than 35 feet from the pin. All each man could do was lag up and save par.

The last, 458 yards long, was the toughest hole during the tournament, with a scoring average of 4.62. Langer missed the green right and Graham sent his second shot into the bunker short and right of the green. There was a small flutter in the Lyle camp when Langer, needing to hole his chip from the light rough, found an accurate line to send the ball rolling towards the hole. It was going too fast, however, and brushed the flag to finish five feet past.

This wasn't a championship for heroics. Graham missed his 15-foot par putt and Langer, from a similar length to that he would face on the final green in far more dramatic circumstances at Kiawah Island six years later, lipped out too. Both men had taken 75 in the fourth round to concede the title, leaving Payne Stewart with a joint-best-of-the-day 68 to finish second, a shot behind the champion.

Lyle's 70 did the trick, yet with typical candour he admitted, 'I thought I'd have to do a 67 or 68 to win today.' The significance of the victory was greater than the manner of it. Langer had won the Masters in April and Europe would regain the Ryder Cup two months later. The balance of power in world golf was shifting.

★ ★ ★

Greg Norman had an astonishing year in 1986. Astonishing in that he was so dominant, winning nine tournaments around the globe and being acclaimed World No. 1 beyond dispute. But astonishing, too, in that he only claimed one major championship. This was the year of the Saturday Slam, when Norman led all four majors going into the last round but contrived to lose three of them in different ways.

His one triumph, the Open at Turnberry, was not only well deserved but emphatically taken. The 31-year-old Australian left no argument about his right to temporary possession of the old claret jug as he swept to a five-shot victory.

Inevitably, in the circumstances, there was no 72nd-hole drama. Norman could have six-putted the final green and still won. Instead he returned a solid par four with two putts from 60 feet to leave all the disappointments, outrageous bad luck and near misses behind him.

Yet there was drama on the 18th. It came on the second day, when Norman laid the foundations of victory with a record-equalling 63. It was a stunning exhibition of the man's talent, containing seven birdies and an eagle. But, remarkably, there were also three dropped shots. One was at the 431-yard 18th. When Norman stood on the tee, he needed a par to break the major championship best for a single round held by nine other players (for the record: Johnny Miller, Bruce Crampton, Mark Hayes, Jack Nicklaus, Tom Weiskopf, Isao Aoki, Ray Floyd, Gary Player and Nick Price). But he didn't know. So when his second shot stopped on the green, 28 feet from the pin, he didn't appreciate that he was two putts from his own place in history. He simply wanted to hole the first one for a 61!

Norman ran the ball three feet past, pulled the one coming back and had to settle for a 63. Caddie Pete Bender recalled, 'Greg said to me, "I want this one. I want a 61."' But it wasn't to be. It would be tough to say he was disappointed with his round, but there's no doubt the last hole left a bitter taste in his mouth.'

For once, though, Greg Norman would experience the sweetest taste of all when he walked off the same green two days later.

★ ★ ★

There are many ways to win at golf. Gloriously, luckily, determinedly, brilliantly. Sometimes, when the pressure is at its greatest, a player just has to grind it out. As Chi Chi Rodriguez once said after a practice-round 64, 'Monday and Tuesday golf out here is like a boxer working on a punchbag. It doesn't hit back.' In major championships, the occasion punches back like a heavyweight champion. The man who can ride the blows will be the last one standing at the end.

So it was at the 1987 Open. The conditions at Muirfield, on Scotland's east coast, dictated a grim struggle against the elements as much as against the course and the rest of the field. The backdrop was grey and forbidding as wind and rain dominated. The bright colours that sunshine brings were banished from the scene. But still drama illuminated the gloom. After four days of an unrelenting slog, two players emerged through the mist to settle the championship, like weary travellers completing a long journey. They were Nick Faldo, an

Englishman who had celebrated his 30th birthday the previous day, and Paul Azinger, a 27-year-old American in his first Open Championship.

With nine holes left, Azinger led by three. But he dropped shots at the tenth and 11th to cling to a precarious single-stroke lead coming down the stretch. Faldo, meanwhile, was like a captain steering a radar-straight course through a storm. He made par after par. Often he found the safe haven of the centre of the green but three times he staved off danger by recovering from bunkers. His 30-yard sand save at the eighth to three feet was probably the outstanding shot of a round remembered for its steadiness rather than its brilliance.

When Faldo came to the last he was still a stroke behind, needing either to birdie the 448-yard hole or to hope that his rival faltered. Azinger it was who gave way. After the Briton had driven down the middle of the fairway, the US Tour's leading money-winner, teeing off at the 550-yard 17th, pulled the ball into a bunker on the left. 'What I did at the 17th was ridiculous,' Azinger confessed afterwards. 'I should never have used the driver. I don't know what I was thinking. It was the shot that cost me the championship.' Pressure might have had something to do with it. All he could do was splash out sideways, leaving himself still nearly 300 yards to the green.

Up ahead Faldo was giving his final approach shot all his concentration. From 195 yards he took a five-iron and struck it as well as he could have hoped. On a perfect line, the ball thumped down on the green 30 feet short of the flag. 'When I saw the ball in the air I thought, "Cor, look at that,"' Faldo would recount later. 'I was so nervous I was almost working from memory, but then in a split second it happens.'

As the Hertfordshire-born professional was receiving a tumultuous reception on the final fairway, Azinger was hitting his third on 17, which finished still 100 yards short of the green. The thin American played his fourth, a good pitch which stopped 15 feet past the pin. He could still save par. First, though, Faldo would putt on 18. From 30 feet he allowed too much borrow; the ball missed by two feet on the right-hand side and ran four feet past. When he needed it most, Azinger's putting touch deserted him. His par putt slipped by on the right-hand side and the two men were level (at five under par).

The pressure that had been building up on Faldo was now condensed into this one teasing putt. Doug Sanders had missed a shorter one on the final green. So had others down the years. But Faldo holed. It was a brave shot, firmly struck into the right half of the cup. The Englishman lifted both arms into the air, nodded his thanks to the crowd and blew out his cheeks in a release of tension.

It wasn't all over yet, though. Azinger could force a play-off with a par at the last. This time he took an iron from the tee and safely found the fairway. But, having learned his lesson from his blunder at 17 and opted for accuracy, he had left himself a long way from the green, probably more than 200 yards. It was a four-iron shot and, in the circumstances, a very difficult one. Azinger could not control his swing, pulled the ball left of the greenside bunker and watched in despair as it ran down into the trap.

Unruly spectators cheered when the ball came to rest in the sand, prompting a subsequent public apology from Alastair Low, the chairman of the R and A's championship committee, for the 'rank bad sportsmanship'. Faldo's caddie Andy Prodger was so disgusted by the behaviour of the fans that he later sought out Azinger and personally apologised. 'You can't help it,' replied the American graciously. 'That's just life.'

Left with a horrid bunker shot, Azinger could not escape. His stance involved placing his right foot inside the bunker, his left bent above it on the steep slope. All he could do was chip the ball over the lip of the trap but 30 feet short of the pin.

As his par putt curled short and right of the hole, ill-mannered spectators cheered again. Azinger let his putter fall to the ground and bowed his head in sadness and frustration. It was all over. Faldo had parred all 18 holes and was champion for the first time. Azinger had dropped shots at both the last two holes and had blown his chance.

Tough game, golf. Cruel game, too. On that misty afternoon, it was anything but a funny game.

★ ★ ★

When Seve Ballesteros says that he has played the best round of his life, then no one should doubt that the golf they have witnessed was something rather special. The ideal finish to such a distinguished occasion could only be provided by a piece of inspirational Ballesteros magic.

The 1988 Open provided exactly that moment. It was treasured by all who witnessed it. Seve, much loved by the British public, had produced a memorable conclusion to his previous Open Championship victory when he birdied the last at St Andrews to beat Tom Watson in 1984. This time Nick Price would be pushed into second place in a head-to-head contest some watchers compared to the Watson–Nicklaus Greatest Show on Earth at Turnberry in 1977.

For the first time in its 128-year history, the Open finished on a Monday because torrential rain at Royal Lytham had washed out Saturday's play. More than 15,000 fans stayed on (or even turned up specially) to take the combined attendance for the championship soaring to a new record 205,285. They were not disappointed.

Price began the round two shots clear of Ballesteros and the defending champion Nick Faldo. In contrast to the weekend storms, it was a lovely sunny day as the three leaders set out together at 12.45 p.m. By the time they reached the turn, two were left in the contest. Ballesteros, playing majestically, was four under par for the round and had joined Price at nine under. Faldo was performing steadily and would complete the 18 holes in level par (71), just as he had at Muirfield a year earlier. But this time par was not good enough. The circumstances were entirely different.

The leaders matched one another birdie for birdie coming down the stretch. It was thrilling stuff. Ballesteros ahead at 11. Price level again at the 12th. Both birdied 13. Both bogeyed 14. Both parred 15. The killer blow came on the 357-yard 16th – the hole which had earned Seve the nickname of the 'Car Park Champion' after he had pushed his drive out among the cars on his way to victory in 1979. This time he played the hole in a conventional manner – and how. His 135-yard nine-iron finished three inches from the pin, for a certain birdie and a one-shot lead.

That was the way it stayed as they played the last. At this point the crowd was to learn – if they didn't know already – why they call Ballesteros charismatic. Not only is he a great player, he is exciting too, with a talent for the unexpected. Seve has never been a straight-down-the-middle man. Now, when he needed a safe par, he got a par. But not exactly safe. Ballesteros missed the fairway. He missed the green. But then he nearly holed a masterly chip which stopped six inches from the flag. In Seve style, it was the only way to play the hole.

The 412-yard 18th hole at Royal Lytham, with its 15 bunkers, is not as demanding as some finishing holes but still takes some negotiating. The drive is the key. Ballesteros let his go out into the right rough. Price struck a beauty into the heart of the fairway. The Spaniard's next shot was not desperately difficult. He had a good lie but a slightly awkward angle to the putting surface. From 170 yards he missed the green left and the ball finished in the thick grass, 50 feet from the flag.

This was Price's chance and he knew it. The 31-year-old from Zimbabwe, remembered for letting slip a three-shot lead over the final six holes of the 1982 Open at Troon, had played splendidly to keep this contest alive. Now he could tie or maybe even win. 'I hit the best tee-shot of my life down that hole,' Price recounted. 'It must have been 290 yards and never left the middle of the fairway. When I reached my ball it was 168 yards to the pin, the perfect six-iron yardage.

'All I could picture in my mind was that I had stiffed that shot. I was so eager to play it. It was funny that in that situation, although there's a lot of pressure and you're a little nervous, once you get over the ball a great calm comes over you because you are in control. You're swinging the way you want to, everything's going not according to plan but within your control. Nothing's out of your reach.

'I was like that. I wanted to hit it too quickly and stiff the shot and I think I rushed my routine. From the time I pulled my club, doing my pre-shot drill and then hitting the shot, I was probably two or three seconds quicker than I normally was. I pulled it. I was so disappointed.

'I know you can't predict making a birdie on the 72nd hole of the British Open, but if ever there was an opportunity for me to win that championship it was right there. Because I think if I had stiffed that iron shot it would have made Seve's chip shot that much harder. But I gave him that opening and I'm sure he would agree. If I had been sitting inside six feet the way I was putting it would have meant he *had* to get up and down to force a play-off.'

Price's approach finished on the left edge of the green, some 35 feet from the hole, making a birdie three unlikely. Yet in order to close out his third Open victory, Ballesteros still had to get down in two shots. Showing the sense of theatre that a Shakespearean actor could not have surpassed, Seve played his masterstroke, delicately extricating the ball from the rough and carrying it forward on an inexorable path towards the pin.

The ball was never going to finish anywhere but close to the hole. The only question was, 'Would it drop?' Gasps of admiration turned to cheers of delight and grew in volume before ending in sustained applause as the ball rolled over the right edge of the cup and stopped like a well-trained dog. It was a shot worthy of winning an Open Championship. 'The lie was difficult but somehow the ball was close enough to the hole to win and I am very pleased,' explained Ballesteros matter-of-factly. It was quite easy, really . . . if you're a genius.

Price could still deny him. But his chance had gone. He gave his long putt every chance but rapped it too hard and to the left of the hole. He even missed the eight-footer coming back. Not that it mattered.

In returning a last-round 69, Price had done enough to win and consoled himself that one day he would. Ballesteros had been simply undeniable. His last-round 65 meant that his 11–under 273 was ten shots better than his winning score on the same course nine years earlier.

It was one of the greatest finishes in championship history. Two years of self-doubt were wiped out as the mighty Spaniard's confidence returned. Ballesteros himself had feared his days of glory were over after he had dunked a four-iron into the lake at Augusta's 15th hole to lose the 1986 Masters. Now Seve was back. There was no question about it.

★ ★ ★

There is a widely held view among followers of golf that Greg Norman threw away the 1989 Open Championship. Such a condemnation is both unfair and unrealistic. Norman played some of the best golf ever seen on that final Sunday at Royal Troon. But so did Mark Calcavecchia, the 29-year-old American who emerged as the surprise champion.

What Calcavecchia achieved – which Norman could not – was a mastery of the 452-yard final hole. During the unrelenting drama of that thrilling last day there were only six birdies scored at the 18th – and two of them came from the man from Nebraska.

He was able to complete the feat twice because of the first four-hole play-off in Open history. This was the first time that extra holes had been required since Tom Watson gained the first of his five titles at Carnoustie in 1975. While the US Masters is decided by sudden death (which critics say is too much of a lottery) and the US Open has an 18-hole play-off (faulted as an anti-climax on the fifth day), the R and A decided on a compromise for the Open. In terms of excitement the new format was an undoubted success. But, ironically, it still came down to sudden death in the end.

Norman was the man to suffer the most, which was particularly unfortunate in view of his contribution to a wonderful day's sport. When it began, Wayne Grady, 31, from Brisbane, Australia, led the tournament by a shot with a posse of Americans on his heels. Calcavecchia was three behind; Norman was nowhere. But the Great White Shark came out snapping to birdie the first six holes. Yes, that's *six* holes. His extraordinary start set up a course-record 64 to lift him from seven shots adrift to be the leader in the clubhouse at 13 under par, 275.

When Calcavecchia came to the last he had to make a birdie three to force a play-off. With an average of 4.23 the hole, which had been lengthened by 25 yards since the 1982 Open, was the fifth toughest on the course that week. There were more than three times as many bogeys or worse (130) returned there as birdies (42). But Calcavecchia had nothing to lose. He went for it.

'Calc' is one of the boys. The son of a former GI from the small town of Laurel, Nebraska (population 1,035), he likes to shoot pool and drink beer with the caddies. In contrast to his designer-clad fellow professionals, Calcavecchia, with his swarthy appearance and shambling walk, could easily be mistaken for a boxer. His swing is not a thing of beauty, either. When he winds up to give the ball a good swipe, every muscle and sinew seems to be straining with effort. But it works.

On the 18th tee he swatted the little white enemy more than 300 yards down the parched fairway to stop just short of the bunker which was later to bring Norman's downfall. From there he heaved a mighty eight-iron 161 yards to within four feet of the flag and rattled in the putt to tie with Norman. It was valiant stuff.

Only Grady could beat them. Two pars would make him the biggest upset winner since Bill Rogers in 1981. But the Aussie-in-the-shadow-of-Norman sent his tee-shot into the right-hand bunker at the 223-yard 17th and took a bogey four. A brave par from the fringe at 18 put him through to the three-man showdown. It was Greg v. Mark v. Wayne over four holes.

Just as he had in the fourth round, Norman made a flying start. He birdied the first from 15 feet and the second from 18 feet. Only a remarkable curling 24-foot birdie putt by Calcavecchia from the back of the second green kept the American in touch. Grady, with two pars, was searching for inspiration.

The third play-off hole, the short 17th, was to prove crucial. Calcavecchia found the green and made a par. Norman and Grady both missed it and dropped a shot. Norman's tee-shot landed on the 'dance floor' but ran through to the fringe at the back. Calcavecchia and his caddie thought he would putt but Norman played a heavy-handed chip which ran ten feet past – and he missed the putt coming back.

So they came to the last with Norman and Calcavecchia level and Grady two shots back. Here the Nebraskan got lucky. His drive out to the right was described by his caddy, Drake Oddy, as 'awful'. The ball hit a cameraman and bounced into some trodden-down rough. Oddy reckoned that if there had been no cameraman and no gallery the ball would have been 25 yards further right in deeper rough.

Norman then stepped up to the tee and, with his adrenaline pumping, walloped a huge drive that took a hard bounce and bounded on across the tinder-dry ground before coming to rest in a bunker 325 yards away. 'I hit the driver there every day,' Norman would say later. 'I didn't think I could reach [the bunker].'

Grady struck the best drive straight down the middle, but it was probably too late to save him. That was certainly the case after Calcavecchia's next shot. He was in the rough 201 yards from the flag and under severe pressure. From that situation the man in the white visor smote a five-iron that rose like a bird and swooped down to the green, coming to rest seven feet from its target. 'As I watched it I thought I can't do better than that,' said Calcavecchia. 'I don't care where it ends up, that's the best shot I ever hit.'

There was no way back for the Australian pair. Norman went from bunker to bunker and then out of bounds behind the green . . . and conceded. Grady hit an excellent second shot to eight feet but his putt lipped out. Calcavecchia had three for it. Just for good measure, like a true champion, he rolled in the birdie putt. Back home in Phoenix, Arizona, his wife Sheryl, expecting their first child, was in floods of tears. At the Cedarview Country Club in Laurel, Nebraska, they were starting a party.

Not only is Calcavecchia one of the boys, he's one of the good guys, too. Amid all the celebrations he remembered to thank his dad, who had died in 1985. 'He gave money when we didn't have money,' said Mark. 'He sent me places to play when we couldn't afford it. I owe him so much.'

Norman, like the sportsman he is, was warm in his congratulations for the victor and in his commiserations for Grady. He might not have realised it at the time, but he would soon be the subject of all the inquests. Why had he driven in such a cavalier fashion at the last? Why hadn't he putted from off the fringe at the 17th? Was he really a champion? Or did he lack the killer instinct to back up his talent?

In this writer's view, Norman was a victim of fortune. If he blundered anywhere, it was on the 17th in the play-off. At the last hole he struck a far better drive than Calcavecchia but with far worse results. Indeed, the American had hit a similar drive to Norman's last at the 72nd hole but his ball had pulled up just short of the bunker. Had it rolled on a few more yards, he would not even have made the play-off.

Fortune, too, was to smile kindly on the eventual champion when he began his charge with a 50-foot putt to save par at the 11th, followed by an outrageous chip that pitched straight into the hole for a birdie at the 12th. It was his lucky day.

Much of the reaction to the latest of Norman's near misses was caused by the desire to see him win. When he followed a final-round 64 with two successive birdies in the play-off, the blond Australian set up the prospect of one of the most remarkable championship victories of them all. When he failed to complete the job, the disappointment was felt not only by the player himself but by historians and followers of golf everywhere. Norman had the potential to be a great player and the sport needs great players. But once again he promised more than he actually produced.

In contrast, Calcavecchia has shown little before or since to suggest that he is destined to be a major figure in the game. Yet that is no reason to begrudge him his glory. Golf is a strange activity full of quirks and unexpected twists to which fairness and justice are irregular visitors. It is a sport for opportunists. When the chance came along for Mark Calcavecchia, he took it . . . twice.

A Burnt-out Case

The moment a tall, handsome Australian broke through the throng of excited spectators on the final fairway of Royal Birkdale to stride expectantly towards his place in history, the world of golf prepared to welcome a new superstar.

There was something special about Ian Baker-Finch. He had style, charm, a film star's looks and a golf game sent from the gods. Nobody could deny his right to the 1991 Open Championship. And as he strolled imperiously to the title on that sunny afternoon in Lancashire, he displayed all the qualities of a man capable of stepping up to join the sport's élite.

But it is fortunate that we do not know our destiny. Luckily for Ian Baker-Finch, as he breathed the sweet aroma of success, he neither knew nor deserved the fate which awaited him. Instead of standing on the threshold of greatness he was to suffer a torment, in playing terms, of the cruellest kind. Golf's equivalent of pulling out toenails with red-hot tweezers. He became a champion who could no longer play the game, at least not in a competitive environment. He was a player trapped by the strange psychological tricks golf can inflict on its hapless victims. The fact that the curse should strike a man who had debunked the theory that nice guys never win merely made his situation sadder to a sympathetic world, willing but unable to provide effective help.

Until he slid from the top of the mountain, Baker-Finch's story had been a heartening saga of a mild colonial boy revealing the steely determination needed to shake off adversity and get there in the end. The youngest of six children, Ian grew up on his father's 20-acre farm in the tiny farming and sawmill settlement of Peachester, on the Sunshine Coast of Queensland. His grandfather, a London solicitor named Arthur, was the first Baker-Finch. He emigrated to Queensland in 1911, returned to Europe to fight in the First World War and later resettled in Australia. He had been given the name Baker by his mother, who wanted to preserve the name of her deceased first husband, and Finch from his father.

He got into golf by playing in the paddock with his father, Tony, using ice-cream tins for holes and dreaming that he was competing against Tom Watson and Jack Nicklaus. He helped the locals create their first nine-hole Beerwah course, playing his part as a lanky little kid by picking up pine cones and twigs from the flat, swampy terrain. He soon displayed a natural talent for the game and at 14 had beaten the adults to take the Beerwah Club Championship. A year later he won the Queensland schoolboy championship and then quit school to begin his professional apprenticeship on the nearby Sunshine Coast.

It took him a long time to make his breakthrough as a player, at 22 winning the New Zealand Open. But, significantly, the promising youngster caught the eye of Peter Thomson, the five-times Open champion and father figure of Australian golf. Thomson invited him to Melbourne for a fortnight around the Christmas holiday to undergo a master class in some of the finer points of the game. He learned, for example, how to play the punch shot under the wind and improve his putting on the true fast greens of the area.

Next, on the recommendation of Greg Norman, Baker-Finch headed for Europe to gain more valuable experience on the tour's variety of courses and conditions. Although it was intended as part of his golfing education, Baker-Finch made an immediate impression. He finished fourth in his second event, in Monte Carlo, and fourth again a week later in the Glasgow Open.

Yet nobody, least of all the man himself, was prepared for the impact he was to have on the sporting world at St Andrews in the summer of 1984. Still only 23, he went round the Old Course in 68 and 66 to lead the Open by three shots at the halfway stage. After three rounds he was still in the lead but now jointly with Tom Watson, his hero from those schoolboy days in the paddock. Last out on the final day, Baker-Finch put his second shot into the Swilcan Burn, finished up with a 79, for ninth place, and wept. He felt he had let down the Australian public who had stayed up through the night to watch him on television. He insisted his failure – which was hardly a shock, given the circumstances – was technical rather than mental. But he had arrived on the world stage and the intriguing question was whether he had the lasting talent to stay there.

The answer came gradually but was eventually an emphatic 'yes'. Over the next five years Baker-Finch won in his native Australia, Sweden, Japan and America. By 1990, at the age of 30, he had served his apprenticeship and was ready to challenge for the Open once more. Back at St Andrews he was again in the last group on the last day, courtesy of a magnificent third round of 64. But this time the pressure was off. He was five adrift of his playing partner Nick Faldo, then at the peak of his powers, who went on to win the championship by five strokes. Nonetheless, Baker-Finch, who carded a 73 to finish sixth, used the day well. Just as Thomson had given him an invaluable technical insight, so Faldo, the ultimate pressure player, showed him how a champion handles the final day of a major championship.

A year later he was to put that lesson to devastating effect. Arriving at Birkdale he was in good form. By now a resident in Florida and playing on the US Tour, he had finished seventh in the US Masters, won a two-day invitational event at Oakmont, twice been runner-up in the New England Classic and only the previous week had lost a play-off for the same event to Bruce Fleisher, a 42-year-old club pro, at the seventh extra hole. In some critics' eyes this was further evidence that he lacked the killer instinct of champions. Ian Baker-Finch may have been a fine player but he was too nice a guy to win an event as big as the Open, they said.

For the first two days of the 120th Championship it looked as if the doubters were right. Baker-Finch was not a factor. He was just cruising along. But there was significant merit in his unnoticed first two rounds of 71. In the first, when calm conditions had allowed Seve Ballesteros to take the lead with a 66, the Australian was heading for a high number when he hauled himself back into the pack by making birdies at the last two holes. That important recovery left him in 20th place, five shots off the lead. The second day was a test of who could cope with a battering from fierce winds and still return a good score. Baker-Finch passed the test after again fighting back from three dropped shots in the first six holes. At the end of the second day he had slipped to 27th place but moved a shot closer to the new leader Mike Harwood, whom he trailed by four. Ballesteros could do no better than a 73, dropping out of the lead.

Saturday is known to be moving day. Baker-Finch made his move. Like a big cat stalking his prey, he suddenly came charging from the undergrowth with three birdies in the first five holes on his way to a course record 64, which included a spectacular eagle-birdie finish. The score was the same as he had posted in the third round at St Andrews to put himself in the final group on the final day. The difference this time was that instead of being five behind, he was sharing the lead with Mark O'Meara, his neighbour and good friend from Florida, who had overcome a sore back to create his own best chance of a first major championship.

As he faced the situation for the third time, had anything else changed? He believed so. Baker-Finch had been taking guidance from the American sports psychologist Bob Rotella, who had imbued him with such positive thoughts as 'Always try to hole every shot'. As the player explained, 'He was talking about every shot from 100 yards in. Since I've seen him, I've never thought about just getting the ball up and down, never.'

His psychological state was also helped by bag carrier Pete Bender, who had shepherded Greg Norman to victory in the 1986 Open. 'Pete's the best caddie in the world,' he said. 'He keeps me in today. He keeps me in the present.'

As Sunday morning dawned, Baker-Finch was relaxed. He woke early in his rented house in Southport, fed breakfast to his two-year-old daughter Haley and for two hours played with her in the garden. When he met his buddy O'Meara in the locker room, the American greeted him with the view, 'It's a great draw – let's go and do it.' But which of them would it be?

In the eyes of the public, Ballesteros was the favourite. The Spaniard had first hit the headlines at Birkdale in 1976 when, as an unknown 19-year-old, he had been runner-up to Johnny Miller. Now 15 years on and recognised as one of the world's greatest players with five major championships behind him, he was back to complete unfinished business. Only two shots behind Baker-Finch and O'Meara, he had offered an opinion before the final round which many observers considered to be an unsubtle attempt at gamesmanship. 'The leaders are not afraid of me,' said the Spaniard. 'Probably they are afraid of the trophy. I'll wait for them to fall.'

The scene on the practice ground reflected the public's support for that theory. Even though Baker-Finch was the joint leader and wearing a bright pink shirt he was virtually unnoticed, while a throng gathered around Ballesteros, whose swing was being carefully monitored by leading coach David Leadbetter.

But Baker-Finch had acquired a strengthened resolve. 'I'll remember the pain of '84 and the experience of last year – and I'll do it,' he said. Crucially, too, he did not need any last-minute tune-up. As Bender later revealed, 'Ian never missed a shot on the range. I knew he was on form and the cream was going to stay at the top.'

Bender was right and Ballesteros was wrong. So wrong. Seve was the one to falter, dropping two shots in the first three holes, while Baker-Finch raced away and was never caught. In one of the best starts a champion has ever made to the last round of a major championship, the six-foot-four-inch bespectacled Aussie birdied five of the first seven holes to reach the turn in 29, having no problems with the spongy greens which leading players from Jack Nicklaus to Ian Woosnam had been criticising all week.

Although he dropped a shot at the tenth, it served merely as a timely warning to maintain his form and concentration right to the end. Only if Baker-Finch's nerve failed him could he lose the biggest prize in golf. It didn't and he didn't. A masterly round of 66 took him to a two-shot victory over his compatriot Mike Harwood, who made up ground with a 67.

But on his imperious march to collect the old claret jug, the champion still had to endure a drama on the final hole. The ceremonial stampede which, at the time, was part of Open Championship folklore was so unruly that O'Meara was sent crashing to the ground and Baker-

Finch was left badly shaken. He hit a bad drive and made a closing bogey, which was not the way a classic round was meant to end. 'I hate making excuses for hitting bad shots,' he said. 'But I felt like I was being stampeded.'

The happiness Baker-Finch experienced that day – as the television viewers saw two-year-old Haley try to lick a microphone she thought was an ice-cream – endeared him to a watching world. He was a man with everything and surely set up for life.

Sadly, no. In one of the most heart-rending declines in modern sport, the Open champion went through a very public collapse. Sensing, perhaps wrongly, that he was on the verge of greatness, Baker-Finch set out to improve his swing and make himself better. Especially he wanted to hit the ball further. Instead he lost everything.

As he lengthened his swing he developed an ugly snap hook. Not all the time but often enough to wreck his card. Then his confidence went and his nerve followed. He was also paying for being Mr Nice Guy, who could not say no. So many people wanted a piece of his time and he was too willing to accommodate them all.

As the downward spiral set in, Baker-Finch tried everything without knowing what was best. He tried hypnosis, self-hypnosis and telephone hypnosis. He took on new caddies, old caddies, even legendary caddies like Bruce Edwards. He had knee surgery and corrective eye surgery. His list of coaches was endless: David Leadbetter, Mitchell Spearman, Butch Harmon, Hank Haney, Jim Flick, Rick Smith, Chuck Cook, Robert Baker, Gary Smith, Ian Triggs and all seven of his own coaches at the Pure Golf Academy on Australia's Gold Coast, near Brisbane. He left Rotella, who had helped him win the Open, and tried sports psychologist Dick Coop and Jim Loehr. None of it worked.

For a long time Baker-Finch refused to give up, although many wished he would at least take a break. They hated to see what he was going through, as one humiliation followed another. At the 1995 Open Championship at St Andrews, when partnered by none other than Arnold Palmer, he pulled his opening tee-shot out of bounds across one of the widest fairways in the sport. Because it was Arnie's farewell Open, the galleries were massive. But that was nothing compared to the agony of the 92 he suffered in the opening round of the 1997 Open at Royal Troon, which left him a shattered wreck.

At the end of that year he decided, at last, to step back, do some TV commentary and put an end to the torture. He had missed 32 consecutive cuts on the US Tour, made only one cut in three years and, since May 1994, earned only $20,000 world-wide. When the Open Championship returned to Royal Birkdale, the scene of his greatest triumph, in July 1998, Ian Baker-Finch was there – but as a commentator, no longer able to trust himself on the course with a club in his hands. 'The tension is out of my body,' he reported. 'I'm having so much fun.' At 37 he was refusing to talk of complete retirement, although his friends and his wife Jennie wished he would.

Back in 1984, after he had messed up the final round of the Open at 23, he had wept for an hour. 'It was painful but also the start of it all,' he said.

By a cruel twist of fate, when he walked down the 72nd hole at Royal Birkdale in a state of euphoria seven years later, it signalled the end of it all. Or, at least, the beginning of the end.

The Iceman Reaches Meltdown

The public was accustomed to seeing Nick Faldo in many guises as he climbed onwards and upwards towards a pinnacle of achievement unsurpassed by a British golfer. This single-minded man with an indefatigable work ethic was, in turn, the steely-eyed competitor, the relentless pursuer, the tight-lipped loser, and the smiling, trophy-hugging champion. Always, it seemed, a sportsman in control of his emotions.

Yet the picture the tall Englishman presented to the world on the final green of the 1992 Open Championship offered such a new insight as to be positively shocking. In the moment of arguably his finest victory Nick Faldo, the ultimate Mr Cool, was a distraught, broken figure crumbling before our eyes under the strain of the most nerve-battering pressure his sport can offer. For just a few seconds Faldo's guard dropped as he bent like an arthritic pensioner to retrieve his winning putt from the hole, his face contorted in pain from the sheer stress of a gut-wrenching finale.

Within minutes the champion golfer of the year was to break down and sob uncontrollably in the privacy of the scorer's hut, hidden from the eyes of the startled spectators. But they had seen enough. They had been left in no doubt about just how much this victory, this courageous comeback, meant to Nicholas Alexander Faldo and what it had taken out of him. Even though he had won the Open twice before and this was his fifth major championship, the importance of not losing an event he had dominated almost throughout was, on Faldo's own admission, so vital to his future well-being and self-belief. Had he thrown it away, who knows what the effect on him would have been? And he so nearly did.

For this was a tournament that the 35-year-old from Hertfordshire had in his pocket for three rounds and even with nine holes to go still looked incapable of conceding. Yet in an absorbing final 90 minutes Faldo and his supporters went through the terrors of a climber losing his grip on the side of the mountain. Just when it seemed he was about to plunge on to the rocks below, a mighty effort of will enabled the desperate man to grab a lifeline and amazingly scramble his way up to the summit.

At the time Faldo was at the peak of his powers. The teenager who gave up cycling and swimming after being spellbound by television pictures of Jack Nicklaus winning the 1972 US Masters had grown into the undisputed No. 1 in the world. He had done so by enhancing an innate natural ability with a monk-like dedication comparable to a champion in any sport. He shared the same philosophy as Olympic decathlon champion Daley Thompson, who used to train on Christmas Day to ensure he did not lose the edge over his rivals. In the process Faldo gained a reputation as a loner, a man who did not seek the casual friendship of fellow professionals. They were not essential to his grand plan of being the best player he could possibly be.

Many would have been proud of the rapid rise which took him from English amateur champion at 18 to a place in the Ryder Cup team as a 20-year-old and a seventh-place finish in the Open the following season. But while his development proved he had enormous potential, this was not enough for Faldo. When, five years later, he could finish no higher than eighth in the Open after fading with a last-round 73 to trail winner Tom Watson by five shots, the seeds of a dramatic reconstruction of his game were already being sown in his mind.

It takes a special character to scrap his swing and effectively start again, particularly when he is No. 1 in Europe at the time. But Faldo found in David Leadbetter a teacher in whom he had absolute trust and agreed that the only way to move to the level of Watson, Seve Ballesteros and his original hero Nicklaus was to place his future in the coach's hands.

The brave decision was to hurt for a while. When Faldo made the change in 1985 he dropped to 42nd in the European Order of Merit and could only watch from the sidelines as his old rival Sandy Lyle beat him to the Open Championship, becoming the first Briton to claim the title for 16 years. Although he maintained his Ryder Cup record by appearing for the fifth successive time, Faldo again had to look on as others stole the glory in Europe's historic victory at The Belfry which ended 28 years of American domination. Captain Tony Jacklin used him in only two matches and Faldo did not contribute a single point.

But his blind faith was to prove fully justified. By 1987 the revamped, tighter swing was ready to stand up to the pressure of final stages of a major championship. The day after his 30th birthday Faldo won the Open Championship at Muirfield, famously playing all the last 18 holes in par to cement his reputation as a relentless grinder. Yet once again the triumph was not enough.

The golfer who was to become the greatest ever to emerge from the British Isles merely reset his sights and aimed higher. The US Masters title of 1989 was followed by a stellar year of 1990, when he became only the second player to defend the Green Jacket successfully before going on to win his second Open Championship at St Andrews.

And so to 1992. When the year began, Faldo's position as the pre-eminent player of his era was confirmed by his record in the majors, which revealed that he had the lowest scoring average for two of the past three years. He was to underline that position emphatically over the ensuing 12 months, which he ended as the unrivalled No. 1 in the world rankings. His domination of his sport was emphasised by the fact that the gap to No. 2 Fred Couples was the same as the gap between Couples and the player ranked 16th (Corey Pavin). During the year Faldo had 19 top-ten finishes from 27 starts and won six times. Nobody was surprised, therefore, when he swept into a commanding lead after three rounds of the Open Championship.

Following a disappointing year by his standards in 1991, Faldo had set himself two goals: to get back to No. 1 in the world and to win a major championship. His renewed ambitions sounded an ominous warning to the other players. A fourth place in the US Open at Pebble Beach a month earlier was a clue that he was running into form. Fond memories of Muirfield, where he had won his first Open five years earlier, and favourable conditions encouraged Faldo to produce memorable rounds of golf over the first three rounds.

After driving into a fairway bunker to bogey the first hole of the tournament, he recovered to a five-under-par opening round of 66 which left him in fifth place, two shots behind the joint leaders Raymond Floyd and Steve Pate.

A second-round 64 left Faldo with a three-shot lead at the halfway stage and in buoyant mood. Never a man to blow his own trumpet, he hailed his play that day as the best round he had ever played in the Open. 'I just felt so good inside,' he said, 'and I kept hitting really good shots, so I thought, "Let's keep rolling on." No matter what club I had in my hand, it felt just right. I've never had that feeling over a whole round. When you consider where we are and what we're doing, and that every shot is marked in history, it really is unique.'

The bookmakers reduced his odds to 4–7 on, and when he kept up the pressure with a third-round 69 to increase his lead to four shots, the odds were slashed still further to 1–7.

The final day was set up as a lap of honour, a seemingly inevitable repeat of his 1990 victory at St Andrews where Faldo led by five going into the last 18 holes and duly won by five with no hint of an upset. The chasing group, led by Pate and compatriot John Cook, paid lip service to their chances but did not really believe they had the slightest hope. As Pate honestly admitted, 'There's no one I like to give a four-stroke lead – and least of all Nick Faldo.' Cook agreed. 'If there's anyone who doesn't beat himself, it's Nick Faldo,' he said.

How little they knew. How little any of us knew.

For nine holes the script had a few twists and turns without promising a surprise ending. Faldo again drove into the fairway bunker on the first to drop a shot but was more troubled by his irons, which rarely threatened the flag and lacked the authority that had so enthused him during the second round.

Still, it hardly seemed to matter because his pursuers were not taking advantage. Cook, an engaging father of three from California, did have the chance to close within a shot of the leader if he could birdie the par-five ninth hole. Instead he drove out of bounds and took a double-bogey seven to remain four shots behind the favourite as he turned for home. When Faldo in the group behind parred the ninth, he was three ahead of his playing partner Pate and four ahead of Cook and Jose Maria Olazabal of Spain, who came charging into contention with a final-round 68 (and was eventually to finish third).

But then Faldo's errant form was suddenly to grab him by the throat. He pulled a simple pitch into a greenside bunker at the 11th and dropped a shot. Another dribbled away when he three-putted the 13th from 30 feet for another bogey.

The tension was now beginning to drain his handsome features, which were screwed up in dismay on the 14th tee when he drove into a steep fairway bunker. Unable to reach the green in two, he dropped his third shot in four holes to lose the lead in the tournament. The old claret jug was slipping through his fingers.

While Pate had offered the early threat, Cook was the man who surged to the front. With perfect timing, the American birdied the 15th from six feet and the 16th from 20 feet. He had moved to 12 under par and was two shots ahead of Faldo with two holes left to play – a stunning swing of six shots in seven holes.

'I knew it was going to be tough and somehow I was making it tough,' Faldo recalled later, 'so I said to myself, "Somehow you had better play the best four holes of your life – right now."' And, somehow, he probably did.

From the middle of the 15th fairway Faldo hit one of the shots of his career, a knocked-down five-iron that pitched short of the green but ran on down the slope and kept rolling until it stopped barely three feet from the flagstick. He had been working on just such a shot with Leadbetter in preparation for the demands of links golf and the hours of practice were about to reap a rich harvest. For the resulting birdie did not simply cut the lead to a single shot, it also put the pressure firmly on Cook's shoulders. The game was back on.

The advantage seemed to have swung back to the 34-year-old former US amateur champion when he struck a fine three-iron to the green of the par-five 17th to set up the chance of an obvious birdie. But after his 30-foot eagle effort had slipped two feet past the hole, Cook brought a gasp of amazement from the crowd as his 'gimme' putt for birdie hit the left lip and spun out. In terms of crucial missed tiddlers, it compared with Craig Stadler's at the 1985 Ryder Cup and Scott Hoch's in the 1989 US Masters.

Now Faldo could catch him if he could succeed where Cook had just failed. He safely negotiated the par-three 16th despite overshooting the green and then kept his promise to himself to play immaculate golf. A sweetly struck four-iron found the heart of the 17th green to leave him a 20-foot putt for an eagle which could put him back in the lead.

By this time Cook was playing the 18th with the tension mounting and spectators desperately trying to divide their attention between the two holes. Those watching on television were able to keep fully in touch with every moment of the drama, while those at the course anxiously peered at the scoreboards and listened for the tell-tale roars of approval or dismay.

As Faldo purposefully strode towards the 17th green, Cook unleashed a well-struck drive down the 414-yard final hole and found the fairway. His approach to the green was 200 yards into a slight head wind, which left him unsure of whether to hit his customary three-iron or take the two-iron instead. Eventually he opted for the two-iron but did not commit fully to the shot and pushed it right into the crowd. As Faldo crouched over his eagle putt, spectators listening on portable radios heard of Cook's botched approach and a murmur went through the crowd. Although their hero subsequently missed his eagle opportunity he safely holed out for a birdie to draw level and the fans knew that their man was back on course for glory.

Cook, needing to get down in two from the rough, was given a free drop in an area trodden down by spectators and played a neat pitch to ten feet past the flag. Facing the most important putt of his life, the American winner of three tournaments that year saw the biggest one of all slip away as the ball stayed out. Given the chance of his first major championship, the stunned challenger finished five, five when he should have taken four, four and he would regret it for the rest of his life.

Faldo had been given the chance to redeem himself. Yet the tension was far from over. An immaculate drive was followed by an equally good three-iron right on line for the flag which ran through the green to stop on the back fringe. This was no certain two-putt. But Faldo coaxed a slick downhill slider to within two feet of the cup. In the circumstances it was wonderfully well controlled, leaving a tap-in to complete the ultimate comeback.

At that moment Faldo was overcome, his emotions spilling out like never before. People could hardly believe it. Not of Nick Faldo. Yet he certainly made people stop and think. Why shouldn't he break down? Why shouldn't the strain have destroyed his composure? He had achieved something truly extraordinary, while being torn apart inside.

'Around 11, 12 and 14 I went to the edge of seeing what failure was – real failure,' he would explain later. 'If it had gone wrong in the end and been a disaster and I had lost, it would have been a tough one to live with.

'I've been very lucky and avoided the major scars in this game. When I lie in bed at night and think about it, it's amazing how it all turned around. I suppose it's part of my make-up. I'd been working on a better mental approach and it was just down to how much you want the darn thing. I was able to put all those mistakes behind me and really pull myself back together. I managed to set myself a goal to go and birdie the last four holes. Just go and do it. And I near as damn did it.'

Some people have said that Cook blew his chance and handed the title to Faldo. But they surely miss the point. Perhaps the Brit was fortunate that the man who came to the front was not Nicklaus, Watson or Ballesteros, who might have handled the pressure more successfully. Yet that same pressure was being applied by the eventual champion, who was a thoroughly deserving winner. In assessing the merit of the victory, his form over the first three days should not be forgotten, and his play on the final four holes surely never will be.

The day Nick Faldo starred in the Great Escape he added to his stature and allowed his fans a rare peep into his soul. From this moment on, they felt they knew the man just a little better.

Failing by Numbers

As with a dame, there is nothing like a scoreboard. In both cases they can have a strange, unnerving effect on people who examine them too closely. But history tells us that, equally, you ignore them at your peril.

Jesper Parnevik blanked them (scoreboards, that is) at the 1994 Open Championship and may even have lost the title as a result. What he certainly achieved was to launch a widespread debate into the tactic of ignoring the on-course scoreboards during the final round of a major championship.

The overwhelming verdict was that the eccentric Swede got it hopelessly wrong. It may be acceptable for a nervous amateur, playing in his club's monthly medal, to blot out all details of his card until the round is over for fear of being adversely affected by knowledge of his progress. But for the professionals it is different. Nobody would deny that the information a player receives by looking at the names and numbers provided for public consumption may induce a feeling of excitement. Yet the champion knows how to deal with those emotions. Part of winning is handling the adrenaline in the final, tense moments of the tournament.

It is the same in any sport. A batsman must go through the nervous nineties to reach a century and, of course, he knows his total throughout. A showjumper knows when he must perform a clear round to win. A tennis player knows when he must serve for the match. Why should a golfer be any different? To pretend that ignorance of the situation is a solution is to withdraw from a crucial stage of the contest. By simply going out to do his best and then hoping for the best, a player is not fully entering into the competition.

For that reason Parnevik earned little sympathy when he lost a thrilling championship on the 72nd hole, partly because he was unsure of what was required. But the Scandinavian's lack of tactical sense should not be allowed to obscure the achievement of Nick Price, who produced one of the great finishes of modern times to secure the 123rd Open Championship. Nick Faldo's comeback in 1992 at Muirfield featured two birdies in the last four holes to overhaul the faltering John Cook. Price did even better, playing the final three holes in three under par to snatch a victory that had seemed Parnevik's for the taking.

The outcome disproved the theory that nice guys never win. Sometimes they do, and sometimes they finish runner-up as well. For Price and Parnevik shared a distinction of being not only fine players but two of the most likeable professionals around at the time.

But that was where the similarity ended. Price was a conventional, short-back-and-sides, collar-and-tie kind of guy. Parnevik was wacky in the extreme. The son of Sweden's most famous comedian was prone to bizarre habits and irregular behaviour. If he was not turning the peak of his cap back to look like a cross between Greg LeMond and Norman Wisdom, he was chewing volcanic dust to improve his blood. A man who once jumped fully clothed into the lake beside the 18th green at St Mellion after a round of 87 later developed the trademark in victory of holing the final putt with a corpulent Havana protruding from his mouth.

Any visions he might have had of a similar celebration in Ayrshire that Sunday afternoon were, though, to disappear in the confusion of drama and misunderstanding. From the beginning the two men, who fought the good fight to the finish, were threatening figures as they took advantage of favourable conditions. Like the other competitors, Price and Parnevik were happy to be spared the vicious winds and rain which had featured so prominently in Greg Norman's 1986 victory at Turnberry, when level par was good enough to claim the old claret jug.

After the first round Parnevik (68) trailed the leader, Greg Turner of New Zealand, by three, with Price usefully placed a further shot back. The Zimbabwean, who had made his major championship break-through two years earlier at the age of 35 when he won the US PGA Championship in St Louis, had taken his game to a higher level. He arrived at the championship with four wins on the US Tour behind him and was to finish the year as the undisputed No. 1 in the world. At Turnberry the golfing community was just starting to learn how good he had become.

Crowd favourite Tom Watson, chasing a record-equalling sixth Open Championship, kept up the pace in the second round with a 65 which launched him to the top of the leaderboard on seven under par 133. The notorious putting problems of the Huckleberry Finn figure from Kansas City were to take their toll as Watson faded to finish in a share of 11th place. But his many British fans enjoyed the 45-year-old's time back in the spotlight.

Parnevik moved into closer order with a 66, which left him just a stroke behind Watson, while Price matched his score to lurk two off the pace.

In the third round another popular figure, Fuzzy Zoeller, the whistler from Indiana who won the 1979 US Masters, jumped out of the pack with a 64 which moved him into a share of the lead with fellow American Brad Faxon on nine under par 201. Price made up his one-shot leeway on Parnevik with a 67 to the Swede's 68 and the two men went into the final day on the same score of 202 – just one shot off the lead. Like athletes in a 1500 metres race they had paced their challenge perfectly, never too far back from the leaders, and were now poised on the shoulder of the pacemakers to make their surge for the line.

It is an old golfing adage that every major championship is won on the back nine on Sunday. Some of the runaway victories of recent years make a nonsense of that argument. Yet it is true most of the time. In this Open Championship Jesper Parnevik both won and lost the event over Turnberry's inward half. He was merely jogging along for the first half of the last round but then amazingly went into overdrive. After playing the first ten holes in a desultory one over par, the former Scottish Open champion began rolling in putts from all over the place to birdie five of the next seven holes and find himself walking down the final hole in the Open Championship with a two-shot lead. The only problem was that Parnevik did not know. How could he, unless someone told him? He had been studiously keeping his eyes off the leaderboards scattered around the course.

Meanwhile, as the rest of the field were burned off by Parnevik's super-charged effort, Price was the only one to take up the chase. Struggling to find his best form, he kept his chances alive with some wonderful scrambling which offered proof of his pedigree. He was also keeping a close watch on the score to know what was needed.

The 410-yard 16th was a perfect example. 'I could have lost the championship right there,' Price was to admit later. 'I walked up and purposely looked at the scoreboard to see what Jesper had done. I wasn't going to try to hit the ball two or three feet from the hole. I played what I thought was a percentage shot and gave myself an opportunity to make a 10- or 12-foot putt. I hit a sand wedge in there right where I aimed. It was a percentage play but I still made the birdie.'

The scenario had a similar script to Faldo's comeback against Cook two years earlier. Price, playing behind Parnevik, was on the 17th as the leader made his way down the final hole, a 432-yard par four. After striking an excellent drive Parnevik was ideally situated to play the 18th the way Price had tackled the 16th – go for the heart of the green and take his chances on either making a safe par or holing a putt which would put the championship in the bag.

Instead, Parnevik went for the flag which was tucked on the left side of the green, inviting trouble for all but the perfectly struck approach. By eliminating any margin of error, the 29-year-old World Cup star was taking a mighty risk. For some reason he thought that nothing less than a birdie was required. How he came to this erroneous conclusion is unclear. If he was not watching the leaderboards, how could he have had a clue?

In the air the shot looked good but it pulled up in rough, short and left of the green. Parnevik had no hope of saving par and crucially dropped a shot. Price, with an obvious birdie opportunity on the 498-yard, par-five 17th, could draw level if he got down in two from 50 feet. But in one of those magic moments for which the Open is famous, he did better than that. As the downhill putt rolled ever closer to the hole, the crowd's low roar of anticipation grew in volume until it exploded like a thunderclap as the ball disappeared from view. An eagle three. What a putt. What a moment.

The likeable Zimbabwean leapt in the air and danced a jig of joy with his caddie Jeff 'Squeaky' Medlen, scarcely able to believe what had happened. In the space of a couple of minutes the tournament had been turned on its head. No longer was Parnevik the obvious winner. Now it was Price, the scoreboard watcher, who had the destiny of the championship in his hands. Unlike the shattered Swede, he knew exactly what he had to do. A safe drive was followed by a conservative six-iron to the heart of the green to leave the ball safely resting below the hole.

As Price and Medlen walked down the fairway with a champion's welcome ringing in their ears, the caddie turned to his player and said, 'This is what this game is all about. Let's make the most of it because we never know when it will happen again.' They were to prove sadly prophetic words.

But on this day the sadness belonged to Parnevik. The man who could have won — or, at least, forced a play-off — was in tears in the scorer's hut as Price safely putted out for his par to claim his first Open Championship. The Scottish Open champion, who had moved to America to make himself a better player and eventually win a major title, had been destroyed by a combination of naivety and inexperience. By keeping his head down and trying to play his own game he had repeated the mistake made by Ernie Els on the final hole of the US Open the previous month. Thinking he needed a birdie on the last, the South African took a driver off the final tee instead of a one-iron and made a bogey.

The difference, though, was that Els did not pay the ultimate price. He still finished in a tie for first place and went on to claim his first major title when he beat Loren Roberts and Colin Montgomerie in a play-off. Parnevik, on the other hand, was left to wonder what might have been. He had two excellent chances to make amends and become the first Swede to join the élite group of major champions, when he was in the final group on the last day of the Open Championships of 1997 and 1998. But each time the comedian's son came up short, failing to come as close as he had done on that fateful afternoon in Scotland when history beckoned — and he was looking the wrong way.

Price simply went from strength to strength. The following month he claimed the US PGA Championship for the second time with a runaway six-shot victory to move up the pecking order of all-time greats with his third major and was installed as World No. 1. For a year or so his fast, rhythmical swing honed under the guidance of long-term coach David Leadbetter made him The Man, a position this genuine nice guy was to lose as he struggled to cope with the pressures. Price simply could not say 'No' to the demands on his time and, as he was stretched in all directions by never-ending requests, lost touch with the cutting edge of his game.

He was also to be devastated by the loss of his caddie, Medlen, who had emerged as one of the characters of golf's travelling circus. Known to all as 'Squeaky' because of a high-pitched voice which some suggested sounded like Mickey Mouse, Medlen first found fame as the bag carrier in John Daly's fairytale breakthrough in the 1991 US PGA Championship at Crooked Stick. Daly, the ninth alternate, only gained entry into the event at the eleventh hour because Price withdrew to be with his wife, Sue, at the birth of their first child, Gregory. As a late arrival and with no caddie, The Wild Thing appointed Medlen for the week and, without having any experience of the course, went out and won the event. Medlen was even involved in controversy when he used the flagstick to point out the line of a putt, causing officials to study videotapes to decide whether a two-shot penalty was appropriate. They ruled no infringement and Daly went on to complete an improbable triumph by three shots.

A year later Medlen successfully defended the title, this time with his regular employer Price, to create his own piece of history. His feat created the unprecedented sight of a caddie giving a press conference to a gathering of hundreds of the world's media after Price's win at the Bellerive Country Club.

The bespectacled bagman was still alongside Price for both of his 1994 victories, adding to his collection of winning 18th hole flags and building the special bond that the two men shared. Amid the Turnberry celebrations, Medlen described Price as 'the nicest man I've ever worked for' and added, 'I don't know if I could caddie for someone else after working for Nick. I don't want to caddie all my life and you never know what will happen in the future. Who knows, maybe Nick and I will just stay together all the way to the Seniors Tour.'

Less than two years later Medlen was diagnosed as suffering from a form of leukaemia. With dignity and courage, he kept working while a suitable donor was sought for a bone marrow transplant. The search proved to be in vain. A transplant was eventually carried out but was unsuccessful and Medlen died at home in Ohio at the age of 43. He was remembered as a decent, honest, hard-working man who had played his part in golf's never-ending folklore.

That afternoon at Turnberry was one of his proudest. For Price, too, it was confirmation that he had finally scrambled his way to the top of the pile after enduring more than his share of setbacks. He knew just how Parnevik was feeling, having let previous opportunities slip through his fingers. In 1982, as a 25-year-old, he led the Open at Troon by three with six holes to play, became too aggressive and lost out to Tom Watson by a shot. Six years later he played well enough to take the title. But despite leading by two at the start of the final day and shooting a creditable 69, he was beaten by Seve Ballesteros's classical 65.

Nonetheless, the experience could not be bought. Price logged the good, the bad and the ugly in his memory bank, learned from his mistakes and was ready when his time came. As a dejected Jesper Parnevik left Turnberry, he could take consolation in the example of his conqueror. One day he would be back and would get it right. He had to believe that.

The Wackiest Open

Face down in the grass, a plump, slightly balding man was frantically pummelling the ground with both fists. Just the sort of scene you would expect from a father playing with his kids in the local park. Or perhaps an excited footballer whose diving header has secured a last-minute winner. But no. This was alongside the final green at St Andrews. This was at the home of golf, traditionally one of the most sacred settings in the sporting world where circumspection is the by-word.

Yet no one minded a jot. In fact, they were delighted. All around people were laughing, cheering, shaking their heads in amazement and generally enjoying a feeling of euphoria they wished would never end. For they had just witnessed a crazy, inexplicable, wonderful moment which sport has an uncanny habit of producing. In the most unlikely circumstances, Costantino Rocca had sunk a 60-foot putt to finish in a tie for first place in the 1995 Open Championship and reality had gone on an extended hike.

Although the anti-climax of a play-off remained, this was the image that will forever remain of the wackiest, most unconventional Open Championship there has ever been. It featured people who neither looked nor behaved like golfers. Pringle-sweatered, clean-cut ex-college kids with textbook swings this lot were certainly not. Instead they seemed to have been recruited from the pages of *Mad* magazine to perform their own version of *Carry On up the Eighteenth*.

The cast list was headed by a reformed alcoholic, a Maori with a piece of bone dangling around his neck, an Italian from a box-making factory, a six-foot-eight-inch Scotsman with red hair, and a Yorkshire-man named Bottomley who seemed to have turned up at the wrong tournament by mistake. Between them they created a colourful pageant filled with vivid images which was appropriately rounded off by a male streaker eluding attempts to catch him as he cavorted around the final fairway to the considerable amusement of the gallery. If it occurred on a regular basis such a scenario might be in danger of bringing into disrepute a sport which takes pride in providing order and sanity in a confusing world. But as a one-off the 124th Open Championship was a sheer delight.

In the early stages the accepted household names of golf had given the tournament a comfortable feeling of familiarity. Arnold Palmer was there to say farewell after providing the inspiration back in 1960 to revive the ailing championship and lift it towards its position of importance on the sporting calendar. So, too, were other past champions Jack Nicklaus and Gary Player, who made the cut for the 30th and 26th time respectively, Player, at 59, being the oldest to do so since the Second World War.

Sixty-five-year-old Palmer failed to survive beyond the halfway stage after shooting rounds of 83 and 75 but was given a wonderful send-off. Mark McCormack, the former lawyer who created a world-wide sports management business after taking Palmer as his first client, tracked his old friend's emotional walk down the 18th fairway with camera in hand to record the final moments. As Palmer walked off the green, Nick Faldo was one of the first to shake him by the hand and thank the great man for everything he had done. 'If it wasn't for Arnold in 1960, who knows where we'd be?' said the then five-times major winner. 'Probably down in a shed on the beach.'

Faldo, the previous winner at St Andrews in 1990, threatened to make another strong challenge after a second-round 67 left him three strokes off the lead. But Britain's greatest-ever faded with two closing rounds of 75 to finish in a tie for 40th place with a group which included British amateur champion Gordon Sherry. The tall Scot (all six foot eight inches of him) had made an impact to match his size, grabbing the headlines in the pre-tournament build-up with a hole in one at the eighth when playing alongside the legendary Nicklaus and five-times Open champion Tom Watson. Sherry was to learn how hard golf can become after he turned professional, but this week he was a happy participant in the engrossing drama.

At the end of the first round, played in mild conditions, the lead was shared by four players on 67, five under par: Watson, Ben Crenshaw, Mark McNulty and John Daly. The sentimental favourites were the veteran Americans, Watson and Crenshaw. Neither had ever won the Open at St Andrews but both were so steeped in the traditions of the Royal and Ancient game that they treasured everything about the small town in Fife. Watson, who won the last of his eight major championships 12 years before, needed one more Open to equal Harry Vardon's all-time record of six and would have loved nothing more than to have made history at St Andrews, where he had lost out dramatically to Seve Ballesteros in 1984. Golf historian Crenshaw, having claimed the US Masters for the second time in emotional circumstances three months earlier, had been in sufficiently good form to suggest he could land a victory which would bring indescribable pride to someone fascinated by the folklore of his sport.

Both men were to be disappointed. Watson immediately fell back with a second-round 76 which featured three double bogeys and eventually had to settle for a share of 31st place. Crenshaw held on until the third round for his bad score, also a 76, and he finished joint 15th.

Yet an American was to maintain his country's impressive record at golf's eternal shrine. Seven of the thirteen Open Championships held at the Old Course had gone to a resident of the United States. But none of them were remotely like John Daly. By adding his name to a list which included Bobby Jones, Sam Snead, Tony Lema and Jack Nicklaus, the hell-raiser from Arkansas, who was trying to straighten out his life, was to pull off one of the biggest upsets the event has known.

St Andrews and Daly did not match. They went together like chalk and cheese, caviar and cold chips, or royalty and an England football fan. St Andrews is old, established, quaint, mystical and approached with awe and respect. Daly was a smouldering volcano, an obsessive man capable of terrifying mood changes, who was − at the time − winning his desperate battle against alcoholism.

A tabloid writer's dream, his extraordinary life was already worthy of Hollywood treatment. Yet the story of his first major championship win at the 1991 US PGA Championship would surely have been turned down by any major studio as too far-fetched to be credible. Not even in films would the ninth alternate drive for seven and a half hours in the hope of being given the last place in the draw, arrive at his hotel shortly after midnight to find that his message light was blinking with the news that he was included, and then go out to win the tournament on a course he had never even seen before. But Daly did. And he did it by booming huge drives more than 300 yards down the course at Crooked Stick, Indiana, which such players as Nicklaus and Ian Woosnam described as the most difficult they had ever encountered.

A new star was born and he was rarely out of the headlines. For Daly's complicated life continued to be an on-going soap opera played out for the benefit of a spellbound audience. There was never a dull moment. His pregnant fiancée turned out to be ten years older than she had claimed to be, a truth which Daly discovered only after they were married. They were to part after he flew into a drunken rage at a party at their home in Colorado, with the divorce papers bizarrely being handed to the golfer at Augusta National during the US Masters. He was involved in a scuffle with another player's father, fell foul of the authorities when he picked up his ball and walked off the course in mid-round and had twice been suspended from the US Tour for his inability to control a volatile temperament.

But Daly, an engaging, honest character at his best, was box-office. Wherever he played, there was an enthusiastic section of fans who loved The Wild Thing, with his uninhibited grip-and-rip-it style. In most people's eyes, though, he was not Open Championship material. Since his breakthrough in 1991 he had won only two events in four years, never finishing higher than 37th on the US Tour, and leading up to St Andrews he had not had a single top-ten finish all year, missing eight cuts in the process. Although he had not touched alcohol for 31 months, the man who began drinking at the age of eight was still suffering withdrawal symptoms. He had the shakes and the sweats and was still enduring headaches when the Open began.

Yet for all those who dismissed his chances, he had one influential supporter, the R and A secretary Michael Bonallack. The game's foremost administrator, a respected judge having won five British amateur championships, had noted Daly's form in the 1993 Dunhill Cup at the Old Course when he played five rounds in one under par. This is a man to watch, suggested Bonallack.

By the time the second round was completed, others were taking notice of Bonallack's tip. While his three first-round co-leaders faltered, Daly held firm with a 71 to share the top place at the halfway stage with compatriot Brad Faxon and Katsuyoshi Tomori of Japan. Twenty-four hours later it was clear that the 25th Open at St Andrews would produce an unexpected winner. Not the conventional legend like a Faldo, a Ballesteros or a Nicklaus (who had won the previous three there).

In the third round Michael Campbell, a 26-year-old New Zealander, had jumped to the head of the field with an extraordinary round of 65 in gusting winds to take a two-shot lead into the last day. A Maori descended from a Scotsman who emigrated in the nineteenth century, Campbell was known as a promising player on the European Tour, having finished runner-up to Bernhard Langer in the PGA Championship two months earlier. Like Daly, the former Australian amateur champion was a long-hitting character-with-a-difference whose true potential was still to be tested. But the merit of Campbell's round could not be overrated. In tough conditions, nobody else scored better than 68, while the eventual champion was eight shots worse. Could young Campbell become the new hero the game was waiting for?

As the final day dawned, Daly was four shots off the lead and in danger of losing interest. A tendency to sulk when things went wrong had blighted his game so often that after he had slipped down to fourth place after having led for two rounds, his detractors were convinced he would continue in the wrong direction. But this particular week his mind was sharply focused.

Somebody had to win, and whoever it was would be a surprise. Perhaps it would be Rocca, whose consistent rounds of 69, 70 and 70 had moved him into second place with 18 holes left. The Italian was another fascinating figure. At Campbell's age he had barely turned professional, having spent his early working life making polystyrene boxes in the local factory in Bergamo, his home town in northern Italy.

The former caddie did not qualify for the European Tour until he was 32 but in the ensuing six years the late-comer made up for lost time, earning more than £1 million and qualifying for the European Ryder Cup team in 1993. A popular, warm-hearted man with a ready smile, he had the misfortune of being best remembered for a mistake. A three-putt on the 17th green of his singles match with Davis Love III – including a miss from two feet – was considered to be crucial to Europe's defeat at The Belfry. Before this day was through, he was to be forever associated with a putt of the much longer variety.

The key factor in the final round was the weather. High winds swept across the Fife coastline, sending scores into orbit and blowing the dreams of many off course. Faldo described the wind as the worst he had known in an Open Championship, while Nicklaus feared for the chances of Daly because of his tendency to hit the ball high. He need not have worried. The 29-year-old simply powered the ball through the elements and on St Andrews' wide fairways, where anything to the left is usually in play, was able to avoid serious trouble.

Yet for Daly to make his strength tell, the others had to falter. And obligingly they did. Steve Elkington of Australia, who was one shot ahead in third place, slipped to a 74, while two players alongside him, Corey Pavin, the newly crowned US Open champion, and Tomori, were round in 74 and 78 respectively. The most important sufferer was Campbell, the leader. As heavy rain lashed the Old Course, the young Kiwi saw his second shot at the fifth blown 100 yards off line on to the New Course. His subsequent bogey was his first for 24 holes, but when he dropped another shot at the sixth it was clear that Campbell was in for a tough afternoon. He could do no better than a 76 to finish in a share of third place, one shot behind the champion.

Alongside him on the same score was a Yorkshireman called Steven Bottomley, whose 69 was not only the best of the day but the round of his life. The 30-year-old from Bingley was a professional to whom the term 'journeyman' was a compliment. Since winning the English Schools' title he had struggled in the paid ranks, travelling around the circuit in a camper van to save money. His best season was in 1994 when he finished 119th on the European Order of Merit and he had been forced to go to the qualifying school seven times to try to retain his card.

Even in 1995 he missed 17 cuts in 29 tournaments and was to lose his playing rights on the tour two years after his Open heroics. But on that final Sunday, Steven Bottomley illogically played better golf than any of the world's top players to earn the unimaginable fortune of £65,666. His cause was helped by a 75-foot putt on the ninth green and a 65-footer at the 15th. Had he not bogeyed the Road Hole, his 71st, he would even have made the play-off for the title. And that really would have been unbelievable.

As things turned out, the actual events strained credulity. I showing commendable determination and exemplary concentra was battling his way through the wind to make up his four-st.... overnight deficit and moved into the lead with his third birdie on the eighth hole. At the turn he was two clear. As the challengers faded, the flaxen-haired heavyweight appeared to be strolling to victory. Then, with the finishing line in sight, Daly stumbled, three-putting the 16th and finding the Road Bunker at the 17th to drop two shots and offer renewed hope to his pursuers.

Rocca was the only one to pick up the baton. After a birdie at the 14th to steady a shaky beginning (in which he dropped three shots), the old boxmaker found himself one behind Daly and needing to birdie one of the last three holes to catch the leader. He went through the 16th uneventfully and then played the first of two incredible shots to save his par at the 17th. After he sent his approach over the green, Rocca's ball came to rest in a small hole on the tarmac road. All he could do was take his putter and hope for the best. As he struck the ball it hopped into the air, bounced crazily up the bank and across the green and stopped four feet short of the cup. The Italian tapped in to leave himself one last chance of glory.

The 354-yard 18th at St Andrews has been the scene of many historic moments. Who could forget Doug Sanders' missed putt in 1970? Or Jack Nicklaus peeling off his sweater to drive the green in the play-off? Now the moment had arrived for Costantino Rocca to add to its history. With the wind assisting him, the swarthy right-hander struck a superb drive across Granny Clark's Wynd to finish 40 yards from the flag.

Clearly the birdie he needed was within reach. But then – calamity. As he attempted what would normally have been a simple pitch across the Valley of Sin – a deep depression in front of the green – Rocca fluffed the shot like a fumbling amateur. The crowd let out a collective groan of disappointment and the ball bobbled barely 15 yards to the bottom of the Valley of Sin. Rocca smacked the side of his head three times in sheer frustration as spectators turned away in embarrassment. On the terrace overlooking the green, Paulette Daly gave her husband a victory hug, believing he had won. Her man wisely urged caution.

Then a strange occurrence took place. Rocca regained his composure, sized up the putt and sent the ball on its way. Up the hill it trundled, over a hump, down towards the hole. On and on. And into the cup.

Pandemonium broke out. A roar of cup final proportions rent the air and Rocca plunged to the ground, unable to contain his joy. In the space of two minutes he had gone from the depths of his most embarrassing blunder to the heights of ecstasy.

Small wonder he had nothing left for the play-off. At other times Daly would have been crushed by having the old claret jug dashed from his lips in such bizarre fashion. But on this day he was cold-eyed commitment personified. After two holes of the four-hole play-off the outcome was obvious, as Rocca three-putted the first and Daly holed from 35 feet for a birdie and a two-stroke lead at the second. A horrible encounter with the Road Bunker on the 17th (where he took three to escape) then left Rocca five behind. By the time he came down the 18th for the second time, there was no drama left.

John Daly really did become Open champion, Costantino Rocca earned a place in the affections of millions and history was suitably served. A year later, golf's most prestigious championship returned to normality.

The Rose Show

When Justin Rose walked into the clubhouse at Royal Birkdale, dusk was descending over the links – and then it dawned on the packed gathering, who were celebrating an unforgettable Open, that a young hero was in their midst. At first, for just a second or two, everything stopped, and then the crowd burst into spontaneous applause. No matter that he was too young to order a drink, no matter either that he was born in Johannesburg. They were claiming him as England's Rose.

An hour earlier Rose had prompted a huge roar from the audience around the 18th green by chipping in from 45 yards for a birdie three. 'It was a tough shot out of the rough and over a bunker and I told my caddie I was going to go for it. I had nothing to lose.'

For the 127th Open, the old silver claret jug was already overflowing with a rare vintage and about the only thing missing was that Rose's miraculous chip did not get him into the play-off. As it was, playing in his first and last Open as an amateur, his final shot was etched into the memory as emphatically as his name had been engraved on the silver medal that he received as the championship's leading amateur.

Leading amateur? Of the original field of 156 of the world's best golfers, only three, Mark O'Meara, Brian Watts and Tiger Woods, finished ahead of Rose. And the 17-year-old (he turned 18 the following week) had battled through two rounds of final qualifying at the adjoining Hillside course.

In his gracious winner's speech, O'Meara had described Rose's performance as phenomenal, a word that had become synonymous with Woods. O'Meara was not exaggerating. Sir Michael Bonallack, the outgoing secretary of the Royal and Ancient who was once Britain's leading amateur, was joint 21st at Carnoustie in 1968 and joint 22nd at Birkdale in 1971 but he did not break 70 on either occasion. When Woods finished joint 22nd at Royal Lytham in 1996, winning the silver medal as leading amateur, it was considered a notable achievement. Justin rose to the challenge at Birkdale with rounds of 72, 66, 75 and 69.

Both the R and A and the USGA are hoping that the Rose–Woods rivalry will be a feature of the game into the new millennium and beyond, even though the Hampshire teenager's introduction to professional golf was somewhat less successful than his experience at

Birkdale. During the anti-climax he suffered missed cut after missed cut.

Had he turned pro a week earlier, Rose would have won almost £70,000 for his Open exploits. 'I don't regret it one little bit,' he said. 'The whole week was unbelievable. I was put at ease by the crowd. The incredible support I received didn't give me time to be nervous. I had a lot of fun and luckily I played well.'

Strolling around the links like Just William, Rose did a lot of smiling which endeared him to the galleries. That and the fact that he was an amateur and a boy amongst men. Few people expected him to remain on the leaderboard but he handled the pressure extraordinarily well. He had the game and the temperament to cope with one of the most dramatic final rounds in the history of the championship.

'To tell you the truth, I wasn't surprised that my swing held up. It's technically pretty sound. In that kind of situation it's your mental state that gives the tell-tale sign. At the beginning of the week I just wanted to be part of it. I didn't realise I would be such a part of it. Going up the 18th I almost had the feeling of being the winner.' At least the 41-year-old O'Meara could use the claret jug for the purpose for which it was intended. It wasn't meant to be filled with lemonade.

To increase the popularity of golf, the R and A made admission free to those under 16 and 20,000 youngsters took advantage of the offer. 'Perhaps we have found a young player who can match Tiger Woods in America,' Bonallack said. 'The comparison is there because both were boy wonders. Justin's been known in junior circles almost since he could walk. British golf has been waiting for somebody after Jacklin and Faldo and in Justin we have someone who is special. Lee Westwood is the heir apparent to Faldo but he is made to look almost old by Justin. No one of that age has done that well in the Open since the days of Young Tom Morris. It is tremendous for junior golf because all the youngsters who saw Justin and Tiger will be asking their parents to let them play golf.'

The careers of Rose and Woods have both been managed and monitored at every stage by their fathers. 'He may look like a gangly kid but he is incredibly strong,' Ken Rose said. 'Just look at his hands. They are capable of strangling a tiger.'

Under normal circumstances he might have alluded to a grizzly bear but the pervasive influence of Woods is everywhere, and nowhere more so than on the career of Justin Rose. Whatever Woods did as a child prodigy, Rose, who is built like a toothpick, did it younger. It seems that he was just a twinkle in his father's eye when he was destined to make a name for himself. 'I don't want to get too philosophical about this but golf seems to have a code of ethics for life itself,' father Ken said. 'I was determined that if I had a son I would introduce him to golf at the earliest opportunity.'

Thus, almost as soon as the umbilical cord had been cut, young Justin, nappy rash or no nappy rash, was hitting a plastic ball with a plastic club. 'He was besotted with it,' Ken said. 'He became so proficient he could hit the ball 30 yards. It was like a cabaret act.' By the age of 11 months, Justin was using a proper club.

When the boy wonder was five, Ken and Anne Rose, whose parents came from London and Glasgow, moved to England from Johannesburg. 'We couldn't afford a full-time coach so I taught him the fundamentals, and that meant a very simple, basic swing. What I didn't know was what a dynamic package I had in terms of talent.'

Whatever else he does, Justin, a member at North Hants who won national under-14, under-16 and under-18 championships, will always be remembered for his extraordinary performance at the 127th Open Championship. It was more a masterpiece from a minor in his first major than a minor masterpiece.

Vintage Claret

Some days you never forget. Sometimes you are fortunate enough to be in a situation which will cause you to repeat, with moist-eyed pride, into your dotage: 'I was there.' Spectators who had the good sense to join the gallery around the 18th green at the Royal Birkdale Golf Club on the afternoon of 19 July 1998, for example, will surely never tire of describing what they saw.

The concluding day of the 127th Open Championship produced an epic contest worthy of the traditions of golf's oldest and most celebrated tournament. Yet it was the amphitheatre of the last hole which burned lasting images into the memory. Moments that make sport – both the taking part and the watching – the fascination and delight that it is to millions around the world. The essence of golf's particular appeal was perfectly demonstrated, as the ponderous, deliberate build-up of tension was like a slow-burning firework suddenly exploding into riotous, colourful excitement.

The record will show that Mark O'Meara became a worthy and stylish champion, claiming his second major title of the year at the age of 41 when he beat fellow American Brian Watts in a four-hole play-off. To do so he twice played the 472-yard 18th on that final afternoon in exemplary fashion when the pressure was at its height, producing controlled, masterful play at the right moment to prove that he really had grown into one of the outstanding professionals of his generation.

The knowledgeable supporters appreciated his talent. But they were stunned and exhilarated by other incidents which they were privileged to witness. Which was the most thrilling? Perhaps it was the final shot as an amateur played by 17-year-old Justin Rose, who pitched into the hole from 45 yards for a closing birdie to send a roar like a thunderclap echoing across Merseyside? Or maybe it was the extraordinary bunker shot of Watts, who conjured the ball to within a foot of the pin when all seemed lost to force himself into the play-off? And what about the fist-pumping celebrations of Tiger Woods after he had holed a 30-footer to keep his slim hopes of victory alive (at least for a short time)? Britain's highest-placed professional, Raymond Russell of Scotland, could not be kept out of the act either, as he struck an immaculate iron shot to three feet for a 66 to clinch his biggest cheque of the year and round off a heartening comeback from illness.

All these images from a glorious day helped to complete a championship which deserves to be remembered as one of the finest of modern times, played out in a variety of conditions testing the skill of the competitors to the full. While O'Meara emerged with distinction to be named 'champion golfer of the year', several among the supporting cast improved their reputations and perhaps even changed the course of their lives through their efforts that week.

Woods, for one, answered a lot of questions. It was hard to imagine that people would have doubted the 22-year-old former US amateur champion in view of how much he had achieved in less than two years since turning professional. But his record in the Open – the event the traditionalists class as the most important of all – had not been impressive and it was something he needed to remedy sooner or later.

His response kept his career right on course. In finishing in third place only a shot behind the champion, Woods produced the lowest scores in both the first and the fourth round, showing that he only needs the consistency that experience will surely bring. What he also revealed to British fans unaware that his three consecutive US amateur championships were come-from-behind victories was a tenacity to make every shot count and to keep fighting to the finish.

The World No. 1 shared the lead with compatriot John Huston after an opening round of 65, six under par, on a calm, windless day when this renowned stretch of Southport links was defenceless against the skills of the world's best. O'Meara, just as in his major breakthrough at Augusta three months earlier, was not a factor on the first day. After a 72 he was seven shots back in a tie for 62nd place alongside the promising English teenager Rose. Watts, a Canadian-born American who made his living on the Asian Tour, was 11th after a 68.

On Friday the wind picked up and so did the scores. Players who had enjoyed a birdie-fest a day earlier were now struggling to keep the ball in play. Huston, for example, slumped to a 77 and down to 23rd place.

The day belonged to Watts and Rose, both of whom were introducing themselves to a world-wide audience. The American was a prophet without honour in his own country, where he was unknown and unsuccessful. He was the original man from everywhere, born in Montreal, raised in Texas, educated in Oklahoma (where he kept a home) and living most of the time in Japan. The 32-year-old moved to the Far East after being unable to make the grade in America. He failed in four out of five visits to the US Tour's qualifying school and, when he could not hang on to his card two years after he finally won it, decided to seek his fortune elsewhere.

Watts had proved an undoubted success on the Japanese Tour, where he had recorded 11 victories and boosted both his bank balance and his confidence. Even so, his name at the top of the leaderboard raised more than a few eyebrows. Surely, we thought, here was a man who had never finished higher than 40th in five previous Opens and who would fade into the pack as the competition intensified over the weekend. How wrong we were.

As Rose amazed spectators and professionals with a 66 which defied the conditions, O'Meara stealthily moved into sixth place, three shots behind halfway leader Watts, with a 68 which put him alongside a dangerous trio of Jesper Parnevik, Jim Furyk and Davis Love III.

Saturday, it could be argued, was the day when O'Meara most showed his mettle. It was a fierce day when he proved his right to take possession of the old claret jug. Gales howled across England's north-west coastline at around 25 miles an hour but gusting up to 35–40 miles an hour, testing the players to the limit. The defending champion Justin Leonard laboured to an 82 and then vowed to go back to his lodgings, put his feet up and laugh at his rivals thrashing around like sailors lost in a tempest. Nick Price, who had started the day a shot off the lead, was blown out of contention after an 82, US Open champion Lee Janzen could do no better than 80 and Phil Mickleson returned an 85.

In the circumstances O'Meara's 72, which was bettered by only two players on the day, showed him to be master of even the cruellest elements. But, as the Florida-based veteran was first to admit, his round contained a moment of controversy which brought him a huge slice of good fortune.

On the 480-yard, par-four sixth hole, O'Meara took a driver for his second shot only to push it to the right into deep rough. A concentrated search by the player, his caddie and a group of spectators found two balls but neither of them was O'Meara's. With a minute to go to the end of the five-minute period allowed to find the ball, O'Meara began to walk back to take a penalty drop from where he had played his previous shot. But as he did so a shout went up: 'We've found it!' Martin Holmes, a ten-handicap amateur, had moved to a higher part of the embankment where the crowd were searching and found the ball straight away, 30 seconds inside the time limit.

O'Meara had previously described the marking on his ball to rules official Reed Mackenzie, a vice-president of the United States Golf Association, as being a Strata with his personal logo on it. Reed examined the ball and agreed that it was O'Meara's, confirmation coming soon afterwards from the player's caddie Jerry Higginbotham. By the time O'Meara arrived back at his ball to identify it himself, the five minutes had passed, prompting at least one rules expert to claim he was out of time and would have to take a penalty. O'Meara offered no argument and agreed to abide by what the officials decreed. He was nonetheless relieved to hear that under an R and A/USGA ruling, if the ball is found within the five minutes it can still be played even though the identification takes place later.

But that was not the end of O'Meara's good fortune. During the confusion over whether he was going back to replay his second shot, Holmes picked up the ball he had found and put it in his pocket. The spot where he had made his discovery was pointed out and found to have been trodden down during the search. When O'Meara tried to drop the ball it rolled more than two club lengths away and he was subsequently able to place it, perfectly legally, in a favourable position on top of the grass. 'I was lucky,' he said, 'because if the spectator hadn't picked up the ball and I'd had to play it from where it had finished I'd probably have made a six or a seven instead of a five.'

Holmes was naturally delighted that he had helped O'Meara to win the Open, wondering later whether the champion might send him a box of balls in gratitude rather than the one which Higginbotham had tossed to him at the time. But he added, 'Now that he's won the title there's no way I'm going to use the ball he gave me. I'll turn it into some kind of trophy.'

With the aid of that important break, O'Meara finished the third day on 212, two over par, two shots behind Watts, who was hanging on bravely, and level with Parnevik and Furyk, with Rose another shot back in fifth place.

As the fourth day dawned, early-morning rain softened the greens and the wind eased, although it still puffed erratically enough to cause a few problems.

If the winner was to come from the leading five, O'Meara did look the best bet. Watts was surely too inexperienced at this level, Parnevik the Swede had blown his two previous chances in 1994 and 1997, Furyk had an improving major championship record but did not look ready, and Rose . . . well, it just wasn't possible. Was it?

O'Meara had the experience and assurance from his US Masters win. And, as he was to prove, he also had the game. But there was nothing boringly predictable about the outcome, as the spectators around the 18th would readily testify. During the early sparring a pattern began to emerge which suggested that nobody was going to take control and run away with the tournament. O'Meara, playing a group ahead of Watts, wiped out the leader's two-stroke advantage on the fourth hole and the battle was joined. Both were playing solidly but not with a brilliance that ruled out the chances of someone leaping from the pack. The charge, in fact, did emerge – from two quarters, one predictable, the other more surprising. Woods and Russell both carded best-of-the-day, five-under-par rounds of 66 and fell just short of the main prize, but they produced some wonderful action in the process.

Woods had fallen back after his bright opening with rounds of 73 and 77 to begin the last day five shots back. His chances had been sabotaged on Saturday when he three-putted four times in the gales. By the time the star of the Nike commercial had reached the 15th tee he was four over par and still on the fringe of the main event.

But Tiger was not to depart without leaving the British public with something to remember. First he devoured the 544-yard, par-five 15th with two mighty blows to set up a birdie and pull back one shot. Then, after a par on the 16th, Woods tried to use his power game again on the 547-yard, par-five 17th, sprayed the ball all over the course and finished up chipping in from 30 feet for another remarkable birdie. So to the 18th, and a drive in the fairway, a four-iron to 30 feet and a putt that fell in on the left side of the hole, sparking the Tiger trademark celebration uppercut to raucous applause worthy of his homeland. Woods had played the last four holes in three under par to finish on 281, one over, and all he could do was wait. Discounting the heckling of a few unruly fans and the injury to his mother, Kultida, who sprained her ankle in a fall near the 18th green on Saturday, Woods had enjoyed his week and acquitted himself well.

Meanwhile, Russell was providing one of the heart-warming stories of the week. The 25-year-old Scot has been regarded as one of the best young prospects on the European Tour having finished in the top 20 of the Order of Merit for the previous two years. But after falling ill with hepatitis at the start of the year, the former World Cup international tried to rush back after three weeks, lost form and confidence and kept missing cuts. He went into the Open with less than £4,000 in winnings for the year, outside the top 150 and facing an uncertain future. But signs of a return to form in the Irish Open and Loch Lomond International culminated in the performance of his life to earn a share of fourth place plus a cheque for £76,666 to secure his tour card for another year.

Russell saved the best till last with a bogey-free round of 66, the highlight of which was a bunker shot which he holed from beside the 14th green. But at the 18th, too, the Edinburgh-born professional showed his class. After driving into the rough and chipping back to the fairway, he was in danger of dropping his only shot of the day until he struck a six-iron 179 yards to stop three feet from the flag and save his par. Magic stuff.

'That last hole leaves a nice taste,' said the delighted Scot. 'I finished the antibiotics five weeks ago. It was just a question of getting my attitude right. And that took a bit longer than it should have done. Hopefully we're getting somewhere near it now and this is probably the biggest thing I've ever done.

'My parents have been tremendously supportive and my girlfriend stuck by me and helped me keep calm during the worst times. It's been tough for her. I've been coming back Friday night like a raging bull, storming round the house and not calming down until Sunday morning.'

While Russell looked forward to happier days, the crowd were treated to strokes of sheer class. Rose holed his final shot from 50 yards for a closing birdie three to launch a week of hype rarely surpassed by Britain's sporting press as he headed for the professional ranks on a wave of hysteria. Watts could hardly expect the same treatment, even if the shot he pulled off was, in its own way, equally brilliant.

As the other contenders faded, the powerfully built American in the white visor had battled with O'Meara all the way. When the veteran birdied the 17th from 15 feet to take a one-shot lead, Watts holed his birdie of similar length to draw level. But down the 18th it looked like his bolt was shot. After pulling his drive into thick, tufty grass on the left, he could only force his recovery into the first greenside bunker. The ball only just reached the sand-trap, trickling in and dropping next to the back lip. As Watts weighed up his options, his task looked impossible. He was forced to stand with his left foot in the sand and his right at an awkward angle on the bank above him. To get the ball out was difficult, but to stop it near the hole was surely beyond him.

Somehow he did it. Chopping down at a steep angle, Watts lifted the ball over the front lip and on to a mound on the left edge of the green, from where it trundled down to stop a foot from the hole. He was into a play-off. 'I just tried to create something in my mind,' he said later, 'and visualised a good shot. Fortunately it came off almost perfect.' Perfection, he admitted, would have been to hole the shot in the same way that Bob Tway did to win the 1986 US PGA Championship.

Sadly for Watts, it was the one way he could have won. Rather like Costantino Rocca, whose astonishing 60-foot putt qualified him for a play-off in the 1995 Open, his finest moment was to mark the beginning of the end. For in the four-hole play-off Watts' putting let him down and O'Meara used the wisdom gained from 17 years on tour to ease to victory. The Ryder Cup veteran was ahead on the first extra hole, the 15th, when he sank a five-footer for a birdie while Watts missed from four feet. Again Watts was near at the 16th but pulled his ten-foot putt, while on the 17th he did finally hole from ten feet – but only to save par after pushing his drive into thick rough.

Back on the 18th tee, O'Meara's slender one-shot lead meant that all around people were feeling the tension. His caddie could be heard pleading, 'Everyone quiet now – and that includes the marshals!' Just as he had in normal play, O'Meara drove securely into the middle of the fairway. So, this time, did Watts. He needed to give himself the chance of a birdie to draw level, but his approach found the bunker and the game was up.

One shot would settle things. O'Meara, with 185 yards to the green, switched from a five- to a four-iron and drew the ball in right over the flagstick to finish 15 feet behind the hole. Peter Alliss, in his BBC TV commentary, described it as a 'glorious, glorious shot'.

Watts' only hope was to hole his bunker shot. He went for it, sent the ball 30 feet past the hole and finished up taking a bogey five. O'Meara, with three shots for victory, took two of them before he was engulfed by his children, Shaun, eight, and Michelle, eleven, and wife Alicia.

The 18th had taken its revenge on Brian Watts, who still walked away with a cheque for £188,000, which was enough to qualify him to play on the US Tour the following year – if he chose to. Then he would not have to stay in Japanese hotel rooms wondering whether his one-year-old son was missing him.

To the victor went the spoils and a special place in the Royal Birkdale story. Back in 1987 in the Lawrence Batley International on this same links course, he had won his first European Tour title and spectacularly holed seven-iron shots from 152 and 145 yards for two eagles in the space of six holes during his final round. Maybe that was an omen.

In the 1991 Open, despite suffering from a sore back which almost caused him not to travel, he started the final day sharing the lead with his good friend Ian Baker-Finch, only to finish third, three shots behind, despite a closing 69. He also suffered the indignity of being knocked down in the 72nd hole stampede, but at least was later to have a slurp from the claret jug back in Florida while thinking that it was, perhaps, the closest he would ever get to possessing golf's most prestigious trophy.

Recognised as a course specialist at Pebble Beach, California, where he has won five times, O'Meara had earned the right to be linked in the same way with Birkdale. 'It's an incredible feeling to win here,' O'Meara said, 'because I love this championship so dearly and Birkdale has been very special to me and my family. This is the world-wide championship. It is played on a difficult links course, in demanding conditions against great players. To have come out on top is an unbelievable moment for me.'

What's that? Great players? If the new champion had beaten some great players, did not that make him one, too? No, he was not claiming that. Just a nice player, who cared for his family.

But at 41 years, six months and six days, Mark O'Meara became the oldest player in the history of golf to win two major titles in the same year. And that had to mean something. Something pretty special.

The Masters

You can buy a country but you can't buy a golf swing

– Gene Sarazen

Sarazen's Resounding Shot

Gene Sarazen missed the first Masters in 1934 because he was touring South America. He made up for it the following year with a shot that was 'heard around the world', a phrase familiar in Concord, New England, the scene of the first hostilities in the American War of Independence.

Old champions and new champions had been invited to Augusta and Sarazen and Craig Wood were installed as favourites. In practice rounds Sarazen had scored 65, 67, 72 and 67. He was long and straight and he had confidence in his putting. He also had confidence in his caddie, a tall Negro who went by the nickname of Stovepipe because he wore a tall silk hat.

Sarazen (he changed his name from Eugene Saraceni) scored 68, 71, 73 and he trailed Wood by three shots. On the eve of the final round a friend gave Sarazen a 'lucky ring'. Although Sarazen was paired with Walter Hagen in the final round, they were followed by a small crowd. The majority were following the leaders.

At the 15th hole Sarazen hit an exceptionally long drive. As he walked to his ball he heard a roar from the 18th green. Wood had holed for a birdie three at the last and finished with an aggregate of 282, six under par. As far as the press was concerned, Wood, three strokes to the good, was the winner.

Sarazen asked Stovepipe what was needed to win. Stovepipe replied, 'Three, three, three, three.' That amounted to eagle, par, birdie, birdie. Sarazen did not have a good lie for his second shot to the 15th and he finally settled on a four-wood instead of the three. 'I knew that the only way I could reach the green with the four would be to toe the club in to decrease the loft and so give me extra yardage.'

In his book, *Thirty Years of Championship Golf*, Sarazen said that as he was standing over his ball, he was suddenly reminded of the lucky ring. He took it from his pocket and rubbed it over Stovepipe's head. 'I suppose the real contribution the ring made was that fooling with it tapered off the tension that had been building up in me. I took my stance with my four-wood and rode into the shot with every ounce of strength and timing I could muster. The split second I hit the ball I knew it would carry the pond. It tore for the flag on a very low trajectory, no more than 30 feet in the air.

'Running forward to watch its flight, I saw the ball land in the green, still dead on line. I saw it hop straight for the cup and then, while I was straining to see how close it had finished, the small gallery behind the green let out a terrific shout and began to jump wildly in the air. I knew then that the ball had gone into the hole.'

He had holed out from 235 yards at the par-five, 485-yard 15th for an albatross two, or what the Americans call a double eagle. When Sarazen reached the green the boy reporting the scores was having trouble making himself believed. The operator at the master scoreboard told the youngster he was mixed up and had obviously meant to report a two on the par-three 16th.

Having made three under par on one hole, Sarazen needed to par the last three to force a tie. He missed from ten feet for a birdie at the 16th and parred the last two, hitting a four-wood approach shot into the 18th.

The next day, when the players were blowing on their hands to keep them warm, Sarazen beat Wood by five strokes over 36 holes, 144 to 149. From the 11th hole through to the 34th, Sarazen had 24 consecutive pars. For his four practice rounds, the four rounds of the tournament and the two in the play-off (180 holes), he never had more than a five on his card.

Bobby Jones asked Sarazen if Augusta National could have the ball, a Wilson three, and the four-wood for display in the clubhouse. Sarazen hoped they would put a plaque on the spot from where he hit his shot. Twenty years later they built Sarazen's Bridge at the 15th hole.

In 1991, Sarazen, at the age of 89, opened the Masters tournament as an honorary starter by playing nine holes with Sam Snead. Sarazen never won the Masters again but Snead won in 1949, 1952 and 1954. In 1953 Ben Hogan established a record aggregate of 274, 14 under par, to win by five strokes after rounds of 70, 69, 66 and 69. Conditions were perfect and at the time Hogan was of the opinion that he played the best golf of his career. The following year he was tied with Snead on a score of 289. The two were considered to be the finest players in the world. Snead shot 72 in the final round, Hogan 75, and the former won an 18-hole play-off with a 70 to a 71.

But the tournament was not remembered solely for the exploits of the two arch rivals. Billy Joe Patton, an amateur, led after the second round and led again during the final round after a hole in one at the sixth. Despite taking a seven at the 13th and a six at the 15th, Billy Joe finished only one stroke behind the leaders. On an extremely difficult day for breaking par, Jack Burke Jnr made up a deficit of eight strokes in the final round to win the Masters in 1956. Burke shot 71 and he beat the amateur Ken Venturi, who scored 80, by one stroke. After 16 holes of the final round Burke was still behind, but at the 17th he got a birdie three and Venturi a five. Cary Middlecoff, who finished third, two strokes behind Burke and one behind Venturi, had a double-bogey six at the same hole. The previous year Middlecoff had won at Augusta by seven strokes after taking 31 on the front nine in the second round.

★ ★ ★

Before Sandy Lyle began to treat the bunkers at the 18th as if they were a mirage in a desert of green, Doug Ford produced a classic thrust to win in 1957. Playing the last, Ford held what he thought was a one-stroke lead over Snead, who was a few holes behind him. 'At the time, the green and bunkering was different from how it is today,' Ford recalls. 'They had the pin on the front left and we all tried to stay short on that hole because it was so fast coming from behind the flag. I hit my seven-iron approach a tad fat and the ball buried in the top of the bunker on the left. I buried it about six inches from the top. I exploded the shot so that it went up the hill to the left of the flag. I only pitched it about five or six feet out of the bunker and it ran about ten feet before making a U-turn. It rolled back down the hill and into the hole. It was kind of a pool player's shot.'

Ford said he went for it. 'I played that shot. At that time I was as good a bunker player as there was around. I never feared the bunker and I was an exceptionally good buried bunker player. I had a great feel for a ball buried in a bunker. I don't know why but ... that's the shot I played.'

The birdie three at the 18th gave Ford a final round of 66 which put him from one over par to five under, and nobody could match it. 'I never thought that was the shot that won it for me. At the 15th I had to hit two of my best shots.' Ford had birdied the 15th, hitting a three-wood across the water. Although he was on the leaderboard after the third round, he was out early and his score of 283 was posted by lunchtime, 20 minutes before television came on the air. 'I was fortunate,' Ford said. 'The field was pretty well spread out and I knew I had a chance.'

His victory was sandwiched between two Masters in which he was not so fortunate. In 1956 he shot 42 on the back nine, six over par, and finished five shots adrift of Jack Burke. He was in the thick of it again in 1958. Arnold Palmer had posted a score of 284 and that included a confusing three at the 12th. He had embedded his tee-shot in the bank at the front of the green. He played his original ball, scored five and then dropped another ball close to where the first had come to rest. With the second ball Palmer scored three and it was that score that counted. A local rule, introduced after heavy overnight rain, allowed him a free drop.

'I came to the last knowing I had to make a three,' Ford said. 'I hit a beautiful drive and a six-iron just to the right of the flag, six feet away.

The pin was in the same place where I had made three the year before.' Ford's putt to tie with the 28-year-old Palmer caught the top lip of the hole and spun out. But for a fraction of an inch, Ford, who won the US PGA Championship in 1955, might have been the first player to win the Masters in successive years.

As it was, winning it once, Ford said, made no big impression on his career. 'We had other tournaments. The Western Open was a bigger event in the '50s. The Masters has become one of *the* tournaments because the media has made it. When I won at Augusta, the US PGA and the US Open were the most prestigious events for a player to win. They gave you a lifetime pass into all our tournaments. I would say the Masters is number two in America. I think the British Open should be ahead of the Masters. But they can make anything if they get the right press. They've done a hell of a job. You can't fault them.' And the 18th? 'It's a great finishing hole. The fellow that hits the high ball has a hell of an advantage.'

Palmer won again in 1960 and it might have been three in a row but for an astonishing recovery by Art Wall in the 1959 Masters. Wall was six shots behind Palmer and Stan Leonard going into the last round yet he won the tournament by a stroke. He shot 66 which included eight birdies, five of them in the last six holes. Palmer shot 74, Leonard 75. Wall was ignored by the television cameras, which were focused elsewhere.

In 1960 Palmer led the field at the end of each round, the only player to do so since Craig Wood in 1941. By now Arnie's Army was on the move and people were queuing to enlist. In fact he owed his lead to an act of sportsmanship by Dow Finsterwald. After missing a putt, he threw the ball back onto the green and tried again. Practice putting was not allowed on the US Tour but Finsterwald thought it was permissible in the Masters. No one had taken a blind bit of notice. When he learned that it was an infringement, Finsterwald reported the incident to officials. He was penalised two strokes, turning his second round of 68 into a 70. He missed tying with Palmer by two strokes.

On the final day, the leader in the clubhouse was Ken Venturi, who finished with a 70 for 283. Palmer needed two birdies from the last two holes for outright victory. At the 17th he got down from 35 feet for a birdie three. 'On the 18th tee a tie was the furthest thing from my mind,' Palmer said. 'I hit a solid drive into the wind down the middle and punched a six-iron under the breeze.' The ball stopped five feet from the pin. 'At that point in my career it was probably the most important putt I'd ever faced and I was very nervous. I read it to break about three or four inches from left to right, stroked it smoothly and watched it catch the left side and drop in.'

★ ★ ★

The Masters again went down to the wire in 1961 when Gary Player, at the age of 25, became the first overseas competitor to win at Augusta National. Player is convinced he did so thanks in no small part to a tenet he received from Billy Graham while he and Graham relaxed in a jacuzzi at the evangelist's home the week before the Masters.

'He gave me a great insight into adversity and how it fits into God's scheme for us,' Player wrote in *Golf Begins at Fifty*. 'In fact without this lesson I would never have won the Masters in 1961. He asked why I had become so successful so early in life and I told him that I was convinced that it was all due to three of my basic beliefs: faith in God, faith in the value of education and faith in physical fitness.

'He thought about that for a while, then said, "I know how badly you want to win the Masters. Now, when you're playing in the tournament I want you to thank God for all the bad shots and all the difficulties you encounter. Any man can thank God for the good things that happen to him but very few can say thank you for the lousy things."'

With rounds of 69, 68 and 69, Player led Arnold Palmer by four strokes on the final day and was still four ahead when he came to the 13th. He pushed his drive into the pine trees on the right, hit a two-iron into the creek, had three putts and took a double-bogey seven. He also made a mess of the 15th, where he missed a short putt and had a bogey six. 'I thought I had blown my lead and that by the time Arnold played the 15th he'd have caught me or even taken a lead. So I said to God, "Well, I'm grateful because now you've really given me a test."'

Player scrambled for par at the 16th and 17th holes but behind him Palmer had taken the lead by a stroke. At the 18th, Player put his approach shot into the right-hand bunker. He came out to six feet and holed the putt for a 74 and a total of 280. Playing the last, Palmer still led by a shot. 'After a great drive my friends in the gallery came up to slap me on the back,' Palmer said. 'I couldn't miss. All I needed was a par four for victory, a five for a tie. With these thoughts in mind I hit my seven-iron, came off the shot and pushed it into the same bunker Gary had been in. Then I blasted over the green, putted 15 feet past the cup and missed the return.'

A double-bogey six in a round of 71 put Palmer on 281, one stroke behind Player. 'It was a marvellous lesson for me,' Player said. 'If I had felt sorry for myself after taking that seven I would probably have lost. It is an experience that has stood me in good stead. It taught me always to try to take adversity on the chin and use it positively to strengthen myself.'

Graham sermon or no Graham sermon, Player told Palmer later that he felt he had thrown the tournament away. 'It was funny,' Player said. 'The next day all the Americans wrote about was how Arnold made a six at the last to lose.' Palmer also learnt a lesson. 'I had made the fatal error of enjoying the victory before I'd earned it and I lost my concentration. Considering the disasters he'd encountered on the back nine, that was some bunker shot Gary played.'

The two were in each other's pockets again 12 months later when Palmer, with a 68, defeated Player, with a 71, and Finsterwald, who had a 77, in a three-way play-off over 18 holes. Playing the 16th hole in the final round, Palmer was two shots adrift of Player and Finsterwald. The pin at the last par three on the course was cut in the back left corner of the green and Palmer pushed a three-iron, putting the ball on the fringe about ten feet from the edge of the putting surface. Palmer played what he described as 'the most important shot of that tournament and one of the most important of my career'.

He faced a dauntingly fast downhill chip. With a wedge, he knew he had to land the ball on the right spot at the right speed to get it close. He succeeded brilliantly on both counts and the ball rolled into the hole for a birdie two. He had another birdie at the 17th to tie the leaders. In the play-off Palmer shot 31 on the back nine after being three down to Player.

When Player contested the 1978 Masters he was 42 years of age, and the only person not in the least bit worried about that was the man himself. He had made his début at Augusta in 1957. Armed with his motto, *mens sana in corpore sano* – a healthy mind in a healthy body – his lack of height had spurred him to work harder at developing strength and flexibility. He found he could still not reach Augusta's par fives in two, so he concentrated more on weightlifting and stretching the length of his swing.

'As I got older I realised the importance of hanging on to the strength I developed. I've thought about those champions who neglected to keep themselves fit and how they always paid the price in the end.' As far as Player was concerned, 'can't' did not exist. The 't' would be crossed out. He would stand in front of a mirror and repeatedly say to himself, 'You're the greatest golfer in the world.'

In 1978 it wasn't just that Player was in his forties. He was also nowhere to be seen on the leaderboard at Augusta. He was seven strokes behind Hubert Green and someone remarked to him that all he needed to stand any chance was eight birdies. 'Don't worry,' Player replied, 'I want to tell you I can get them.'

With nine holes to play he was still five shots off the pace. At the ninth he got down from 12 feet and he had another birdie at the tenth, where he stroked in a putt from about 25 feet. He single-putted the 12th green for a two, and the par fives, the 13th and 15th, both yielded birdies after he had hit the greens in two.

He made a 15-footer for a two at the 16th and when he stood on the 18th green he looked up at the scoreboard. It told him that Tom Watson, the defending champion, Green and Rod Funseth were level with him.

'I knew I had to get a three,' Player recalls. He hit an accurate drive and a six-iron to about 18 feet above the hole. The putt dropped.

It was Player's ninth birdie, his seventh of the last ten holes in a round of 64. He had come home in 30. His playing partner, Seve Ballesteros, threw both arms around Player, although at that stage it was by no means clear that the South African had won. A par at the last would have earned Watson a tie; instead he bogeyed the hole, the memory of which would haunt him when he stood on the 18th tee with Ian Woosnam 13 years later.

Funseth missed his putt for a birdie but it seemed that Green, at least, would take Player into a play-off when he put his approach shot to within three feet of the flag. As he was about to putt, though, he was distracted by the voice of a television commentator. He backed off and went through his preparations again. He missed. He had, he said, only himself to blame. Player was on 277, Green, Watson and Funseth on 278. Green had won the US Open and would go on to win the US PGA. He would not win the Masters.

'The 18th is a deceptively difficult hole,' Player says. 'It has ruined a lot of people. Look at Greg Norman. The green is narrow. It's very slopey, and if you miss it to the left you are in trouble, and if you miss it to the right you are in trouble. It doesn't look like it's a back breaker but it really is.

'When I think of the finishing holes in my career, when I say a prayer and thank God for the talent He's given me, I could think of the British Open or the US Open or the PGA, but it's amazing how every time my mind goes back to the 18th at Augusta and I'm playing with Ballesteros and I've got this downhill putt. I look at the scoreboard, I know what I've got to do . . . and in it goes. My caddie jumps up. I've got a picture in my office with my caddie jumping up and the people with their hands in the air. Those are the things you cherish.'

★ ★ ★

In 1979 the Masters experienced its first sudden-death play-off and Frank Urban Zoeller, or Fuzzy, emerged as the champion on his début at Augusta. At the end of 72 holes Zoeller, Tom Watson and Ed Sneed were level on 280. When the fourth round had started, Sneed had been five strokes ahead of his nearest challenger, but he bogeyed the last three holes to finish with a 76. 'On the 18th tee I was two shots behind but by the time I got to the green I discovered that Ed had three-putted the 17th,' Zoeller said. 'When it went up on the board the crowd kinda roared a little.'

There was nothing wrong with Zoeller's drive at the last but his second shot would have delighted the society of duffers. 'I was trying to force a pitching wedge,' Zoeller recalls. 'I was kinda in between clubs and when I'm like that I'll go with one less and hit hard because the adrenaline usually takes over. I hit it fat. I don't mind telling you it does happen out there. We do hit crappy shots and that was just terrible.' His ball finished short of the bunker on the right but he got up and down to save par. He chipped to about four feet and made the uphill putt. 'I hate to think about the tension now. When I was young I had good nerves.'

The three players had pars at the tenth and Zoeller won it at the 11th, thus setting a trend (subsequent sudden-death play-offs did not reach the 12th), with a birdie three from eight feet.

★ ★ ★

The pen, as Roberto de Vicenzo discovered in 1968, is mightier than a three-iron. This was the finish to end all finishes. The popular Argentine, who the year before had won the Open Championship at Hoylake, tied for the Masters but wrote himself out of the play-off.

The final round coincided with de Vicenzo's 45th birthday and he began with an eagle two at the first hole. He shot 65 for a total of 277 and only Bob Goalby, who had a 66, could match it. However, down at the recorder's tent, all was not well. After de Vicenzo's card had been signed and handed in, an official noticed an embarrassing discrepancy. Tommy Aaron, de Vicenzo's playing partner, had marked him down for a four at the 17th instead of a three. De Vicenzo had correctly scored 65 but the scores on his card added up to 66. The rule books were thumbed through before a group of officials consulted Bobby Jones in his cabin by the tenth tee. Jones, who was then confined to a wheelchair, could only confirm that the four at the 17th had to stand because de Vicenzo had signed for it. A 65 went down as a 66 and an own goal. 'What a stupid I am,' de Vicenzo said. His aggregate was adjusted to 278 and Goalby won the tournament by a stroke.

★ ★ ★

The '80s began with a runaway victory by Ballesteros, at 23 the youngest winner. He followed it up with another four-stroke triumph in 1983 and two years later Bernhard Langer maintained Europe's presence and finally made the sports editors in Germany realise that golf was not an alien sport.

Langer began the fourth round two strokes behind Ray Floyd, one behind Curtis Strange. 'More significantly,' Langer wrote in his autobiography, *While the Iron Is Hot*, 'I was tied with Seve Ballesteros and so he and I had to play together in the final round. Significant because Seve is a difficult man to partner. It is not his fault, it is just his way.'

The last time the two had played against each other was in the final of the World Matchplay Championship the previous year, when Langer said that Ballesteros intimidated opponents on the course. In the 1985 Masters they shook hands on the first tee in the last round, wished each other luck, and the next time Ballesteros spoke to Langer was on the 18th tee. 'Well done,' he said. 'This is your week.'

Langer's plan was to safely negotiate the front nine holes and he did not look at the leaderboard until the tenth tee. It told him that Curtis Strange was the leader at seven under after picking up four strokes on the front nine. 'I felt myself begin to crumble inside,' Langer said. 'Then I thought, nobody cares whether you finish third or tenth or 25th. You want to win a major, so go for it.'

For a man for whom putting had provided the cruellest handicap, Langer's stroke at Augusta was as confident and as sure as anybody's. He holed from 13 feet for a birdie two at the 12th, from shorter distances for birdies at the 13th and 15th and from 14 feet for a three at the 17th.

Langer's progress coincided with Strange's collapse. The American, three strokes ahead with six holes to play, put his ball into the creek at the 13th and took six. As Langer stood on the 15th tee, a spectator shouted to him, 'You can win. Curtis is blowing up.' Langer recalls, 'I wasn't sure what he meant exactly.' Whereas Langer birdied the 15th, Strange subsequently took another six after again finding the water with his approach shot. What had promised to be the greatest recovery in the history of the Masters – Strange had shot 80 in the first round and had booked a flight home – was finally submerged.

When Langer walked to the 17th tee he led the Masters for the first time in his life. He finished with a 68 for 282, two ahead of Ballesteros (70), Floyd (72) and Strange (71). By the 18th green, Ballesteros put his arm around Langer. 'He told me I was a great champion and that I had played really well,' Langer said. 'And he meant it. Apart from anything else, Seve loves to see Europeans beat Americans.'

Jack of All Trades

Jack Nicklaus, the son of a pharmacist from Columbus, Ohio, began playing golf at the age of ten and not long after that was battering his way around one of his father's haunts, the Scioto Country Club. Bobby Jones knew Scioto. He had won the US Open Championship there in 1926. Nicklaus would repay the compliment by winning, repeatedly, on Jones's course, Augusta National.

Nicklaus won his first Masters in 1963 when he was 23, with an aggregate of 286, one stroke ahead of Tony Lema. Two years later he won with a score of 271, beating Arnold Palmer and Gary Player, who were joint second, by nine strokes. He scored 64 in the third round. Jones witnessed the massacre and was prompted to remark that Nicklaus had 'played a game with which I am not familiar'.

However, even the compilation of that record aggregate (it was beaten by Tiger Woods in 1997) did not compare in Nicklaus's mind to his fifth Masters triumph in 1975: 'The most exciting tournament I've ever played in.' Nicklaus was fighting his corner against two of the finest players of the day, Johnny Miller and Tom Weiskopf. The scores posted after the third round were, Weiskopf 207, Nicklaus 208 and Miller 211. 'I never doubted I would win,' Weiskopf said. Miller had gone to the turn in 32 against Weiskopf's 34 and Nicklaus's 35.

The Masters is unique in many ways and one of them is the spine-chilling roar of the crowd that erupts around the greens in response to an outlandish shot or putt. Nicklaus heard such a noise as he advanced down the fairway of the long 15th. He was about 250 yards from the flag on the par five. He had the pond to carry and it was into a breeze. He took out his three-wood, twice, and put it back into the bag. He wanted to hit an iron. He waited until the breeze died, settled over a one-iron and let fly. 'The finest one-iron shot of my life.' Everybody in the stands knew it was good because Nicklaus was striding after the ball while it was still in flight.

The scoreboard by the 15th green was not up to date. Officials did not put up Weiskopf's birdie at the 14th because they did not want to distract Jack. Jack may be colour blind – a glance at his clothes (that day he was wearing green stripes and, uncomfortably, white trousers – 'they have to be lined or my underwear shows through') usually gives the game away – but he could just read the scoreboard by the sixteenth green.

Nicklaus missed his eagle putt at 15 but was level again with a birdie. At the short 16th he was faced with a 40-foot uphill putt for a birdie. First, though, he watched Weiskopf and Miller get birdies on 15. Then they watched Nicklaus roll in his 40-footer. They were still watching when he did the most un-Nicklaus-like thing. He leapt into the air and danced around the green. 'I knew that Tom was going to have a hard time playing that hole after watching somebody make two,' Nicklaus said. Weiskopf three-putted and lost the lead for good. Miller remarked later, 'I was happy to walk through the Bear prints.'

Standing on the 18th green, Nicklaus was 12 under par when he heard another of those communicative responses from the community. Nicklaus waited for the scores to go up. His situation, regarding his putt, would have changed had it been Weiskopf who had birdied the 17th. But it was Miller, and he and Weiskopf, going to the 18th, were a stroke behind. Nicklaus safely two-putted for his par at the last and a round of 68 put him on 276. Both his rivals had good chances to force a play-off, Miller pitching his second shot to about 15 feet and Weiskopf to eight. In the scorer's tent Nicklaus was getting prepared for a play-off. He said that one or the other, not both, would hole out for a birdie. Both missed. At least the Bear's green stripes would go with the jacket.

When Jack Nicklaus says things like, 'That was the most exciting tournament I've ever played in,' you have to be wary of making it a definitive statement. The man has a long playing record – some would claim he *is* a long-playing record – which spans four decades. Eleven years after he had seen off Weiskopf and Miller to win his fifth Masters, he won his sixth. He was aged 46 and he became the oldest winner by nearly four years.

Anybody who writes Jack Nicklaus off is asking for trouble. Tom McCollister, of the *Atlanta Constitution*, wrote him off the week before the start of the 1986 Masters and was responsible for lighting a fire beneath the Bear which roused him from hibernation. McCollister told his readers that 46-year-old men don't win the Masters and the article was taped to the door of Nicklaus's refrigerator. It gave the Bear a sore head. He kept reading the cold print. 'I thought about it all week,' Nicklaus said. 'Done. Through. Finished. Washed up. Sometimes you need something like that to get you going.'

Nicklaus shot 74 in the first round, 71 in the second and 69 in the third, by which stage he was tied ninth and was four shots adrift of the leader Greg Norman. McCollister, of course, was right. Nicklaus had spent more and more time designing and building golf courses and less time playing on them. He had not won a tournament of any kind for two years. In seven tournaments that season he had won only $4,403. His best finish had been a tie for 39th. He had missed the halfway cut three times and was 160th on the money list. He was 157th in the putting statistics. He had not broken 70 since February. 'I really have played just awful,' he said. 'As many people have said, this is the December of my career. Maybe I should quit right now. Maybe I should say goodbye. But I'm not that smart.'

He was smart enough, on the morning of the final round, to calculate that he would need to score 66 to tie, or 65 to win the tournament. All week he had been complaining that the putts wouldn't drop. He was still complaining when he missed two putts from around four feet going out in the final round. At the eighth hole he pulled his tee-shot into the woods. Then he hit a three-wood through a four-foot gap in the trees 40 yards ahead and escaped with a par five.

At the ninth he hit a wedge to ten feet and twice he stepped back from the putt, disturbed by roars from the crowd around the eighth green. Tom Kite had chipped in for an eagle from 80 yards, followed by Seve Ballesteros, who got down from 50 yards. 'Let's see if we can make a roar of our own,' Nicklaus said to the spectators who remained loyal, before making the putt for a birdie. He went to face the back nine with a score of 35 over the front, one under par for the day and five behind the new leader Ballesteros. At the tenth he holed from 20 feet for another birdie. 'Go get 'em, Jack,' they cried.

Peter Higgs, the co-author of this book, followed every shot of the crusade, not, initially, to watch Nicklaus but to monitor the progress of his playing partner Sandy Lyle, who was not a million miles removed from the leaderboard. 'As I stood there impassively [at the tenth green] I knew that this man could not possibly win,' Higgs wrote. 'His fans were just making fools of themselves.' They made fools of themselves again at the 11th, where Nicklaus forced in another long putt for a third successive birdie. However, at the 12th, the Golden Bell, the hole tolled for the Golden Bear. His tee-shot went through the back of the green, his chip was weak and he took a bogey four.

From that point, Nicklaus would say later, he decided to play aggressively. He was on in two at the par-five 13th, with the severe dog-leg left, and a birdie ensued. When he walked over the brow of the hill at the 500-yard 15th, the murmurs had merged into a groundswell of support. Soon there would be a crescendo.

He had just over 200 yards to the pin. He smacked a four-iron and the ball came to rest about 12 feet from the hole. By the time he stood over the putt he was still four shots behind Ballesteros. The Spaniard had gone to nine under with an eagle at the 13th and from his reaction, and that of his brother and caddie Vicente, the Masters was as good as won.

Nicklaus's putt was almost identical to the one he had missed in the final round of his last victory in Augusta in 1975. Recalling that that one had been underhit, he stroked the ball firmly into the cup. When his five-iron tee-shot at the 16th finished three feet from the hole, if Augusta National had had a roof, it would have come off.

In the early part of his career Nicklaus was not easy to love. For one thing, he was unattractive: a podgy kid with a crew cut who looked as if he should be shifting sandbags in the US Army. For another, he upset Arnie's Army by beating the legend when Palmer was at the height of his popularity.

Now, though, Ohio Fats, as Nicklaus had cruelly been called, was from another time. Now the roar was for the Golden Bear. A 46-year-old part-timer he might have been, but in the southern sunshine that Sunday afternoon, the famous concentration, the management of his game and the rock-like resolution he applies to the closing stages of a major championship were all sharply in focus.

With his son Jackie carrying his bag, they walked less than 200 yards from the 16th tee to the green through a wall of noise. Nicklaus, his figure reflecting in the lake, waved and waved again. 'The sound was really deafening,' he said. 'To have these things happen to you and to have them happen again, and at a place like Augusta, which means so much to me, well, I was close to tears.'

He wasn't going to win his 20th great championship by crying, so he reminded himself, 'Hey, you've still got a lot of golf to play.' He tapped in the birdie putt (no dancing with the Bear this time), and whilst he was waiting to drive at the 17th tee he heard another sound, one that, for most people, came not from the heart but from the pit of the stomach. Ballesteros, who still led by two shots, hooked his four-iron approach into the water at the 15th. Perhaps the noise, and/or the sight of Nicklaus's name at eight under par, unnerved him. Whatever, Nicklaus birdied the 17th from ten feet and was in the lead for the first time in the tournament. He had gone eagle, birdie, birdie. He had shot seven birdies in ten holes. 'The more nervous I got, the better I putted,' he said. 'At my age I should have been incapable of even getting the putter back. Somehow I began to draw it back straight.'

Nicklaus walked up the 18th fairway to another shattering encore. His mother was in the gallery. She had not seen him play at Augusta National since 1959, when he was an amateur. Her son was about 40 feet from the flag and he needed two putts to keep the lead. Her grandson tended the flagstick. The ball finished a few inches from the hole and thousands of throats rose again, this time to acknowledge one of the great rounds of the Masters and one of the great achievements in sport. Jack fell into the arms of Jackie.

Nicklaus had covered the back nine in a record-equalling 30 strokes for a round of 65, a score he had predicted would make him the winner by one. When Ballesteros took three putts at the 17th, his chance had gone. Tom Kite missed from 12 feet at the last – had he made it he would have forced a play-off – and then there was Norman, who had led going into the final round. After a poor start he got back to nine under with four successive birdies and needed a par at the 18th to tie. Just a par. He hit a four-iron into the spectators on the right (Norman often plays to the gallery) and all he could manage was a bogey five.

Once again Nicklaus, who had been pacing the floor of the Bobby Jones cabin, too nervous to sit down, was the winner by one: 279 to 280 by Norman and Kite and 281 by Ballesteros. Nick Price, who established a course record of 63 in the third round, was on 282. The previous record of 64 had been set by Lloyd Mangrum in 1940 and equalled by, among others, Nicklaus in 1965.

Nicklaus was so animated that you couldn't get him to leave the press centre. Tom McCollister duly took his share of the credit for an achievement which Herbert Warren Wind, in the *New Yorker*, described thus: 'Jack Nicklaus's quite unbelievable drive to victory on the final ten holes at the Augusta National Golf Club must be regarded as nothing less than the most important accomplishment in golf since Bobby Jones's Grand Slam in 1930.'

Nicklaus was wearing a yellow shirt, with the golden bear motif over the left breast, and a gaudy pair of check trousers. The shirt in that colour would sell well, but not half as well as the extraordinary putter he was using. Nicklaus had said that Augusta National was a young man's course, with the hardest greens to putt on and hard hills to climb. Anybody who wins the Masters must have an exceptional week with the putter. Nicklaus had an exceptional wand in his bag. It was called MacGregor's Response ZT and the head of the club was approximately 30 per cent larger than conventional putters. Throughout his career Nicklaus had putted with a Wizard 600, a club he obtained in 1962 from George Low, one of the game's geniuses on the greens. Why on earth would Nicklaus, at the age of 46, dispense with the services of his Wizard? 'I had fallen into the habit of decelerating the putter head at the moment of impact. I should have been accelerating. I had to find something that would help me do that.'

On the back of Nicklaus's charge in 1986, MacGregor, in the space of two years, sold well over 300,000 of the monster putters. At the time MacGregor was one of Nicklaus's companies and the putters were snapped up at about $90 a time.

Ten months later the Golden Bear was fitted with contact lenses. 'It doesn't matter that I can't follow the ball in flight,' he said. 'Hell, compared to me Tom Watson's blind.'

His Masters triumphs are spread over 23 years, his US Open and US PGA victories over 18 years and the Open over 12 years. At Augusta

National on that Sunday evening in 1986 he said, 'This was probably my finest round of golf.' When Jack Nicklaus says things like that, you have to be wary. The man is an LP.

In the spring of 1999, McCollister was killed in a car accident, aged 61. Nicklaus said, 'Through the years people called me about Tom, simply because of that Masters story. It gave me a little needle and a little inspiration. I always enjoyed seeing Tom and we always had a good laugh over that story. I always felt Tom was a very fair guy when he was writing and, more important, a good guy.'

Of Mize and Men

If gambling were allowed on American courses, which it is not (try telling that to some of the good ol' boys in the bleachers), you could have had any price on Larry Hogan Mize winning the Masters in 1987. Not just on the morning of the first round when he had 84 other players to contend with, but also on Sunday evening when it became a three-man and then a two-man contest.

Mize, a 28-year-old Augustan, did not break 70 in the four rounds of the tournament and found himself in a play-off against two of the game's most charismatic and successful players, Greg Norman of Australia and Seve Ballesteros of Spain. It was no contest.

There was a lot of praying in the colourful wooden churches of Augusta on that Palm Sunday morning. People were encouraged to attend the early service in casual dress so they could go straight from church to the Masters. Larry Mize, the local boy, was on the leaderboard going into the fourth round. Ben Crenshaw and Roger Maltbie were on 212, Norman on 213 and Ballesteros and Mize on 214.

The pace of the greens in the first round of the 51st Masters frightened most of the players to death. Billy Andrade, then an amateur, was already nervous on account of playing with Arnold Palmer. On the first tee, Arnie winked and smiled at his young partner. Billy the Kid shot 74, Arnie 83.

No matter how gently it was hit, the ball, like *The Mousetrap*, just ran and ran. A feather duster was required for putting, not a metal object. Only eight players bettered par on the first day and Mize was one of them, getting a birdie on the 18th in the process. (A few weeks before, Mize had changed his putter, reverting back to an old Wilson he had used in college.) Tom Watson was of the opinion that an aggregate of 284, four under par, would win it. He was out by one. In the second round Mize had a level-par 72, finishing with a bogey five at the closing hole. Jumbo Ozaki, who was wearing a fetching pair of check trousers with a matching cap, should have dressed like a frogman. He took 11 at the 15th, where he hit four balls into the pond.

Norman made his move in the third round with a 66 and Ballesteros, who missed all but five greens, putted brilliantly for a score of 70. 'We love ya, Larry,' a group of spectators shouted as Mize made his way to the first tee on the last day. He had produced another 72 in the third round, finishing, significantly, with a birdie at the 18th.

After taking bogeys at the 14th and 15th in the final round, Mize, at two under par for the tournament, realised he would have to recover a stroke at the last if he was to stay in contention. He hit a nine-iron approach from approximately 140 yards. The ball pitched near the flag, rolled cautiously up the hill and then came back down to finish six feet from the hole. He made the putt to finish with a 71: 285, three under par. His birdie at the last was his third there in four rounds.

There were others immediately behind him who would have given anything for a three at the 18th. Ballesteros had birdied the 17th to move to three under, as had Norman. The Spaniard hit his approach shot at the last into the bunker on the right of the green and he did remarkably well to get up and down to save par. While Ballesteros was being escorted to the Bobby Jones cabin to join the awaiting Mize, Norman was playing the 18th. He needed a par to get into a play-off, a birdie to win outright. The same mathematics had applied at the same stage 12 months earlier. His drive was left of the fairway and, with the front bunker to carry, he played a beautiful wedge shot to about 22 feet below the flag. The putt that would win him one of the few things in the world that he cannot buy, a Green Jacket, looked good from the outset. The Shark bit his bottom lip, went into a crouched position and was ready to do the Fosbury flop in the middle of the green. Norman was convinced it was in, so was his caddie, so was the gallery. The ball flattered to deceive. Like Norman, it paid lip service to the hole. Somehow it did not drop.

So it was a par for Norman and a walk to the Jones cabin. Crenshaw and Maltbie, the last pair, needed birdies on the 18th to join the play-off. Neither managed it, and in Crenshaw's case he knew that he had kissed his chance goodbye when he left a six-foot putt on the lip at the 17th. It cost him a bogey five and he and Maltbie finished on 286, one stroke outside the membership required for the Jones cabin.

Earlier in the week Norman had re-emphasised one of the Masters' unwritten commandments: the tournament begins on Sunday over the back nine holes. Norman had in mind the tenth tee but not for a second time around, and he certainly did not envisage it finishing at the 11th.

The third sudden-death play-off in Masters history featured the dark conquistador, the Great White Shark and a 28-year-old with goose bumps, arthritis in his left hip – he was taking pills three times a day – and no reputation whatsoever other than that he had shown a propensity for snatching defeat from the jaws of victory.

His only professional win had come four years earlier in the Memphis Classic. In 1986 he squandered a lead in the final round of the Tournament Players Championship and in the Kemper Open he took three putts on the final green to let Norman into a play-off which the Australian won. When he stood on the tenth hole, Camellia, all that was behind him. Mize played it impressively, outdriving his opponents and hitting a seven-iron to 12 feet below the hole. Ballesteros and Norman were on the back fringe.

Ballesteros, putting first, drifted the ball three and a half feet past the hole. And he missed that coming back. The experience, he acknowledged subsequently, would haunt and debilitate him for years to come. Mize and Norman had par fours and adjourned to the 11th, the White Dogwood, where the tee is set in a cathedral of a dozen tall pines 100 years old and 100 feet high.

Ballesteros retreated in the opposite direction, back up the hill towards the clubhouse. He was in tears and inconsolable, despite words of comfort from Ken Schofield, the executive director of the European Tour. After frittering away the lead in the Masters the previous year and the year before that, Ballesteros had been determined to redeem himself. 'Winning is everything, losing is nothing,' was all he was heard to say. He refused to come into the interview room.

Seven days later he emerged from a somewhat less consequential play-off to win the Cannes Open from Ian Woosnam. He was able at last to talk of Augusta. 'In the play-off I hit my second shot perfectly but I found I had a difficult downhill putt. I kept saying to myself that I shouldn't leave it short. It went three and a half feet past and with the setting sun in my eyes I must have aimed left. It is ridiculous that the Masters should be decided on one hole. It is like throwing a coin in the air and guessing. I said the same thing in 1979, so it is not because I lost that I am saying it.' He believes that in the event of a tie the major championships should be decided, like the US Open, over 18 holes. 'I believe I was also the champion with Larry Mize at Augusta.'

If Ballesteros was crestfallen, imagine the feelings of Greg Norman. He was safely on the green at the 11th in two while Mize had gone way to the right with his five-iron approach shot. Norman, runner-up to Jack Nicklaus in the Masters 12 months earlier, had been on the point of winning another major championship when Bob Tway blasted out of a bunker and into the 18th hole to capture the US PGA title. Now Norman was poised for his first Masters triumph.

Mize reached for his sand wedge. 'I was disgusted with my second shot and my faithful caddie Scottie told me to calm down. I knew I would have to make a firm, low, aggressive chip and to pitch it just short of the green. I had to get it close.' It was all of those things and more.

The ball took two bounces through the fringe and faced a long journey, right to left, downhill towards the flag. The distance from Mize to the hole was approximately 140 feet. Norman estimated that it would finish at least five feet past the hole. However, he could not see the line.

Mize could and so could thousands of people assembled in Amen Corner.

A growing murmur exploded into a roar when the ball disappeared into the cup. The amazed Mize, in one unchoreographed action, hurled his club and himself into the air. When he remembered that Norman still had a putt to tie, he attempted to quieten the crowd. Norman would not have heard them in any case. The colour seemed to drain from his face. He was gutted. Mize had snatched victory from the jaws of the Shark.

'I couldn't believe it,' Norman said. 'I thought he would struggle to get up and down in two. If he stayed down there and played that shot for three days he would never be able to do that again.' Three days? Norman was obviously not thinking clearly. Three years, more like. In fact Mize returned to the spot some months later and attempted, for the benefit of a sports magazine, to repeat the shot. But how can you repeat a stroke of genius?

From the age of nine the local boy had started playing golf at the Augusta Country Club, just over the fence from Augusta National. As a youngster the only way he could get into one of the world's most exclusive clubs was as one of the tournament's volunteer workers. His particular chore at the Masters was to work on the scoreboards, and on 12 April 1987 his name was at the top of them. The great American dream was fulfilled when Jack Nicklaus helped Mize into the Green Jacket.

'When I worked in the tournament,' Mize said, 'I used to idolise Jack Nicklaus, so you can imagine what all this means to me. I always fantasised about winning the Masters and I get goose bumps every time I come here.'

A Sandy Lie

When Sandy Lyle walked to the 18th green for the fourth and last time, his immediate feeling was one of relief. In the horticultural lexicon that gives Augusta National the unique distinction of sounding, and looking, like a cross between a golf tournament and the Chelsea Flower Show, the last hole bears the innocuous name of Holly, the shortest hybrid (in title) on the card.

Holly is, after all, a pretty straightforward climax to Augusta National's blaze of glorious green. That, at least, is what Lyle was telling himself in April 1988. When he stood on the tee he did not think long and hard about what club to select. Holly is 405 yards long, uphill. No water to drown the hopes of those dreaming of wearing a Green Jacket. Trees to the right, bunkers just left of the fairway. No need to flirt with danger by lashing out with the driver. Lyle had played the hole either with a one-iron or a three-wood and he had no serious doubts about what club to use in the fourth round. He reached for the one-iron.

David Musgrove, who was then Lyle's caddie, wrote in his book *Life with Lyle*, 'I thought about giving him a three-iron but if he had hit a three-iron that would have given him a longer club to play into the green and therefore less chance of getting the ball close enough to get a birdie. He suspected he needed a birdie to win, though he wasn't sure. He could have hit a driver and cleared the bunkers but then he'd have had a difficult place to approach the green from. You're at a bad angle to the flag if you do that. You're coming in across the green and there's not much landing area.'

Lyle was as formidable with the one-iron as many others with the driver. 'I had the shot visualised in my mind,' he recalls. 'The pin was at the front and if I'd hit the driver I'd have probably been faced with a downhill lie for my second shot. It is much easier to be on an uphill lie, 30 yards further back. I felt at ease. You can make four at the 18th and there's a chance of a birdie. But it doesn't mean that you can't take six there also.'

In a matter of moments Lyle's emotions ran the gamut from relief to despair and back again. His tee-shot started off on what seemed the perfect line but the ball drifted left and rolled into the front bunker. Like a cat on a hot tin roof, Lyle began to hop from one foot to the other.

'As I walked up the hill I thought that was it. I'm dead. The second bunker isn't as bad but the front one has a steep face.' Lyle was convinced he'd been caught in Holly's ivy. When he reached his ball his mood changed. 'It had rolled into the face and stayed there. It gave me a launching pad. I could have hit a five- or six-iron, that's how good the lie was.' Before deciding on what club to hit, he asked how Mark Calcavecchia, who had just walked off the 18th green, had finished.

After his prayers had not been answered at Amen Corner, Lyle had lost the lead for the first time since the ninth hole on the second day. He hit it into the water on the 12th and held his head in his hands. Calcavecchia was the leader in the clubhouse – except that he wasn't in the clubhouse. He had posted a total of 282, six under par, and he couldn't tear himself away from the scene around the 18th green. Lyle knew he needed a par to tie and force a play-off, a birdie to win. But he was bunkered. Only Lyle knew how nicely.

He had 142 yards to the front of the green, 150 to the flag. 'I thought to myself, I've had a break here. I've got a great chance of getting on the green. The distance was right for the eight-iron but I would have had to have hit it 100 per cent. If I'd hit it 95 per cent it wouldn't have carried enough.'

For the seventh time that afternoon he took a seven-iron to play his second shot. 'I hit it almost too well,' he recalls. 'I was not trying to be fancy, just a clean hit and I would take it from there.' He hit it so cleanly he could almost count the grains of sand that were disturbed. The result was what one seasoned American observer described as the greatest bunker shot in the history of golf. As soon as he had struck the ball, Lyle knew it was good. He ran out of the bunker and began leaping up and down. The cat was back on the roof.

He threw down his sun visor, but to those around the green, including Calcavecchia, it looked like a gauntlet. The ball flew past the flag, bounced onto the bank of the two-level green and stopped at the top. For a few heartbeats it seemed it would stay there, but then it began to obey Isaac Newton. While Lyle was striding towards the green, his ball began to roll in his direction. From being almost stationary, it gathered pace down the hill and came to rest ten feet from the hole. Ben Crenshaw, his partner, was faced with a shorter putt. 'Would it be better for you to putt out?' Lyle asked him. 'Whatever you like, Sandy,' Crenshaw replied.

Musgrove was thinking of something else. 'I had started to get backache on the last three holes and I didn't want to go down that bloody tenth hole in a bloody play-off, not for anyone.'

The line of the putt facing Lyle was normally right to left but the grain of the grass would influence the ball left to right. Lyle reasoned it was a straight putt and 'I hit it smack in the middle, as good as I can hit'.

It gave him an aggregate of 281, seven under par. Not since Arnold Palmer in 1960 had a golfer made a birdie on the final hole to win the tournament while playing in the final pairing of the day. When the world was watching.

'I was stunned,' Calcavecchia said. 'I didn't expect him to get a birdie on that hole. Another couple of inches and the ball would have stayed up the hill. It was an incredible shot. A lot of people panicked out there but Sandy's got a great head on his shoulders. He is unflappable and what he did in the final round was awesome.'

Lyle, who won the Greater Greensboro Open in North Carolina (in a play-off) prior to the Masters, was at the height of his mental and physical powers. He had acquired a badge which read, 'It's not important whether you win or lose, it's important whether I win or lose.' His status as a millionaire had been assured when he won the Open Championship in 1985. On that occasion he finished with a bogey five and others with better chances failed to take them. His first major title was not won in classic style; the Masters was.

Lyle had reached the turn in 34 and was leading the field by three strokes. Then Calcavecchia went through Amen Corner in three, three, four to Lyle's five, five, five. Calcavecchia, who made three tricky and courageous putts to save par at the 15th, 16th and 17th holes, did not waver, and he reproduced that quality on a major stage a year later. Lyle, unlike at the Open three years earlier, could not rely on others' mistakes. Instead he produced a masterstroke when anything less would probably not have sufficed. He does not, however, watch it at home on the video. 'I would probably start sweating if I saw that again.'

For Lyle at that time, golf was no sweat. When he led going into the last round he asked, 'Is it right that a Scotsman has never won the Masters?' It was. But now in Augusta, which was captured from the British by Light-Horse Harry Lee in 1781, there would be haggis, neeps and tatties on the menu at the champions' dinner.

That same week Ian Woosnam, then the European No. 1 shot 81, 74 and headed straight for the airport. Lyle commented at the time, 'There were many times when I felt like quitting and going for the easier money in Europe. I am sure Mr Woosnam feels like that now but he could do well here if he perseveres.'

Nick Faldo finished with an aggregate of 296, 15 strokes behind Lyle. The Englishman's time would come. So too would the Welshman's, and they would not have long to wait.

Faldo's Sudden Glory . . .

Nick Faldo and Sandy Lyle enjoyed a symbiotic relationship in that their strengths and weaknesses were of mutual benefit. Although they did not eat together, certainly not as friends, they fed off each other. Contemporaries and teammates, they could almost have come from different planets.

Lyle, from Shrewsbury in England but a Scotsman by blood, is the son of a professional, hence the presence in his hands at the age of three of a wee golf club. Faldo's nature is such that from an early age he realised that team games were not necessarily good for the soul, or perhaps the sole, especially if the individual was talented and most of the others were not. Faldo homed in on golf at the age of 13 when, on a television set in Hertfordshire, he saw Jack Nicklaus playing a round of the Masters. He had never heard of Nicklaus; he had never heard of Augusta. He had barely heard of golf. The picture bedazzled him. The rest is geography: from Welwyn Garden City to the Garden City in America's deep south.

Lyle won the Open Championship at Royal St George's in Kent in 1985, Faldo followed him at Muirfield in 1987; Lyle became the first Briton to win the Masters in 1988, Faldo became the second. Then he accelerated out of the slipstream and watched the rest of the world from his rear-view mirror.

The final day of the 1989 Masters, the 53rd, was fraught and fractured. Rain and lightning ruined the symmetry of the tournament, interrupting the third round on Saturday and meaning that those with unfinished business had to rise and shine early on Sunday morning. There were 14 players who had an uncomfortable Saturday night/ Sunday morning and Faldo was among them. He was not finished. Not by a long chalk.

Faldo had to resume his third round with a pitch onto the 13th green. He bogeyed the 16th and 17th and slid home in 39. Looking more like a fisherman's friend than a man enjoying a round of golf in Georgia, Faldo finally came off the 18th green with a score of 77. His mood was blacker than the weather and he directed some of his thunder towards a pressman. 'You're always asking me ******* questions,' Faldo shouted. 'It's all up there on the ******* leaderboard.'

A cathartic experience, perhaps. When Faldo went out in the

afternoon for the final round he was five strokes adrift of Ben Crenshaw. For those on or near the leaderboard, there was time, or a reporter or two, to kill between the full stop at the end of the hyphenated third round and the beginning of the fourth. Some players, like Crenshaw, had a nap. Faldo, armed with five putters, went to work on the practice green. He settled on a different model, a Taylor Made, and in his hand and in his mind he went from purgatory to purgative.

At the first hole he made a putt of about 55 feet for a birdie. As the putts went down, Faldo's name went up. At the 16th, Redbud, he hit his tee-shot to the back of the green, which is not the place to be. 'I immediately thought of Sandy last year,' Faldo said. Lyle had holed an improbable putt at the same stage and Faldo did likewise. 'You just don't hole those,' he said.

Nor do you make putts like the one he made at the 17th. He was about 30 feet from the flag but it had a break of about four feet. Faldo did not stroke the ball, he punched it. If it hadn't disappeared into the hole it would have raced off the green. He shot 65, the best score of the week, and posted an aggregate of 283, five under par.

He retired to the Bobby Jones cabin to wait and watch. One by one they fell short. The rain continued to fall, it was past happy hour and the lights were visible in the clubhouse. Seve Ballesteros, who had reached the turn in 31, led at that point but then the fireworks petered out. The water at the 16th drowned him. The Spanish tear ducts flowed in sympathy.

Greg Norman moved to five under for the tournament with one hole to play. He was level with Faldo and he could beat him by a stroke with a birdie. The Australian, who is regarded as a Floridian by most people who watch him on the US Tour, had faced the same situation three years earlier when Jack Nicklaus had been ahead of him. Once again the Great, or Lesser, White Shark managed to snatch defeat from the jaws of victory. He drove from the tee with a one-iron and left himself an approach shot of about 190 yards. He opted for a five-iron instead of a four and the ball hit the bank in front of the green and rolled back onto the fairway. His pitch to the flag was 15 feet short and he missed the putt. Par would have got him into a play-off but, when it really mattered, he fell short on every shot. Later, Norman insisted that the five-iron was the right club. If so, it was the wrong player. It was his third near miss at Augusta National in the space of four years.

Ben Crenshaw and Scott Hoch took up the Stars and Stripes. Crenshaw, the winner in 1984, was three behind when he played a near-perfect tee-shot at the 16th. He was eight feet short of the hole with an uphill putt and he knocked it in.

They went to the 17th with Hoch at six under, Crenshaw at four under and Faldo, in the dry, at five under. Both Americans caught a tree with their drives at the 17th and neither could see the green. Crenshaw hit a fairway wood onto the left of the green and Hoch a three-iron which soared to the right, kicked off a bank and rolled 20 yards down and away from the green. Hoch, instead of flighting the ball onto the green, chose a chip and run off the bank and he played it magnificently. It flirted with the flagstick before slipping three feet past.

Crenshaw was 25 feet from the hole but even so he gave his putter the touch of a butterfly and the ball floated on and on and, with its last revolution, fell gratefully into the cup. There was a thunderous roar from beneath thousands of multi-coloured umbrellas. A minute later the same voices could only choke a sympathetic sigh when Hoch's putt for par stopped on the left lip.

While the umbrellas descended on the 18th, Faldo left the cabin and went to the practice ground to prepare for a play-off. Crenshaw and Hoch, now both five under, drove safely up the 18th. It was nearly 7 p.m. Crenshaw hit a five-iron and, he would say later, his club slipped. His ball flew left into the greenside bunker, while Hoch was safely on in two. Crenshaw, still wearing the obligatory sun visor, came out of the bunker too strongly (no excuses there), went 15 feet past and missed the return. Like Norman, Crenshaw lost his grip at the ultimate moment and paid the ultimate price. Holly again reminded them that she is not as accommodating as she looks.

Hoch, though, made his par and Faldo, who had been picking mud from his sweater (Pringle were happy to clean up), was waiting for him. They made the short journey to the tenth, Camellia, for a sudden-death play-off. By the time they had reached the tenth green a gambler would have given 20–1 against Faldo. The Englishman won the toss, drove first and pushed his shot into an awkward downhill lie. Hoch hit a perfect drive with a slight draw. Faldo drilled his second into the right greenside bunker; Hoch found the front of the green, 30 feet or so short of the hole. Faldo came out 20 feet short, left that putt three feet from the target and swallowed a bogey five.

Hoch's putt was bold – a shade too bold, it can safely be said in hindsight. It went an agonising two feet past. It would have been better if it had been two feet short. Hoch was faced with a downhill putt with a slight break from left to right. And he seemed to take forever. He stalked the hole like a man from the bomb disposal squad. Crouched, he studied it from every angle.

'I'm still in this, I can still win this,' Faldo kept saying to himself. He had been chanting a similar mantra since the age of 13. Anyhow, the putt was left lip. It also needed a stiff upper lip to make it. When Hoch finally steeled himself to pull the trigger, he aimed too far left. Hoch hurled his putter in the air and, like a distracted majorette, only just managed to catch it on the way down with the tips of his fingers of his right hand.

Now he had his back to the hole and when he turned around he was faced with an even longer putt coming back. He took no time at all in potting that. Bobby Jones, who did not regard himself as a particularly good putter, was fond of quoting a contemporary Alex Smith: 'Miss 'em quick!'

Hoch missed it slow, but more of that later. The hole was halved in fives and it was on to the 11th, the White Dogwood, the introduction to that trinity of watery hell holes known, thanks to Herb Warren Wind, as Amen Corner. Faldo drove right of centre, Hoch a bit longer and left of him. Faldo found his ball in casual water and took it 15 steps to the right, his nearest point of relief.

The 11th, a par four, had dogged Faldo all week: he had scored five, five, five, five. This time it was different. Despite the pond on the left and the creek winding its way around the back, Faldo told himself he had to follow the direction of the dog-leg – down and left to the heart of the green. He had about 210 yards to go and he attacked the hole with a three-iron. What the hell? On the previous hole he had been facing a life sentence when the jailer's keys landed in his lap.

Faldo found the heart of the green on a hole which is only ten yards shorter than the par-five 13th. Hoch missed the green on the right, which is the only place to miss this green. Hoch had spent nine of his 33 years on tour and was no spring chicken, but even the wisest of old birds could not help reflecting on what Camellia had done to him, and before that Nandina, that other seductress par four, the 17th in the last round. Faldo, remember, had rocketed in a putt from 30 feet; Hoch missed from three.

If the one going like Concorde hadn't dropped and the one that didn't had . . . Hoch was now in a position not dissimilar to that which had confronted Larry Mize two years earlier. America, and Hollywood, expected nothing less. They got a lot less. The pitch was short, short enough to leave Hoch wondering whether he could match Faldo's par. Faldo rubbed a bag of salt into Hoch's gaping wound by knocking in a putt from about 25 feet. A birdie three after four fives. It was his ninth birdie of the day and he had completed 26 holes.

He didn't hurl his ball into the crowd, he didn't throw his putter. Faldo gives nothing away. He raised both arms and, although he had said from the start that he believed he was destined to win, he wore the look of a man waking from a dream. Eighteen years after seeing Nicklaus on television, Faldo was being fitted for the Green Jacket by Lyle, clad in a kilt and bearing a Scottish flag.

Perhaps Faldo was right. He was destined to win from the moment he changed his putter after faltering over the closing holes in the fourth round; from the moment when everything he touched on the greens produced a magical result; from the moment when those who could do him the most harm proceeded to do him the most good; and from the moment when Scott Hoch missed a heartbeat and joined the all-time losers.

'I'm glad I'm not carrying a gun,' Hoch said later. Whether he would have pulled the trigger on himself or Faldo is not clear. If it had been a double-barrelled model perhaps both would have got it.

The capricious nature of the game will dictate that the short putt Hoch missed on the first hole of the sudden-death play-off will be remembered by many long after the 25-foot putt Faldo sank to win it. Faldo has watched the incident numerous times on television. 'He was aiming too far outside the left edge,' he argues. 'The putt should have been left of centre. He tried to dolly it in and you can't swing it that slow. Even from that distance you have to accelerate through the stroke. Something was seriously wrong, perhaps his alignment or the tension.'

Sandy Lyle, who was commentating for the BBC, was of the opinion that Faldo would win the play-off. 'Scott took far too long over the putt, more than double his normal time,' Lyle said. 'He lost his normal rhythm. When you're thinking that this is to win the Masters, you don't want to add to the pressure. When I won at Augusta I didn't waste any time over my putt.'

To complement his Green Jacket Faldo donned a Union Jack cap. He needed no motivation to put one over the host nation after watching a preview of the Mike Tyson–Frank Bruno heavyweight fight on American television. 'You should have seen it,' Faldo said. 'It opened with film of the Heysel Stadium disaster and went on to say that Britain no longer had any leading sportsmen. No mention of our achievements in golf.'

From Augusta Faldo went to Hilton Head Island in South Carolina for the Heritage Classic and one of the first players he bumped into was Hoch. 'I'm not sleeping very well,' Hoch told him. 'Neither am I,' replied Faldo, referring to all the calls and messages of congratulation he had been receiving. It was not what Hoch wanted to hear. He had to be reassured by Craig Stadler that it was not Faldo's intention to gloat. 'I played really well for 72 holes and a lot of other guys screwed up before I did,' Hoch said. 'Faldo was all over the place and his 65 was full of luck.'

. . . Floyd's Sudden Death

Raymond Floyd had been one of a host of Americans who, 12 months earlier, had recoiled in disgust when Scott Hoch had failed to finish off Nick Faldo at the tenth, the first play-off hole. Floyd, captain of the United States Ryder Cup team in 1989, now had a glorious chance to strike a blow for Old Glory.

At the age of 47 he had the 54th Masters in 1990 in the palm of his hand. The palms, though, began to sweat. Floyd had won the Masters once before, 14 long years ago, when, wearing a pair of trousers straight out of Dean Martin's wardrobe, he had almost lapped the field with a record-equalling aggregate of 271, 17 under par.

This time, however, he had the defending champion breathing down his neck, and when the going gets tough, Faldo gets tougher. Unlike the 53rd Masters, the tournament was blessed by the weather, and although an early spring meant that many of Augusta National's flowering shrubs were in full bloom a week or two before their cue, the fairways and greens were magnificently verdant. The scoring would prove to be lower than the previous year and Mike Donald's 64 in the first round was one off the course record. As Peter Jacobsen remarked, the slums of Chicago are full of first-round leaders.

Floyd was the only player to break par on each of the first three rounds and on Sunday afternoon he was ten under and 15 years and three strokes in front of Faldo. Then he saw the Englishman take a double-bogey six at the first. At that point Fanny Sunesson, Faldo's young Swedish caddie, understood the vicarious nature of her job. 'She was fabulous,' Faldo said. 'She told me not to worry about it, that everything would be all right. I need that sort of encouragement on course.' She told him on the fourth tee to use a three-iron instead of a one-iron and he hit it to eight feet.

Destiny was riding with Faldo again. His playing partner was Jack Nicklaus, who in 1966 had become the only man to successfully defend the Masters. Nicklaus, of course, is also the man who was responsible, albeit inadvertently, for introducing Faldo to golf. It was a demonic seed he planted, and in the last round of the 54th Masters he was on hand to reap the return. Faldo shot 69, Nicklaus 74.

'I thought when I saw the pairings on Saturday night that maybe it was a great omen,' Faldo recalls. He is a great believer in omens (thank goodness his parents didn't christen him Damien), and it was at Jack's tournament, the Memorial, and at Jack's course, Muirfield Village, that Faldo had his first full session with David Leadbetter, the man who engineered Faldo Mark II.

While Nicklaus dropped down a few rungs, Floyd, the renowned frontrunner, was holding fast at the top of the ladder. As is so often the case, the 12th, the Golden Bell, played an inordinate part in the proceedings. First Faldo. His tee-shot found a bunker at the back and, from an awful lie, he somehow managed to save his three. 'The 12th did it for me,' Faldo said. 'The ball was plugged in the sand and all I could see was water. I thought, "I could play a career-best shot here and it could still go in the water."'

Then it was Floyd's turn. He too overshot the green but then rolled in an 18-footer for a birdie two. Now he was four strokes ahead with six holes to play. 'I honestly didn't think I could lose,' Floyd said.

Faldo's strategy all along had been to attack the par fives and, providing his tee-shots were good enough, he would go for the green in two at the 13th and 15th. While Faldo had birdies at both, 'hitting hell' out of a two-iron at the 15th, Floyd played safe, laid up and settled for par fives. He was still three ahead with four to play. When Faldo had a birdie two at the 16th, just as he had 12 months earlier, he was one stroke behind. When Floyd pulled his nine-iron approach to the 17th and, just as Hoch had done 12 months earlier, took a bogey five, the scores were level. Faldo had picked up four strokes in five holes.

The news was flashed to the 18th green, where Faldo had gone to the back fringe with his approach. He was 30 feet from the flag. According to Faldo's then wife Gill, there were American players and their wives around the green who were praying that Faldo would chip instead of putt. They knew that if he did the former instead of the latter, the odds were he would finish much further from the hole, thus increasing his chances of taking a bogey instead of par and therefore opening the door for Floyd.

Faldo putted, accepted a four and, after a 69 put him at ten under par, watched Floyd make a near-miraculous par at the 18th. His drive found a fairway bunker and from there he flew into a greenside bunker on the right. He had to get up and down for a round of 72 to go into a sudden-death play-off. Under the circumstances, Floyd, from the sand, played a most courageous, most professional shot. The ball rolled to within six feet of the flag and his nerve held to hole the putt. He and Faldo were tied on 278, five strokes better than Faldo's four-round total the previous year.

They headed for the tenth tee, Faldo bidding to emulate Nicklaus in back-to-back victories, Floyd dreaming of becoming the oldest Master.

In Faldo's case vicissitude equals *déjà vu*. His drive at the tenth was too straight and he did not work the ball around the corner, just as he had against Hoch. Similarly he put his approach into the right greenside bunker. Against Hoch he had taken three more shots to get down, as indeed he had done at the same hole earlier that day. Floyd, with the better drive down left of centre, hit what appeared to be the winning shot. He rifled his approach at the flag and the ball came to rest about 12 feet from the hole.

Faldo played as good a shot from the bunker as Floyd had done at the 18th. He came out to four feet. 'I think that shot rocked him,' Faldo said. 'There he is thinking maybe he has two putts for it and suddenly he realises it's time for that magic phrase: "I have to hole this to win." It meant his cushion had gone.'

Floyd's putt died inches short. He tapped in, Faldo holed out and they moved on to the White Dogwood, the 11th. According to Faldo, 'Now Ray has to be thinking, "I had a putt for it and I didn't hit it hard enough. Why didn't I hit it a bit harder?"'

The sun was setting, giving the pines a golden tinge. Their shadows now covered the fairway. Faldo, perhaps crucially, outdrove his opponent, who then briefly disappeared to answer a call of nature. When Floyd arrived at his ball, Faldo thought that he was out of breath. He also thought that he hurried the shot, making it without even taking a practice swing. Floyd's chosen weapon from about 170 yards was a seven-iron, and although he had a clear line to the flag he pulled the shot. The ball flew progressively left until it splashed into the blue–dyed pond that etches into the front left of the green. Floyd on fish. His heart sank with the ball.

Faldo, and countless Americans, could not believe it, not of the old pro, the old grisly, the renowned frontrunner, the man who would not break under pressure. Floyd, like Hoch, had cracked.

'What has he gone and done now?' Faldo thought to himself. As he had done earlier that day, he reached for his eight-iron (the previous year he was hitting a three-iron into the same green) and faded his ball to within about 20 feet of the target. 'It was a professional shot,' he recalls, 'a darn good shot.'

Floyd took a penalty drop, chipped to about 12 feet and the best he could hope for was a five. He never had the chance to putt. 'It was the most devastating thing that has happened in my career,' said a pink Floyd, a veteran of 27 Masters. 'I don't think I've ever had anything affect me like this.'

Floyd's first mistake was to win the par-three contest on the Wednesday. Nobody who has won the prelude has gone on to win the opus. Floyd said he had 'drawn lightning from the jug' after his positive performance in the third round. On Sunday he drew water.

No play-off in Masters history has gone beyond the 11th, and prior to the introduction of sudden death Ben Hogan and Gary Player failed in 18-hole play-offs to win the Masters back to back. Faldo's play from tee to green throughout the tournament was hugely impressive. He avoided all the water and visited only two bunkers in three rounds. About the only thing that did not go his way was his wish to be presented with the Green Jacket by Jack Nicklaus. Tradition holds that it is the past champion who plays the role of valet. Faldo could not be both the gentleman and the gentleman's gentleman and it was left to Hord Hardin, the chairman, to do the honours.

Reflecting on what actually transpired, Floyd said, 'It wasn't the waterlogged approach shot at 11 that cost me the title. It was the fact that no one came out of the field and made a charge at me on the front nine. It dictated play. I started playing for par. I don't feel that I lost it. Faldo won it by the way he played.'

Meanwhile, Faldo had gone up in Scott Hoch's estimation. They met again at Hilton Head Island a few days after the Masters and the former Walker Cup player from Orlando approached Faldo on the practice ground, offered his congratulations and warmly shook his hand. 'I was not a fan of Faldo's. He wasn't my favourite person,' Hoch said, 'but I have to admit I was really impressed by what he did. I still think he was lucky against me, but what he did against Floyd was no fluke. You don't get lucky twice.'

Iron Woosnam

Early in 1987 Ian Woosnam was complaining, with some justification, that he had never been invited to the Masters tournament. Twelve months later the man who had plundered Europe wished that he had never heard of Augusta. The No. 1 on the European Tour missed the halfway cut and then booked himself on the earliest possible flight to Britain. There is no greener course than that at Augusta National but all Woosnam was interested in, as his fellow Welshman Tom Jones might have put it, was the green, green grass of home.

Woosnam's four-week introduction to America had been a disaster: the wrong man in the right country at the wrong time. He was 17th at Bay Hill and missed the cut in his next three tournaments. 'It has done me no good at all,' he said. 'I have learnt absolutely nothing.'

In his first round in his first Masters he scored 81. In the second round he stood an outside chance of surviving until he came to the 18th hole. He drove into a bunker and then cut a five-iron short and to the right of the green. He tossed the club away in disgust. He chipped into another bunker and finished with a double-bogey six in a score of 74. He beat a hasty retreat but, like General MacArthur, he would return. And the 18th would be the scene of his greatest victory.

By April of 1991, Woosnam had finally awoken to the American dream. He went into the 55th Masters ranked No. 1 in the world despite the fact that he had never won a major championship. This time Woosnam was ready. His preparatory work in America had been excellent. He had already won in Europe and was joint seventh, with Nick Faldo, in the Nestlé Invitational at Bay Hill. Rain washed out the last round. While Faldo returned home, Woosnam went on to the USF and G Classic at the English Turn Golf and Country Club in New Orleans. It was the Welshman's turn. He secured his first US victory, after which he spent some time on vacation in Florida with Greg Norman.

Meanwhile, Faldo's game plan was badly diluted. He spent a frustrating week in Houston, where the Independent Insurance Agent Open was closed. He and everybody else had to take a rain check as The Woodlands became submerged under a relentless downpour.

When the cast assembled at Augusta National, people were not talking about Ian Woosnam, they were talking about Nick Faldo, and for two reasons. First, the talk of the locker room was of an article on Faldo that had appeared in *Sports Illustrated*. The contents were hardly as explosive as the allegations, that appeared the same week, that Nancy Reagan had had a fling with Frank Sinatra, but they made life uncomfortable for Faldo in a week when he was determined to enter the Masters with as little fuss as possible. In the article Faldo was critical of several fellow professionals including Greg Norman – 'his swing is way too loose' – and Paul Azinger – 'it's hard to have a great champion with bad technique'. Azinger, whom Faldo had defeated by a stroke to win the Open at Muirfield in 1987, responded, 'I find it all very sad. We all want to be successful but most of us have a bit of fun along the way. It's a pity that Faldo can't be like Sandy Lyle, who is one of the most delightful and unselfish players on the tour. If you compliment Faldo on playing a good shot, he will reply "yeah", as if to say "I know". Faldo is obsessed with the idea of being remembered for having the greatest swing in the world. It's a bit too early for him to start thinking about immortality.'

Faldo said he had been 'stitched up' in the article, but then he would say that. He was also the centre of attention for another reason, though. Having won the 53rd and the 54th Masters, he had the chance to become the first player to complete a hat-trick, if that is the correct way to describe hanging three Green Jackets in a row. Jack Nicklaus, who had inspired Faldo to take up the game, had back-to-back victories in 1965 and 1966 and the following year missed the cut. Faldo, with only seven competitive rounds under his belt, wanted his place in history – but history, not to mention a little Welshman, was against him.

Nobody in their right minds would have backed Woosnam to win the tournament after the first round. He shot 72, level par, but said he had no confidence whatsoever on the greens. He experimented with a new, heavier putter, discarding the ladies' model he had been using for the past year, and played serenely for the next two rounds. He scored 66 and 67 to lead Tom Watson by one stroke and Jose Maria Olazabal by three going into the final round.

On Saturday night Woosnam and Olazabal, in near darkness, were the last to leave the practice putting ground. Woosnam's play had been of such a high standard in the third round that he could have put more distance between himself and the field. He had birdied the 12th, 13th, 14th and 15th and had had great chances to pick up further strokes at the 16th and 17th. 'Neither Tom nor I is the best putter in the world at the moment,' Woosnam admitted. He was 33, had been a phenomenal money-winner over the last four years but had never won a major and had never led one going into the last round.

For the second day running he was paired with the 41-year-old

Watson, who had last won the Masters in 1981. Steve Pate gave the leaders something to think about by posting a 65 to finish at nine under par. Woosnam, who carried two wedges in his bag at the expense of a one-iron, reached the turn with a three-shot lead, 12 under to Watson and Olazabal's nine under, but that cushion, over the back nine holes of Augusta National on a Sunday afternoon in April, did not make the ride any easier.

The emotions of Watson and Olazabal were following the contours, one minute up, the next down. The young Spaniard had drawn level after seven holes with three birdies and followed it with three bogeys when he began to visit the azaleas. At the tenth Watson was within a stroke of Woosnam but he had a bogey at the 11th and a double-bogey five at the 12th, where he found water. As he walked to the 13th tee Watson told himself he would have to eagle the 13th and the 15th to get back in the hunt. He did so with a series of outstanding shots. 'We're rooting for *you*, Tom,' yelled a spectator.

Woosnam, after what seemed an interminable wait on the 13th tee, clattered his drive into Rae's Creek and people cheered. You do not applaud a man's misfortune, certainly not at Augusta. Bobby Jones would not have approved. 'That was bad sportsmanship,' Woosnam said. 'Some people were trying to give me a hard time. The more aggressive I become, though, the better I play. I was more determined after that.'

After taking a six at the 13th, Woosnam's lead was one. On the 14th tee a loud voice informed him that this was 'not links golf, this is Augusta National'. Watson told Woosnam a story about the former tour player Don January. When people said anything to him, January would turn to them and say, 'Thank you very much, thank you very much.' Woosnam smashed his drive down the middle of the fairway, turned to the heckler and said, 'Thank you very much.' In fact, January's riposte was not so gentlemanly. The first word ended with a 'k' but was preceded by three letters, not four. Said quickly, it sounded like 'thank'!

With three holes to play, Olazabal, who had had birdies at 13, 14 and 15, and Watson, who had duly eagled the 13th and the 15th, had drawn level with Woosnam at 11 under. The 18th hole was the tie-breaker, or, in the case of the 41-year-old from Kansas and the 25-year-old from Spain, the heart-breaker. Olazabal, playing immediately in front of Woosnam and Watson, hit his tee-shot into the second fairway bunker on the left. 'I was trying to fade it,' he said. 'I didn't think I was capable of getting over the bunker. I was just trying to make four.' Now he had 151 yards to the flag, he went for it with an eight-iron and deposited his ball in the left greenside bunker. His shot from the sand nearly reached the top tier of the green but rolled back down the slope and came to rest about 40 feet from the flag. His putt for par was two feet short. 'I would love to be able to hit that tee-shot again,' Olazabal said. From the first bunker did he not think of playing short and then pitching and putting? 'No,' he replied, 'I had to go for the green.' Olazabal would also painfully recall the seven he had taken at the short sixth earlier in the tournament.

Then there were two. On the 18th tee Woosnam had already decided on his strategy, a courageous attack with the driver, irrespective of the fate of Olazabal or Watson. Watson had been driving brilliantly all year but when it mattered he went for the safer option and paid a terrible price. He hit a three-wood into the trees on the right, from where it was impossible to reach the green in two.

Woosnam chose to hit his ball as hard as possible in an attempt to clear the hazards. He cleared the bunkers all right. He cleared every-thing. He drove it way to the left onto a piece of redundant practice ground. If it was an unconventional, not to say unique, route to the green, at least he had a shot. There are those who believe that Woosnam deliberately took that path. They are almost certainly right. After his six there in 1989 he had learnt to play the hole (getting three birdies and a par at the 18th in 1990) and he did not do so by hitting the ball miles left.

In any event, Woosnam and Watson parted company. If there had been no crowd, Woosnam would still not have been able to see the green. With the marshals having difficulty controlling excited spectators on the side of the fairway, he had trouble finding his caddie. Woosnam, all five feet four and a half inches of him, had to repeatedly leap into the air like a performing dolphin to get a glimpse of the flag. Finally he hit an eight-iron from about 140 yards onto the fringe of the green. Watson, meanwhile, went from wood to sand near the greenside and his recovery flew past the flag.

Woosnam's first putt finished about six feet to the right of the hole; Watson charged his about four feet past. Had he putted out for a five, the pressure on Woosnam would have been that much greater. 'I had dreamed of sinking a putt at the 18th to win the Masters,' Woosnam said. 'I told myself that this was the time to show my bottle. I had holed this putt so many times in practice. This is the Masters and now is the time to do it.'

He consulted with his caddie Phil Morbey and they agreed that there was a slight swing from right to left. 'I aimed for the right lip. I concentrated on keeping my head down and I thought I might have hit it a little soft, but with three feet to go I could see that it was in.'

Before the ball hit the bottom of the cup Woosnam was dropping onto his right knee, simultaneously delivering a fierce right uppercut to nobody in particular but several targets in general. To the course, which had once embarrassed him, to those spectators who would have given anything to see Watson win, and to those who had doubted that he would ever become a major champion. During the final round Glendryth, Woosnam's wife, had hidden her badge, which carried her name, and closed her ears. 'I didn't want to hear people say bad things about my husband,' she said.

To some in the deep south that day Woosnam was about as popular as General Sherman. The majority, not unnaturally, wanted to see a Watson renaissance. Another factor was that Woosnam's victory repre-sented Europe's fourth successive win in the Masters and the seventh since Seve Ballesteros won in 1980.

Watson, alas, took three putts at the last for a double-bogey six to finish tied third. Later he would find time to console Olazabal (he gave him a hug), who was runner-up on ten under par. Who would console Watson, who had gone through a similar experience when losing to Gary Player in 1978? 'I played well enough to have a chance of winning but I didn't do it. I just wasn't good enough. The cup wasn't full, I guess.'

Woosnam had no such reservations. 'I told my friends I was going to show America how I can really play. I realised it was time I believed in myself. I had always thought I was second class.'

A tall Scotsman had previously slipped the Green Jacket onto the shoulders of a taller Englishman who, in the 55th Masters, in turn acted as valet to a diminutive Welshman. Faldo's Jeeves to the honourable Woosie.

Ben's Sentimental Journey

Harvey Penick had been Ben Crenshaw's coach for 37 years and it seemed inevitable that the Texan would take a sentimental journey in the 59th Masters in 1995. 'I believe in fate,' Crenshaw said, proudly displaying his Green Jacket. 'Fate dictated another championship.' From the age of six Crenshaw had come under the guidance of Penick at the Austin Country Club and the University of Texas. Penick died, aged 90, a week before the Masters and, on the eve of the tournament, Crenshaw left Augusta National to serve as a pall-bearer at the funeral.

When Crenshaw arrived in Georgia he was complaining of a toe injury and had just missed the halfway cut in New Orleans. 'From just a few practice days I got some confidence,' Crenshaw said. 'I don't know how it happened. When you're 43 you don't know how many chances you're going to get.'

Crenshaw, who won the Masters in 1984, certainly played some inspired golf, perhaps the best of his career, and he won in style. His aggregate of 274 was one of the lowest in the history of the tournament. He was also the oldest winner since Jack Nicklaus, who was 46 when he won in another emotional affair in 1986.

Crenshaw began the final round as joint leader at ten under par and he finished at 14 under, a stroke in front of Davis Love III and three in front of Greg Norman and Jay Haas. Love, the last man to qualify for the Masters after winning in New Orleans in a sudden-death play-off, was the leader in the clubhouse following a 66 that contained seven birdies. Going down the final stretch, Crenshaw responded with a birdie at the 16th, where he hit a peach of a tee-shot to within about six feet of the flag, and another at 17, where he rolled in a curling 15-footer. 'It was just meant to be that Ben would play well,' Love said. 'He was driven. All I could do was watch him putt and I just knew he was going to make them.'

Crenshaw, who has always been acknowledged as an outstanding putter, did not three-putt a green in the entire tournament. 'I played the 17th like a dream,' he said. 'It was the prettiest putt I think I've ever hit.' Love had also birdied the 17th but it was at the penultimate hole that Norman, once again, came up short, in every sense. He played a poor approach shot, missing the green on the left, took five and was resigned to a place in the shadows. 'Maybe there was something in the wind,' Norman said. 'Maybe Harvey's up there saying, "Hey, Ben, I'm going to help you do this." You've got to admire what Ben did. It takes a lot of nerve.'

Penick – his *Little Red Book* of golf tips became a bestseller – had given Crenshaw a putting lesson two weeks before the championship. A favourite piece of advice was 'Take dead aim'. 'It means much more than how to hit a golf shot,' Crenshaw explained. 'It means to trust yourself and not think of anything that is going on in the world at that particular moment but letting your muscles and instinct take over.

'Whatever I have accomplished I owe to Harvey. When I was six he cut down a mashie, put my hands on the club and my grip hasn't changed since then. Whenever anybody went to see him for a lesson, they got a large dose of golf and a larger dose of love.'

There was a growing impression that the 59th Masters had been scripted by Mills and Boon. Indeed, Love was all around. Davis Love III pointed out that his father, the late Davis Jnr, had been coached by Penick in college.

Love III, from Sea Island in Georgia, had, up to that point, a miserable record in the majors. His highest finish had been 25th in the Masters in 1992. 'Davis is fabulous,' Crenshaw said with the almost obligatory winner's generosity. 'He's going to win many coats here. He's so loaded with talent.'

Crenshaw won $396,000 and a small percentage of the purse went to Carl Jackson. Harvey Penick may have been Crenshaw's 15th club but it was Jackson who had to carry the bag. Whenever Crenshaw plays at Augusta National he teams up with Jackson, who has more than 30 years of Masters experience. A native Augustan, Jackson, who caddied in his first Masters in 1962, was a former butler to Jack Stephens, the then club chairman. Jackson's knowledge of the greens was invaluable to Crenshaw and the caddie was often consulted.

Jackson also came up with a catchphrase: 'Reach deeper.' It was mentioned several times in the final round and by the time they reached the 18th green the tank was nearly empty. Crenshaw had to take dead aim for the final time to coax in a two-foot putt, and when the ball dropped, so did he. Jackson walked over to lend a helping hand. 'Everything's all right, Ben,' he told him.

Crenshaw received the Green Jacket from Jose Maria Olazabal, who had begun the defence of his title with a 66 in the first round. On a day of low scoring, Nicklaus had posted a 67 but in the second round had retreated with a 78 that included a shanked tee-shot at the 12th. Nicklaus barely made the cut, which came at 145.

As Crenshaw made his move with a 67 following a 70, the lone amateur survivor was the 19-year-old Tiger Woods. Crenshaw had a bogey-free 69 in the third round and was tied at the top of a congested leaderboard with Brian Henninger, an unheralded Oregonian who was playing in his first Masters.

A dozen golfers were bunched within three strokes of each other and, as Crenshaw noted on the final day, Augusta was the 'most tempting golf course in the world'. As his rivals, with the exception of Love's 66, fell away, Crenshaw found the temptation irresistible. His 68 meant that Love was unrequited, by a single stroke.

The Lion King

In the spring of 1998 Mark O'Meara arrived at the Augusta National Golf Club with the reputation of being the tiger's minder. He left six days later looking like a lion. A plump creature, slightly greying around the temples. But a lion nonetheless.

At the age of 41 this admirable, unsung and largely underrated golfer had not simply claimed his first major championship. He had won it in the grand manner by birdieing three of the last four holes to snatch victory away from the world's finest as his 20-foot curling putt dropped into the cup on the 72nd hole.

That delicious sweet moment on an April afternoon in Georgia brought O'Meara's life to a pinnacle of achievement in the way that revealed golf at its most sublime. Four days of sporting action, avidly followed by millions of devotees across the globe, decided by the final roll of a small white ball into a hole four and a quarter inches wide on the very last green. Idiotic, really. Yet wonderfully compelling.

Almost inevitably, because this was Augusta and this was the US Masters, there was a fascinating, almost fairytale story behind O'Meara's long-awaited emergence among the game's élite.

The build-up to the first major of the year had been all about Tiger Woods, whose performance 12 months earlier had prompted what now seem ridiculous calls to change the lay-out of Augusta to stop the young champion dominating the event for years to come. Woods's victory, at 21, had been so extraordinary, so emphatic, as to induce a state of panic among some golf traditionalists who should have known better. His record-breaking 12-shot victory in his first Masters appearance as a professional with a score of 18-under-par 270 indicated to their anxious minds that the only way to prevent him from winning repeatedly – and consequently destroying the charm and mystique of this celebrated tournament – was to drastically amend the masterpiece Bobby Jones had created.

The staid old Green Jackets of Augusta are not renowned for hasty actions, however. So they paid no heed to the clamour, added a few minor alterations (as is their wont) and waited to see what happened. Their wisdom was vindicated. Woods could not repeat his wondrous feats, finished a creditable eighth and Augusta's honour was restored. A sense of reality returned to a somewhat relieved sport, the champion's fall from grace being anything but a disgrace as it simply underlined the true merit of his 1997 achievement.

In the process, Tiger's legacy was to be the inspiration for his friend O'Meara. Among all the theories expounded about how the young phenomenon could be denied a successful defence, nobody had suggested that his regular practice partner might have been taking notes. Youngsters are, in the time-honoured tradition, supposed to learn from their elders. Yet sometimes the pupils teach the teachers, if the teachers are smart enough to help themselves. Mark O'Meara, it should be said, is a shrewd cookie.

Handed the task of acting as a big brother for Woods in the minefield-strewn, banana-skin-laden world of the US Tour, the veteran had proved an admirable choice. Both men were clients of Mark McCormack's International Management Group, they lived close to each other in the gated celebrity community of Isleworth in Orlando, and when Woods made the step from brilliant amateur into the professional ranks, O'Meara was ideally situated to keep a watchful eye on him.

As his achievements in living up to the hype merely increased the frenzy around him, Woods was grateful for the rock of O'Meara's solid values. The experienced professional's been-there-done-that approach offered a powerful antidote to the perils of fame. In 17 years on tour he had won 14 times, played in four Ryder Cups and accumulated $9 million but he still put his family first. Woods was able to tap into the senior professional's vast knowledge of life on the road and come back down to earth among the homely companionship of O'Meara's eight-year-old son Shaun, eleven-year-old daughter Michaelle and wife Alicia.

Yet the partnership was a two-way street. As Woods boomed his colossal drives 70 yards past his initially startled friend in their many practice rounds together at Isleworth, the shorter hitter had to devise ways of overcoming the disadvantage. In the process the old dog learned some new tricks and his game developed.

But there was even more to it than that. The vitality and energy of youth rubbed off on him too. 'There are so many things I've learned from Tiger,' O'Meara explained in the afterglow of victory. 'He has tremendous personal drive and has brought my game on, too. It's like playing tennis with a better player. You have to improve or keep being beaten.

'Spending so much time around Tiger has also rekindled my passion and given me a zest to keep trying for things that had passed me by.'

What had most notably passed him by were major championships. He had had his chances but never revealed the decisive quality needed to come through on the really big occasion. He had led the field after two rounds of the 1995 US PGA Championship at Riviera but faded to finish sixth behind play-off winner Steve Elkington of Australia. He was third in the 1988 US Open and third in both the 1985 and 1991 Open Championships (in which he shared the lead at the start of the final round). At Augusta his best year was in 1992 when he was fourth, five shots behind Fred Couples, his only top-ten finish in 14 attempts to win the US Masters.

Altogether O'Meara had teed the ball up in 56 major championships with a conspicuous lack of success, which had prompted regular questioning about this shortfall in an otherwise proud career. The cagey interviewee fielded such probing with the reasonable response that he had been blessed with a talent which had brought him inestimable rewards and he had no intention of beating himself through failing to meet other people's expectations. Privately, as he later admitted, he did worry about the missing ingredient in his game.

When he opened the 62nd US Masters with two-over-par 74, there was not the slightest reason to believe O'Meara was about to strike a vital blow for the older generation and halt the bandwagon the new breed had set rolling in the previous year's majors. He was five shots behind first-round leader Couples and having problems with his putting, which he knew would have to be in perfect working order if he was to have any chance of succeeding on the slick, marble-fast greens.

But O'Meara still had faith. His long-time coach Hank Haney had been offering soothing words of encouragement throughout pre-tournament practice in the belief that his charge's time was close at hand. Now he introduced some practical advice. During a session on the practice green after the first round, Haney suggested he change his alignment by moving his head more directly above the ball so that he could take the putter head back in a straight line. O'Meara has long been regarded as one of the best putters in the game and this timely tip was all he needed to get into the groove. 'The speed of my putts was fabulous over the next three days,' said O'Meara. 'The best it has ever been.'

During the four days he took a total of 105 putts, compared with a total of 144 if he had two-putted every green. In contrast, the two players who finished only a shot behind him could not match these figures and unquestionably lost the title on the greens. Couples had 114 putts. David Duval, the joint runner-up, took 111.

But before O'Meara could make his mastery tell, he had to work his way into the tournament. A second-round 70 moved him through the field but at halfway he was still five adrift of Couples, who now shared the lead on five-under-par 139 with Duval, the shy 26-year-old in the wrap-around shades, fast emerging as one of the rising stars of the game.

At the weekend O'Meara made his move. A third-round 68 swept him into a share of second place, two behind Couples, who was clinging tenaciously to the lead he had held from the start. He stood alongside a revitalised Paul Azinger, enjoying his best major tournament since recovering from lymphoma in his right shoulder in 1994, and was a shot ahead of Duval and Jim Furyk, the Ryder Cup player with the unconventional swing. The scene was set for a memorable last day, during most of which O'Meara did not look the likely winner. Another near miss seemed the most probable addition to his curriculum vitae.

But before the main course reached its lip-smacking conclusion, spectators were able to whet their appetites on some savoury moments. Out of nowhere came David Toms to create his own entry in the record books. Out of history came Jack Nicklaus to extend his reputation as the Golfer of the Century at the age of 58.

The previous claim to fame of Toms, a 31-year-old journeyman from Shreveport, Louisiana, was a victory in the 1997 Quad City Classic. Pleased to have survived the halfway cut, he hoped a decent last round would give him a healthy pay cheque and push him up the money list. After 11 holes of the final round he was way down the field, making no impression on the event. Then two things happened. His wife Sonya left to catch the plane home and Toms birdied six holes in succession. He completed the back nine in 29 strokes to equal the record on his way to a 64, which gave him a share of sixth place alongside the indefatigable Nicklaus.

The Golden Bear just continued to amaze. How could a man with a sore hip, less than two years away from his 60th birthday, outscore and outshine his playing partner, Ernie Els, the 28-year-old reigning US Open champion and world No. 2? Obviously he could not. Unless he is Jack Nicklaus, and then anything is possible. How the fans loved every moment of his last-round 68, sending cheers echoing through the pines as they recalled the Sunday of 1986 when the Bear rampaged to an improbable final-round 65 to gloriously claim his sixth Masters at the age of 46 (while Els departed to re-evaluate his game and his approach to a major in which he regularly fails to do justice to his elegant talent).

To have pulled off number seven would have stretched the bounds of golfing credibility just a little too far. Not even Nicklaus could score the 64 he needed to finish at the top of the heap this time. But he provided another matchless performance to set alongside so many others which have made this man a sporting figure of incomparable magnitude.

Even though Nicklaus disappointed himself by falling four strokes short of glory, his contribution to a Masters tournament which deserves to be ranked among the finest of recent times could not be under-valued. To suggest he was a warm-up for the main act is less of an insult than a compliment to the quality of the concluding drama. Both Couples and Duval will know they could have won. Furyk had visions of at least taking the contest to a play-off. But none of them could compete with O'Meara's fabulous finish.

Couples was the first to make a decisive move for the Green Jacket. After eight holes the 1992 champion was three shots clear and threatening to pull away from his playing partner O'Meara. Two holes were to wreck his dreams. On the ninth O'Meara hoiked his drive into the trees only to scramble a par, while Couples, from the middle of the fairway, tried to be too cute with his second shot, left it short of the green and made a bogey. Instead of extending his advantage, faltering Freddie was pegged back. Worse was to follow on the 13th, where he pulled his tee into the trees in the corner of the dog-leg, recovered and then put his third into Rae's Creek in front of the green and took a double-bogey seven. Although he was to valiantly regain the dropped shots with a magnificent eagle three at the 15th, Couples was never to recover from those setbacks.

As he fell away, Duval took up the challenge. Since winning his first event on the US Tour at the 87th attempt in October 1997, the professional's son from Jacksonville had made it such a habit that a major championship was the next logical step in his career. Aficionados of the sport were not surprised in the slightest when Duval moved smoothly to the top of the leaderboard and seemed to have victory in his grasp. A run of six birdies had taken him to nine under par, like Couples three clear of the field, but in his case with only three holes to play. Maybe it was no foregone conclusion, but something extraordinary needed to happen to keep Duval's name off the growing list of exciting new major champions. Being Augusta, something did happen.

First Duval three-putted the 16th from the back fringe to offer his pursuers renewed hope. O'Meara, the old lion stalking his prey, needed no further encouragement. A competent two-putt birdie at the 500-yard, par-five 15th was followed by a safe negotiation of the par-three 16th. Two holes to play and the realisation dawned on O'Meara that this was the time to strike. If only he could distil all those years of practice into a handful of flawless strokes, he would make his ultimate dream come true.

As the sun began to set and he strolled up the hill past Ike's Tree on the 17th fairway, two thoughts came vividly to mind. Firstly, despite the tension, he could appreciate the beauty of the setting and his good fortune in being at the heart of a situation that made the senses tingle. 'Jerry,' he said, turning to his caddie, the faithful Higginbotham. 'You know, this is what it's all about.' But mindful of getting lost in a wistful reverie, he brought them both back to reality by adding, 'If I could birdie the last two holes I might just win this thing.'

Easier said than done. But this is Augusta, where mighty deeds are enacted. This was a man with the eye of the tiger, a man whose time had

RIGHT: Seve savours a classic moment: victory at the last in the 1984 Open at St Andrews

BELOW: Rocca roll: Costantino Rocca celebrates his amazing putt on the 72nd hole of the 1995 Open to force a play-off

Walking on water: John Daly toasts his Open victory at
St Andrews in 1995

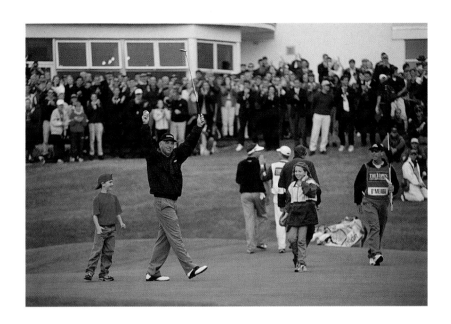

ABOVE: A family affair: Mark O'Meara celebrates his triumph in the Open at Royal Birkdale

RIGHT: Sunday best: Gary Player is congratulated by Seve Ballesteros on a stunning finale in the 1978 Masters

Jack Nicklaus stoops to conquer at the 17th in the final round of the 1986 Masters at Augusta

A great escape: Nick Faldo's outstanding bunker shot at Augusta's 10th during his 1990 play-off victory against Ray Floyd

You beauty! Ian Woosnam wins his first major as he holes out on Augusta's final green

The moment of truth: Mark O'Meara's last-hole birdie putt, which brought his first major title at the age of 41

LEFT: Brothers in arms: Fuzzy Zoeller and Greg Norman after the 18th hole in the play-off for the 1984 US Open at Winged Foot

BELOW: Hale the champion: Irwin putts to win the play-off against Mike Donald in the 1990 US Open at Medinah

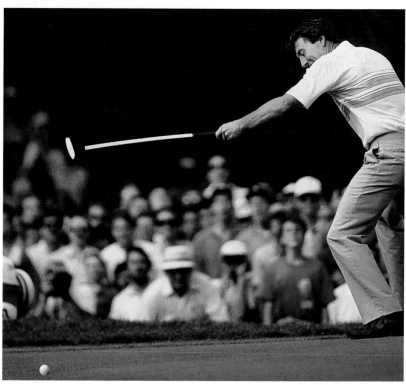

A shot in a million: Bob Tway holes from a bunker to win
the 1986 US PGA Championship

Zinger up for the cup: Paul Azinger with the 1993 US PGA
Championship trophy

arrived. O'Meara struck an imperious approach to the ideal spot seven feet below the flag on the 17th green. In any other circumstances the putt was almost a gimme for such a wielder of the blade. Not now. The putt had to be holed and so it was, with the calm assurance of a man on a mission.

So to the 18th, which many a luckless challenger has had reason to curse. It is the perfect stage for such a moment of theatre. Steeply rising through an avenue of pines before bending to the right, where its green sits below the clubhouse, this 405-yard-long stretch of land is both dangerous and enticing. In recent times the failures of Greg Norman in 1986 (who pushed his second shot into the crowd and missed out on a play-off) and Tom Watson in 1991 (who pushed his drive into the trees and made a double bogey) have been offset by Sandy Lyle's birdie three from the fairway bunker for his thrilling 1988 victory. The drive is a true test of a player's mettle, needing to avoid the two large bunkers on the left without going too far right to block out the approach to the green. Some players opt for a three-wood for accuracy, leaving a long approach to the green. O'Meara, now on the same score as playing partner Couples and having caught Duval, knew that this was no time to be timid. He took the driver and landed the ball in the perfect spot 148 yards from the pin. Couples found sand and knew his chances were fading.

When Couples sent his recovery into another bunker beside the green, the advantage was with O'Meara – if only he could take it. His seven-iron was sweetly struck and finished pin high 20 feet to the right of the hole. Couples came out of the bunker to four feet, knowing the best he could hope for was a par and a play-off. If O'Meara missed and Couples holed, they would join Duval on eight-under-par 280 and face a three-man sudden-death play-off.

Yet O'Meara had it in his power to make extra time unnecessary. What he did not know was that minutes earlier Duval had missed an almost identical putt for possible victory and Furyk had also failed from a similar situation to finish one behind Duval. In both cases they had underestimated the borrow of the right-to-left putt and the ball had slid past on the left side. Although ignorant of this potentially vital piece of information, O'Meara did have the advantage of some inside knowledge. As part of his meticulous planning he had rehearsed the putt from that spot several times during practice. But still he was unsure of the line. 'It had been a long day out there,' he recalled. 'I looked at the putt the first time and it looked as if it was going to break a little to the left. But then I saw that the cup was slanted a little more and I recommitted myself when I was behind the ball to play outside the hole.'

All he had to do now was stroke it in. That's all. The long journey from Orange County, California, where the 13-year-old boy first took a golf club in his hand and was set up for life, would be complete. 'I took a couple of deep breaths and tried to soothe myself a little bit,' he said. 'You want to win it now. I knew that this was my opportunity and fortunately I took it. I hit a pretty good putt and saw it breaking down there. I was concerned with the last foot and a half whether it would hang in there and not lip out on the low side. Fortunately it did that and went on in.'

O'Meara thrust his right arm into the air in a gesture of triumph while his features remained poker-faced. Even as he hugged Higginbotham in celebration, there was no delirious grin, no whooping and hollering that some players could not have resisted. It was as if O'Meara was saying, 'There you are, I've done it. What's the big deal?' Duval, watching on television in the Jones cabin, was not surprised. He had partnered O'Meara in America's President's Cup team and knew what to expect. 'Mark's one of the best putters out there and he makes an awful lot of those,' said the runner-up ruefully.

Couples appreciated O'Meara's muted reaction, while admitting that in the same circumstances he would have been running around the green. 'I felt like scooping my stuff up, walking to the tent and getting the hell out of there,' said the man who knew his Masters was effectively over. But he still had to hole his four-footer, did so and left the stage clear for the champion.

Fate had at last smiled on Mark O'Meara, and he accepted his elevation in golf's pantheon with the same dignity he had displayed in past failures. 'I think it's timing,' he said after being helped into the Green Jacket by his young, old buddy Woods. 'To win a major you need a little luck and to do the right thing at the right time.'

Insisting that he did not qualify to be a great player, O'Meara – who used to be mistaken for fellow professional Mark McCumber – suffered no illusions about his new status. 'I don't need to be a superstar,' he said. 'I want to be a nice player and a good father to my children, to take care of my friends and try to treat people with respect. That's what my father taught me. I don't mind if people recognise me. I think it's flattering. I just hope they get my name right.'

Inevitably, life did change for O'Meara. One of the first consequences of his star status brought attention to a simmering dispute between him and the Swedish golfer Jarmo Sandelin over an incident in the 1997 Lancôme Trophy. A Swedish TV viewer had spotted that on the 15th green in the final round O'Meara, facing a two-and-a-half-foot putt, had replaced his ball half an inch closer to the hole than had been indicated by his marker.

After the incident had been replayed on Swedish TV, Sandelin, who finished runner-up to O'Meara in the tournament, had written to

O'Meara, through his manager, sent a video recording of the incident and asked for an explanation. O'Meara was unable to offer a full explanation but insisted that he had not intended to gain any advantage and, in the meantime, had sought advice from the US Tour and the European Tour. When he was told that the tournament was over, the results had been posted and could not be amended, he hoped the matter would be allowed to rest.

But his Masters triumph led to Sandelin making his grievance public. The controversy hit the headlines and led to the giant Scandinavian confronting O'Meara at the TPC of Europe in Hamburg. The American continued to protest his innocence and steadfastly refused Sandelin's demands to hand back the trophy, while, no doubt, reflecting on the pitfalls of success.

The many friends who backed O'Meara's acknowledged integrity and dismissed the allegation against him as completely unfounded point to the well-deserved breakthrough of one of the most popular US Tour players. The old kid on the block finally made it. In doing so he went to joint 68th on the all-time list, sharing the position with 109 players who won a single major championship.

Little did he know that this was just the beginning. Before the year was out he would leave them all behind. Even, for the time being, a one-time winner named Tiger Woods.

The US Open

Golf is played one stroke at a time but it took me many years to realise it.

– Bobby Jones

A Bobby Dazzler

The dapper Willie Dunn Jnr, who taught golf to the aristocracy in Biarritz, was the game's first playboy. The Vanderbilts invited him to tea in America, where, in 1894, Dunn may have been the first US Open champion. Scotsmen can be relied upon to sniff out a greenback from 100 paces and Dunn was one of a legion who crossed the Atlantic, if not to relieve the natives of their money, then to introduce them to golf.

It was all Robert Lockhart's fault. An immigrant Scot, in 1888 he returned to New York from a visit home, armed with a supply of clubs and balls. It was just what the American yuppie had been waiting for. The next thing, the St Andrew's Golf Club was founded. Like its forefather, the Royal and Ancient Golf Club of St Andrews, it had Scottish members. However, it had something else: an apostrophe. It signified, at least in terms of punctuation, that there was only one St Andrew.

In 1894 St Andrew's Golf Club in Yonkers, New York, held an open championship (match play) and Dunn won, defeating Willie Campbell two up in the final. There were four entrants. Dunn won a hundred dollars and a gold medal, and if it was argued that no single club could arbitrarily run a tournament to decide a national championship, Dunn could have pointed out that Willie Park Snr had won the Open Championship at Prestwick in 1860, when the R and A had nothing to do with it. What Park Snr had done in Britain, Dunn Jnr had done in America. In any case, the fledgling United States Golf Association was formed shortly after Dunn's victory and their records have the diminutive Scotsman, who could not be separated from his medal, as their first champion.

After ill-fated Johnny McDermott (his career was finished at 23) became not only the youngest player at 19 to win the US Open but also the first American-born champion, Francis Ouimet confirmed the maturity of the home-grown response by driving the Brits out of Boston in 1913. The US Open, with one or two notable exceptions, would become an all-American show. And all-American stars were lining up on the tee, including Walter Hagen, Gene Sarazen and Bobby Jones.

In the 1919 US Open at Brae Burn Country Club near Boston, Mike Brady led Hagen by five strokes after 54 holes but shot 80 in the final round to finish on 301. Hagen, who needed to birdie the 18th to win, hit his approach pin high about eight feet to the right of the cup. As he walked towards the green, Hagen sent word ahead for Brady to leave the clubhouse and watch the climax. Hagen's putt caught the lip and spun out. They were tied.

Hagen won the play-off 77–78 thanks to a spot of gamesmanship at the 17th. From his drive Hagen found his ball embedded four inches into the soft turf. He argued that a spectator must have stepped on his ball and asked for a free lift. It was denied him, at which point Hagen insisted he had the right to identify his ball. He picked it up, wiped off some mud and carefully replaced it. He had a shot and the championship was as good as his.

Three years later Gene Sarazen won his first major when the US Open moved to Skokie Golf Club near Chicago. Sarazen, four strokes behind the leaders after the third round, shot 68 for 288 to beat Bobby Jones by a stroke. Playing the 18th, a par five of about 485 yards, Sarazen was tempted to play for par until his caddie told him to go for broke. Into the wind, Sarazen hit driver, driver and the ball finished 16 feet from the cup. He got his birdie, while Jones, who needed two fours to tie, took five on the 17th. When he returned to Pittsburgh, Sarazen, aged 20 (he told the press he was 21 – 'I thought the champion should be a man, not a boy'), was fêted at a victory dinner. He made his entrance in a giant golf ball, and when the band struck up 'The Star-Spangled Banner', the 'ball' swung open and out stepped Sarazen, waving the cup aloft. For 1922 the style was perfect.

Bobby Jones would not have to wait long for his first US Open triumph, although at Inwood, near New York, in 1923 he made heavy weather of it. Believing he had the championship in his pocket, Jones eased up in the final round, and when he took six at the last he had lost four strokes in three holes. He shot 76 for 296. The 18th, a formidable hole, measured 425 yards and in front of the green was a lagoon. Only Bobby Cruickshank, who, as a British soldier, had endured the horrors of the First World War, could catch Jones and to do so he had to birdie the last. His mid-iron approach shot covered the flag all the way, cleared the water and stopped six feet from the hole. It was one of the finest shots ever played in championship golf. Cruickshank holed the putt to tie. 'It gave me a chance to get square with myself,' Jones said. 'I'd never have felt I had won that championship. I finished like a yellow dog.'

The following day they were all-square playing the 18th but Cruickshank half-topped his drive, and when Jones hit an approach that was as impressive as his opponent's had been at the same hole in the last round, the amateur from Atlanta was hailed as the champion. 'I don't care what happens now,' he said. Later he would be recognised as the champion of champions.

Jones was runner-up in the US Open over the next two years but in 1926 he became the first player to win the Open and the US Open in the same year. After winning at Royal Lytham, he sailed on the *Aquitania* to New York, enjoyed a parade through Broadway and caught the sleeper to Columbus, where the US Open was being played at the Scioto Golf Club.

With seven holes to play, Jones trailed Joe Turnesa by four strokes; playing the 18th, Jones needed a birdie to win. The hole was a 480-yard par five, and, with 10,000 spectators lining the fairway and crowding around the green, Jones got the four he needed, ripping an iron to the heart of the green, ten feet from the cup. 'Don't tell me it isn't destiny,' Jones said. 'Do you think I fancy for an instant I could ever do it again?' Jones and the US Open were heart to heart.

At Olympia Fields near Chicago in 1928, Jones and Johnny Farrell were tied on 294 after 72 holes but the title seemed destined to go to Roland Hancock, a 21-year-old professional from North Carolina. Hancock needed only fives on the last two holes to win. As he walked over a footbridge to the 17th tee, passing over a brook reeking with the overflow from bootleggers' stills upstream, Hancock heard a spectator yell, 'Make way for the new champion.' The leader took six at the 17th and six at the 18th to finish a stroke behind Jones and Farrell. The play-off was over 36 holes, the USGA deciding that 18 was not a fair test. Jones bogeyed the 34th to go one stroke down and he holed from 30 feet to match Farrell's birdie at the 35th. At the last Farrell made a putt from eight feet to preserve his one-stroke advantage.

Since 1922 Jones had been beaten over 72 holes in the US Open on only two occasions, and at a time when the bricks in Wall Street resembled gold, the amateur from Atlanta was more popular than a silver dollar. As far as the public was concerned, Jones was a blue-chip investment. He played only weekend golf until he arrived at Winged Foot in the suburbs of New York City for the US Open in June 1929. A.W. Tillinghast, one of the greatest designers in America (his courses stood the test of time even if his name, shamefully, did not), had been asked to produce a 'man-sized course'. Winged Foot, cut through forests, was 6,786 yards long.

Jones's favourite playing partner was Old Man Par. 'He never shoots a birdie and never incurs a buzzard,' he said. 'He's a patient soul, Old Man Par. And if you would travel the long route with him, you must be patient too.'

In the first round, Jones did not appear to be on speaking terms with the Old Man. He began double bogey, par, double bogey but played the rest so aggressively he finished with 69, the best score of the day. Then he shot 75, 71 and went into the last round leading Al Espinosa by five strokes.

Espinosa posted a score of 294 and then watched Jones play on a banana skin. He flew from bunker to bunker at the eighth hole and took seven, and another seven at the 15th meant he needed three pars to win by a stroke. Instead he took three putts at the 16th and at the 18th he needed a par to tie. He pulled his approach into rough on the bank of a bunker and, with his niblick, left his third shot 12 feet short of the hole. The putt had a break of about a foot from left to right and Jones holed it. In the play-off he shot 72, 69 and Espinosa crashed to 84, 80.

In 1930, at the age of 28, Jones dramatically increased his workload. He played in the Savannah and Southeastern Opens, then sailed to Britain and competed in the *Golf Illustrated* Gold Vase and the Walker Cup before gorging himself on the major championships. By modern standards it was not at all dramatic but by Jones's standards it represented overtime.

From 1923 to 1930 he entered a total of 28 tournaments, an average of only 3.6 per year. In all, 21 of those tournaments were major events and he won 13 of them. He won the US Amateur five times in thirteen attempts; the US Open four times out of eleven; the Open three out of four and the Amateur once in three appearances. When he won the last at St Andrews in 1930 it started the ball rolling for his Grand Slam. By now, the bricks in Wall Street had crumbled, but Jones was more solid than ever. He won the Open at Hoylake, the US Open at the Interlachen Country Club, Minneapolis, and the US Amateur at Merion, Pennsylvania.

The US Open was played in a heatwave and this time there would be no tie, in more senses than one. After shooting 71 in the first round, Jones perspired so heavily that the red dye from his tie stained his shirt. The knot was so tight that the tie had to be cut off.

He followed with rounds of 73, 68 and 75 but once again the final round was traumatic. The 17th was a throat-clearing par three of 262 yards and Jones missed the green way to the right. His ball hit a tree and was never seen again. He asked for a ruling and the referee, assuming the ball had gone into a dried-up water hole covered by swamp grass, ruled that Jones could take a drop opposite the point where the ball had crossed the margin of the hazard. He took a one-stroke penalty, pitched onto the green and made five. The ruling was to Jones's benefit and many people felt that, since no one had actually seen the ball fall into the hazard, it should have been declared lost and Jones should have played another ball from the tee.

Jones, now only one stroke ahead of Macdonald Smith, felt he needed a birdie at the last and he got it with a putt from 40 feet that ran over two slopes. His 287 was two strokes too good for Smith and one off the record set by Chick Evans in 1916. At Interlachen, Jones decided that, win or lose in the Amateur, it would be his swansong from competitive golf. At Merion he won the Amateur without breaking sweat and announced, at the age of 28, his retirement.

★ ★ ★

Jones's departure coincided with several changes – a new, improved ball, steel shafts instead of hickory – and the result of the US Open at the Inverness Club in Toledo, Ohio, in 1931 prompted another. It came down to a contest between George Von Elm and Billy Burke. Von Elm, a talented amateur, announced that he had become a businessman golfer. He said he was not qualified to call himself a professional but, on the other hand, if there was money to be won he'd take it, just like any other business income. Burke came in with 292 for 72 holes and Von Elm, who dropped four strokes in five holes, needed a birdie at the last. He holed from 12 feet to force a 36-hole play-off. The next day Von Elm again birdied the last hole to tie. After another 36 holes Burke won with 148 to 149. It had taken 144 holes and the USGA had seen enough. From then on, play-offs would be restricted to 18 holes.

As the Depression bit, most professional golfers endured a hand-to-mouth existence, but the dog days were enlivened by the appearance, from out of the hills of western Virginia, of Sam Snead. He owned a rag-bag of clubs (eight in all, while most players carried more than 20) until Dunlop offered him a contract worth $500, two dozen balls a month and a new set of clubs.

Slammin' Sam was colourful, humorous and a natural. His driving was spectacular and they reckoned that from within 100 yards of the flag he'd get down in two. He was the biggest crowd-pleaser since Jones and when he entered the US Open at Oakland Hills in 1937 he was expected to win. Especially when he produced an eagle three on the last hole in the last round for a five-under-par total of 283.

Snead, though, would always find that, in the US Open, anything he could do someone else could do better. Ralph Guldahl, who two years earlier had announced he was retiring from golf at the age of 23, shot 69 in the final round to deny Snead and the following year became the fourth player to win the US Open in consecutive years. Guldahl was in prime form from 1936 to 1940 (he won the Masters in 1939), but when his game deserted him he finally quit.

Snead began 1939 with three victories and was second in the Masters, beaten by a stroke by Guldahl. The US Open title again beckoned when Snead went into the final round at Spring Mill, Philadelphia, a stroke off the lead. Byron Nelson, who had been five strokes off the pace, finished with a 68 for 284. It was in Snead's hands, for, playing the last two holes, an innocuous par four and a par five, he needed only to par them for a round of 70 and 282. He dropped a shot at the 17th, where he went through the green, but even so a par at the last would have been good enough.

He drove nearly 280 yards into rough on the left and attempted to reach the green in two. He topped the shot and the ball disappeared into a bunker about 110 yards short. With an eight-iron he failed to get out. Then he hit it into another bunker, from where he put the ball 40 feet beyond the hole. He putted three feet past and left his next putt short. Snead was left staring at a figure of eight. It is said that women's eyes watered and men patted him softly on the back. There was no back-slapping a year later, either, when Snead, one stroke behind after three rounds, shot 81.

The first post-war US Open in 1946 was Byron Nelson's last. At the age of 34 he retired to his cattle ranch in Texas. The previous year he had won 18 tournaments, 11 of them in a row. He had a wonderful chance to bow out on a high note when he needed par on the last two holes at Canterbury in Cleveland to win the US Open. But he three-putted the 17th and dropped another stroke at the last and was tied with Vic Ghezzi and Lloyd Mangrum, the latter winning the play-off by a stroke. But for a penalty stroke in the third round when his caddie fell onto his ball, Nelson would probably have won it.

At St Louis in 1947 Snead had another chance to win a championship that seemed to mock him. After he bogeyed the 17th in the last round, he needed a birdie at the 18th to tie Lew Worsham, and he did just that with an 18-foot putt. In the play-off Snead was two strokes in front with three holes to play but Worsham holed from 20 feet for a birdie at the 16th and had drawn level going to the 18th. Snead played a lovely approach to the 18th green, about 20 feet from the flag, while Worsham was off the back edge. His chip rolled 29½ inches past the cup. This we know. Snead left his putt short and was about to address the ball again when Worsham stopped him. 'Are you sure you're away?' Worsham asked him. An official measured the putts: Snead's was 30½ inches from the hole, Worsham's 29½. Snead missed, Worsham didn't. Worsham won with a 69 to a 70.

Snead played in 31 US Opens over 40 years. He won the Masters three times, the US PGA three times, the Open once and 78 other events. Only the US Open rejected his advances.

★ ★ ★

Ben Hogan, on the other hand, enjoyed a passionate affair with the national championship. He won it in 1948 but in February 1949, driving home to Fort Worth, was fortunate to survive a head-on collision with a Greyhound bus. An injury to his left leg was particularly serious, but nothing would stop him from playing in the 50th US Open at Merion in Philadelphia in the summer of 1950. Hogan, his legs bandaged from thigh to ankle, shot 72, 69 but on the final day faced the ordeal of having to play two rounds. He scored 72 in the morning and was three strokes clear of the field playing the back nine in the afternoon.

By that stage his legs were ready to give way and he was in such discomfort he could not pick his ball from the cup. By the time he had limped to the 18th, his lead had gone and he needed a par to tie George Fazio and Lloyd Mangrum. He made a four-foot putt to do so and spent the night in a hot bath to prepare for another 18 holes the next day. Fazio was the first to succumb, and over the closing holes it was between Hogan and Mangrum.

Playing the 16th, Mangrum was one stroke behind, and as he was about to putt he saw an insect on his ball. He lifted the ball, blew the insect away, replaced the ball and made the putt. He had also blown away the title. On the 17th tee he was informed he had incurred a two-stroke penalty for cleaning a ball on the green and his four became a six. Hogan, now three strokes clear with two holes to play, sank a 50-footer for a birdie two at the 17th and won with a 69 to a 73.

Having reached his nadir in 1938 when his wretched form and lack of income had reduced him to virtually living off oranges, Hogan rejoined the Tour in 1951 but his legs forced him to be selective. A feature of the US Open that year was the severity of the course, considerably stiffened by Robert Trent Jones, at Oakland Hills. Hogan shot 76, 73, 71 and 67, the lowest score of the week and arguably, over a brutal course, the greatest finishing round in the championship's history.

It was his third triumph but his *annus mirabilis* was 1953, the year he won the US Open, the Masters and the Open. At Oakmont his aggregate was 283, 16 strokes better than the total with which Sam Parks had won the title on the same course 18 years earlier. Hogan finished six strokes ahead of Snead, the runner-up for the fourth time.

When the US Open was held at the Olympic Club in San Francisco in 1955, Trent Jones was again called in to arm the course to its teeth. In the first round, of the 162 starters 82 failed to break 80. After rounds of 72, 73 and 72 Hogan shot 70, prompting Gene Sarazen, commentating for television, to congratulate him on winning his fifth US Open. Hogan gave his ball to an official and said it was for the USGA museum.

They'd forgotten about Jack Fleck. A former caddie from Iowa, Fleck had played in 41 tournaments and had won less than $7,500. In San Francisco he played with a new set of Hogan clubs and after three rounds was three strokes behind the leader – Hogan. In the final round Fleck went out in 33 and he needed a birdie three at the last to tie with the man whose name was on his clubs. Fleck's seven-iron approach to the 18th green finished eight feet right of the hole and he applied the perfect stroke to the downhill putt.

Fleck had gone round in 67 and Hogan had to unpack his bags. In the play-off the next day Fleck held a one-stroke lead playing the 18th and it was more than enough. Hogan hit his drive into deep rough and took three more strokes to get out. Fleck shot 69, Hogan 72. When the US Open returned to the Olympic Club in 1966, Hogan, then 54, finished 14th. Perhaps four US Opens is the most any man can hope for.

Cary Middlecoff, who became the new champion in 1956, put up a splendid defence the following year at the Inverness Club in Toledo. Jimmy Demaret, at 47, was the leader in the clubhouse on 283 and he watched through the window as Dick Mayer came to the 18th needing a birdie three to beat him. Mayer played the hole flawlessly and holed an eight-foot putt to draw the curtains on Demaret. Middlecoff, who heard the roar, had scored 68 in the morning and needed another 68 to tie. He had to get two birdies in the last three holes and he did just that, making putts of 20 feet at the 16th and nine feet at the last. He was never the same again and in the play-off he shot 79 to Mayer's 72.

★ ★ ★

Arnold Palmer, who birdied the last two holes to win the 1960 Masters, was one of the favourites for the US Open at Cherry Hills, Denver, but not after three rounds. He was in 15th place, seven strokes adrift. The first hole was a par four of 346 yards and, with the ball travelling further at altitude, Palmer drove the green. With six birdies in seven holes he went to the turn in 30. Jack Nicklaus, a 20-year-old amateur who was paired with Hogan, led by a stroke after 12 holes but three-putted the 13th and the 14th.

Both Hogan and Palmer were four under par playing the 17th. With Palmer waiting on the tee, Hogan's pitch to the island green on the par-five 17th was too short and it spun back into the water. With his drive, Hogan found water again at the 18th, where he took seven to finish in 284, level par. Palmer, a witness for the prosecution, knew he could play the last two holes conservatively and he did so for a round of 65 and a total of 280. Two strokes further back, in second place, was Nicklaus. Hogan was impressed. 'I played 36 holes today,' he said, 'with a kid who should have won this thing by ten strokes.'

When the championship returned to Oakmont in 1962, the USGA had the dream ticket of Palmer–Nicklaus. Palmer, with the Masters already won, was playing on a course he had frequented as an amateur and in front of people who idolised him. Nicklaus had turned professional in the winter and the king and the pretender were paired together in the first two rounds.

On the final day more than 21,000 people, most of them paid-up members of the Palmer fan club, invaded the course, shattering the attendance record. Palmer shot 71, 68, 73 and Nicklaus was two strokes adrift after rounds of 72, 70 and 72. The greens were as difficult as any in America and nobody putted them better than Nicklaus. In 54 holes he did not take more than two putts.

Palmer, who had three three-putts in the first round, opened up a four-stroke lead over Nicklaus after the fourth hole in the final round but that soon evaporated. Nicklaus was in first with a 69 for 283. Palmer had chances for birdies at the 17th and 18th but missed from eight feet and ten feet. The two players were tied, and in the play-off the next day Nicklaus shot 71, Palmer 74. In 90 holes Nicklaus three-putted once. Palmer did it ten times.

Before the 1964 US Open at the Congressional Club in Washington, Ken Venturi received a letter from a family friend, Father Francis Murray, which included the lines, 'If you should win you would prove to millions everywhere that they, too, can be victorious over doubt, misfortune and despair.' Beset with a back ailment, Venturi's fortunes had plummeted and at the age of 32 he appeared to be finished. In a qualifying round his partners had to plead with him to continue when he threatened to walk off the course. At the halfway stage of the championship Venturi was six strokes off the lead after rounds of 72 and 70. On Saturday morning he went to the turn in 30 and by the time he finished his round he could barely stand. The temperature climbed into the nineties and Venturi, dehydrated, bogeyed the 17th and 18th for a 66, two strokes behind Tommy Jacobs.

During a 50-minute break Venturi rested in a bedroom in the clubhouse, drank lemon tea and took salt tablets. When he went back to the first tee in the afternoon for the final 18 holes, a doctor accompanied him. Ice was placed against the back of Venturi's neck. The temperature reached 100 degrees but he did not melt. He went round in 70 for 278, four strokes clear of the field. At the end of the year he developed a problem with his wrists through poor blood circulation, and his renaissance amounted to one sticky but glorious week in Washington.

By the summer of 1966 Arnold Palmer was 37 years of age and he had not won a big one since the Masters of 1964. At the Olympic Club in San Francisco, Arnie's Army was back on manoeuvres. Palmer led by three strokes from Billy Casper going into the last round and when he went to the turn in 32 he was seven in front of Casper, his playing partner. But Palmer then became sidetracked, his thoughts firmly on breaking Ben Hogan's record of 276.

Palmer's lead over Casper was five strokes with four holes to play. The 15th was a par three, 147 yards, with a slightly elevated green surrounded by bunkers. The pin was positioned tightly to the right, close to the hazards. Casper hit a safe seven-iron to the left of the flag. 'Preoccupied with beating Hogan's record, I went for the perfect shot, right at the pin,' Palmer said. 'Had the ball hit an inch to the left of where it did it would have stopped near the hole, but it didn't. The ball trickled down into the right-hand bunker. I hit a good sand shot to within eight feet of the pin. Then Billy delivered his *coup de grâce*. From 20 feet he aimed well left to allow for the break and holed the putt. I missed my putt and for the first time I realised that Casper could catch me.'

At the next Palmer took six to Casper's four and at the 17th they were level. Casper made up seven strokes in eight holes, five of them in the last three. Palmer, once again in trouble off the tee, played the 18th heroically to save par. He shot 71 to Casper's 68 and both men finished with 278.

The play-off was almost an action replay of the fourth round. Palmer went to the turn in 33 to Casper's 35 but again it all went wrong for him over the back nine. He scored 73, Casper 69. The Olympic champion's putting, as it had been when he'd won at Winged Foot seven years earlier, was slick, silky and crucial.

Palmer would suffer at the hands of another glossy finisher at Baltusrol 12 months later. In the final round Palmer and Nicklaus were again locked in combat. Playing the seventh, a long par four, Nicklaus, a stroke in front, was 30 feet from the hole with his approach while Palmer had drilled a one-iron to ten feet. Nicklaus holed out; Palmer never gave his putt a chance. The 27-year-old Nicklaus went on to score 65. He finished four strokes in front of Palmer – and one stroke better than Hogan's record aggregate of 276.

Another 27-year-old was fifth at Baltusrol. He had a flat, unorthodox swing but he said he could hit a one-iron 260 yards through a doorway. From 1960 to 1967, Lee Trevino, who grew up in a shack near Dallas with no electricity, no plumbing and no father, played golf 15 hours a day. 'You don't start playing at 5 a.m. every morning and hit a thousand practice balls a day for seven years just to win a two-dollar bet,' Trevino said. He was ready to win the US Open. At Oak Hill in Rochester he scored 69, 68, 69 and 69 to become the first player to achieve four sub-70 rounds. He tied the record of 275 set by Nicklaus, who, at Rochester, finished second, four shots behind.

Trevino's grandfather – a surrogate father – was a gravedigger who shifted earth and booze in equal measure. In the space of a couple of years Trevino won more than $400,000. Not that he saw a lot of it. 'I got it all too fast,' he said. 'It went to my head.' He had business problems, personal problems, he drank, he burned the midnight oil, he missed tee times and withdrew from tournaments. In the locker room at Doral in early 1971, Nicklaus remarked to Trevino, 'I hope you go right on clowning and never learn how good you are, because if you do the rest of us might just have to go home.'

Trevino won in April and won in May but the favourite for the US Open at Merion was Nicklaus. He had already won the PGA Championship and was second in the Masters and Merion was the course where, in 1960, he had scored 269.

In June of 1971 Merion was considered to be a mind-boggling test, the thinking man's course. Nicklaus said he would use his driver on only three holes. Trevino said it was the hardest course he'd ever seen. Par was 70 and in the third round Nicklaus shot 68 to stand at 209, Trevino 69 for 211. Going to the 18th, Trevino held a one-stroke lead and a par four there would give him 279. He missed the green with his approach shot and took a five for 69, 280.

Merion's famous finish also tested Nicklaus to the limit. He had to hole three putts from around six feet to save par at the 15th, 16th and 17th and he came to the last needing a birdie to beat Trevino by a stroke. His drive found the centre of the fairway, from where he hit a four-iron that seemed to cover the flag. His ball came to rest 14 feet short of the cup. His putt trimmed the right edge. Nicklaus shot 71 for 280 and the two most irresistible golfers in the world returned the next day for an 18-hole play-off that entranced the audience.

Trevino had a bogey at the first but then Nicklaus became entrapped by sand. As he attempted a recovery at the second, his ball hit the bank of a bunker and rolled back in. A bogey six. At the short third he again left his ball in a bunker and took a double-bogey five. Trevino went out in 36, Nicklaus 37. Trevino kept his nose in front.

When Nicklaus birdied the 11th, Trevino birdied the 12th, and when Super Mex overshot the 14th green, he chipped on and got down from eight feet to save par. He applied the stiletto at the 15th. Trevino was 25 feet from the hole, Nicklaus eight. Trevino rolled in his curling putt and although Nicklaus sank his, he was still two strokes adrift. When Nicklaus hit his tee-shot into a bunker on the 17th, the game was well and truly up. Trevino shot 68 to 71 and the Golden Cub looked crestfallen. In three big plays that year Nicklaus had finished first, second, second. To emphasise there had been nothing fortuitous about his victory, Trevino won the Canadian Open a few weeks later, followed by the Open Championship.

The championship returned to Oakmont in Pennsylvania in 1973, the course on which Nicklaus had beaten Palmer 11 years earlier. They were both in contention again but on the final day the field was stunned by a tall, thin Californian. Johnny Miller had dropped out of Brigham Young University to join the tour in 1969. After the third round he was six shots off the lead, but this was not the Oakmont of old. The sting from its fearsome greens had been drawn by heavy rain and the course was there to be attacked.

After shooting 76 in the third round, Miller told his wife to pack and be ready to leave Pittsburgh. He then went to the turn in 32, one under for the championship. All eyes were on the 43-year-old Palmer, and when he played the 11th he was four under and he missed a four-foot putt to go five under. On the 12th a scoreboard told him that somebody was five under and it came as a shock to the system. Palmer bogeyed the 12th, the 13th and the 14th. Miller ground Oakmont into submission. He came back in 31 and 63 was the lowest score ever shot in the US Open. He hit every green and missed only one fairway; he had nine birdies and one bogey, a three-putt on the eighth. He finished with a winning score of 279, four strokes better than Hogan had shot at Oakmont in 1953 and than Nicklaus and Palmer had scored in 1962.

Hubert Green won the US Open at Southern Hills in Tulsa in 1977 but he was not everybody's choice. Whilst playing the last round Green was told that he was the subject of a death threat. A woman had telephoned the FBI in Oklahoma City with the message that three men were on their way to Tulsa to kill Green. Were they only 24 hours from Tulsa? The police took no chances. Uniformed officers joined Green's gallery and detectives scoured the crowd. As Green left the 14th hole, his lead reduced to a stroke, officials informed him of the threat. Green could withdraw, ask for play to be suspended or play on. He elected to play on, shot 70 and won by a stroke from Lou Graham.

As the 1980 championship approached, Jack Nicklaus had turned 40 and 21 years had passed since he had won the 1959 Amateur, his first national success. When he arrived at Baltusrol in New Jersey he was, for a man who hadn't won anything in 23 months, in remarkably good spirits. There were those who thought his powers had waned, but for one thing Nicklaus had been working furiously, with the help of Phil Rodgers, on his short game, and for another Baltusrol was where he had won in 1967 with a 72-hole record.

Thirteen years on, Nicklaus had a three-foot putt at the 18th in the first round for a record 62. He missed. After 54 holes Nicklaus was on 204, level with Isao Aoki of Japan, and when the last pair went out in the final round it was estimated that the television audience had reached 90 million homes.

When Nicklaus reached the turn in 35 he was ahead by two strokes, but although he played almost flawless golf over the back nine, Aoki stayed with him. At the 17th (630 yards), Aoki was five feet from the hole in three, Nicklaus 22 feet. Nicklaus holed his putt for a birdie, as did Aoki, and they also birdied the 18th. Nicklaus shot 68, Aoki 70, for 272 and 274 respectively. The record had been 275. The scoreboard carried another message: JACK IS BACK. It was his fourth US Open victory and he had caught Anderson, Jones and Hogan.

It was four more than Tom Watson had won. Watson kept heading the money list and he kept winning Opens in Scotland, but the US Open remained aloof. At Baltusrol Watson was in the hunt but he finished four strokes adrift of Nicklaus. Their rivalry had an edge. Some observers reckon that it took Nicklaus a long time to recover from his epic duel with Watson for the Open at Turnberry in 1977. Before the final round at Baltusrol, Watson ventured the opinion that 'if Jack wins, I think he might retire from golf. That is why there's a lot more pressure on Jack Nicklaus than there is on Tom Watson.' Nicklaus thought the remarks ill-considered and ill-timed. 'It's a ridiculous thing for him to say.'

The 1982 US Open at Pebble Beach, California, where Robert Louis Stevenson described the Monterey Peninsula as 'the greatest meetings of land and water', produced another great meeting, of mind and matter. Pebble Beach, or the Cardiac Cliffs, as they are called in Thomas Boswell's *Strokes of Genius*, is probably the most breathtaking place on earth to play golf. Watson played there often during his college days at Stanford. 'It reminds me of a lot of Scottish courses,' he said.

The crashing surf of the Pacific does not have a pacifying influence. 'I must win the US Open to be considered one of the great players,' Watson said. After rounds of 72, 72 and 68 he was three shots ahead of Nicklaus and tied for the lead. The next day Nicklaus went out and birdied five consecutive holes from the third to take, momentarily, a one-shot lead. He went round in 69 and 284 and then waited for Watson. At the 16th Watson, at five under for the championship, led by one but after he drove into a bunker he and Nicklaus were level.

Watson then faced two of the most beautifully dangerous holes in the world. The 17th, a par three of 209 yards, has a green shaped like an hourglass with a ridge in the middle. The hole protrudes into Carmel Bay and is perched above a rocky beach. Watson hit a two-iron into the breeze; the ball hit the left edge of the green and bounded into rough between two bunkers. Nicklaus, watching on television, thought it would be impossible for Watson to get a three from there and calculated that he would have to birdie the last to get into a play-off.

Watson had other ideas. 'Get it close,' his caddie said. Watson replied, 'I'm not going to get it close. I'm going to make it.' On the 10th, 11th and 14th holes he had made improbably long putts. Now he relied on his sand wedge and he had a better lie in the weeds than he could have hoped for. He opened the face, sliced across the ball and slid the edge of the club underneath.

'As soon as it landed on the green I knew it was in,' Watson said. It broke a foot and a half left to right and disappeared. He had turned a probable four into a delicious two and ran around the green, grinning maniacally. Watson also birdied the 18th, shot 70 and his 282 beat Nicklaus by two strokes. 'You son of a bitch,' Nicklaus said as he gave Watson a bear hug. 'You're something else.' Later Nicklaus said, 'That is one of the worst shots that ever happened to me.' One man's chip-in is another man's trap-door.

'This makes me feel that my career is one plateau higher,' Watson said. 'I don't think you could have a better scenario than Pebble Beach and Jack Nicklaus, the greatest golfer of all time.'

When Fuzzy Zoeller stood on the 18th fairway at Winged Foot, he was prepared to concede the 1984 US Open to Greg Norman. Norman had just holed a putt from around 40 feet and had run a lap of honour across the last green. Zoeller took a white towel from his bag and waved it in surrender.

But Zoeller had only been winged, not mortally wounded. He was unaware that Norman's putt was for par, not a birdie. The Australian had hit his approach shot into the stands on the right. No one had ever birdied the 72nd hole to win the US Open; Norman hadn't and Zoeller needed a par four to tie, on 276. He got it, and by the time they walked up the 18th fairway again the following day, the crowd was chanting, 'Fuzzy, Fuzzy!' Norman waved a white towel. In the play-off Zoeller shot 67, Norman 75.

After Fuzzy, the championship seemed set for a Chinese takeaway when it moved to Oakland Hills in 1985. T.C. Chen, a former sailor, shot 65 in the first round of his first US Open, the highlight of which was an albatross (or double-eagle) two at the second, where he holed a three-wood from 240 yards.

Going into the final round, Chen, on 203, was two strokes ahead of Andy North. Albatrosses and sailors, however, are not good travelling companions. When he birdied the second, Chen's lead was four strokes, but the fifth, a par four of 457 yards, stopped him in his tracks. He took eight, including a penalty shot for hitting the ball twice on the same stroke. He continued to drop shots and within four holes crashed from four strokes ahead of North to three behind. North also faltered but despite scoring 74 – he had done so in the last round to win the US Open at Cherry Hills seven years earlier – he won by a stroke from Chen and two others.

Everybody scratched their heads. North had made only two birdies in the last 36 holes and in the last round had hit only four fairways. Yet on the leaderboard nobody had made the move that would have sent North southwards.

Olympic Silver for Watson

In the summer of 1987 Scott Simpson emerged, as Larry Mize had done in the Masters, from beneath the sun-visored anonymity of the rank and file of American golf to become the US Open champion. No disrespect to Simpson, but the groans from the press tent could be heard in Sausalito.

Tom Watson was the hot favourite going into the final round at the Olympic Club in San Francisco. Watson was not only popular, he also had the sympathy vote. The advantage he held over Simpson and a few others on the leaderboard was that he had been winning major championships while they were still drinking at the soda fountain. Watson, though, had suffered a drought and his last victory had come in 1984. Prior to that he had won eight majors and had been top of the money list for four consecutive years. 'I know how to win,' he said. 'I know how it feels and I know how it's done. I'd rather be in the lead than coming from behind. It's anybody's guess what's going to happen.'

Twenty players were within four shots of Watson and what happened did not follow the path of the romantics. In the final round Simpson, 31, from San Diego, California, shot 68. It was by far the best round of the day from anybody who had a prayer of landing the championship.

Simpson's other similarity to Mize is that he is a devout Christian, a non-smoker and a non-drinker who was converted from Buddhism in 1984. He prayed on Saturday night, Sunday morning and again during the final round. 'I didn't pray to win, I just prayed that I would do my best,' Simpson said. 'In previous tournaments I tended to lose my temper and I made a commitment to the Lord not to get angry. Christianity is the most important thing in my life and I give thanks to God for the opportunity to compete and do my best. My belief helped when the pressure was on.'

But did he believe he could win the US Open? 'To tell you the truth, I am surprised. There have been so many great champions and I didn't think I was good enough.'

Watson is one of those champions, and he would have won the title again but for a nervous start which cost him two strokes when he three-putted the first two greens. He did so again at the fifth. When he dominated world golf he never three-putted anything – or at least never seemed to.

Simpson went into the fourth round one under par after scores of 71, 68, 70, one stroke behind Watson, who made 72, 65, 71. It was the third occasion the Olympic Club had hosted the US Open and the result was as surprising as the previous two. In 1955 Jack Fleck birdied two of the last four holes to force a play-off with Ben Hogan which Fleck won. In 1966 Arnold Palmer blew up over the back nine and lost a seven-stroke lead to Billy Casper. Fleck and Hogan tied on 287, Palmer and Casper on 278. Simpson surpassed Fleck's performance by birdieing three of the last five holes, the 14th, 15th and 16th, and Watson had very little room for manoeuvre.

Watson had birdies at the eighth, ninth and 14th holes but when he reached the 18th tee he knew he had to get a birdie three to force a play-off with Simpson. He hit a perfect drive but was short with his second when he used a pitching wedge instead of a nine-iron. 'I thought the wind was at my back but when I hit the shot the breeze was in my face,' Watson said. He had a 45-foot putt and thousands of people standing ten deep around the 18th green were willing the ball to drop into the hole. The putt was on line but stopped, agonisingly, two inches short. Simpson, already in the clubhouse, finally accepted that it was a day of thanksgiving.

Watson's cause had not been helped when a huge balloon alongside the 18th fairway broke loose and got caught in the eucalyptus and cedar trees. 'I didn't know what the hell it was,' he said. 'It made a hell of a racket and I thought something was dropping out of the air.'

In the end Watson shot 70 to finish on 278, one stroke behind Simpson. Seve Ballesteros was in third place, four strokes further back. 'It felt good to be back in the hunt again,' Watson said. 'I had to win to prove I was back. It was one of the most important rounds of my career.' As it was, of course, for Simpson. No longer would he be mistaken for his fellow tour professional Tim Simpson. 'People keep mixing us up,' said Scott. 'During the tournament I received cries of, "Go on, Tim!"'

To many Europeans the US Open is closed. The field of 156 included a solitary Briton, Sandy Lyle (by virtue of winning the Open at Royal St George's in 1985), and three other Europeans. While the R and A is more generous in accommodating Americans than the US Open is in inviting players from overseas, the USGA can defend itself against charges of nepotism. The qualifying list at the Olympic Club began with 5,400 entries, whittled down to 600 golfers who competed for places on 12 courses. Arnold Palmer was a casualty, while Johnny Miller, the only golfer to win the US Open and Junior Open titles, had to qualify the hard way after being refused a special exemption.

Bobby Jones observed that nobody wins the US Open; everybody else just loses it. America has produced some forgettable golfers and Andy North is one. North has won two US Opens, which is one more than Palmer and two more than Sam Snead, which is all the more remarkable considering that Snead completed 72 holes on 27 occasions.

Four years after San Francisco, Scott Simpson had a gilt-edged chance to follow North's direction. The 91st US Open in 1991 was held at Hazeltine National near Minnesota and the European entry was considerably healthier than it had been at the Olympic Club.

Hazeltine had been the venue in 1970, when Tony Jacklin became the first Englishman to win the US Open since Ted Ray. Ray had won at the Inverness Club in Toledo, Ohio, in 1920. In Ray's day there was an entry of 265 players. On the day of the Jacklin, the figure was 3,605 – but there were more Europeans competing in 1920.

In the Swinging '60s Tony Jacklin, a young man from Scunthorpe via Carnaby Street, decided to head west and take on the Americans. He went to the qualifying school, gained his card and in 1968 won the Jacksonville Open in Florida. 'Nobody remembers but I was the first European to win a four-round tournament in America,' Jacklin recalls. 'Nobody had ever done it, not even Henry Cotton.' Jacklin became a pioneer because he found the golf scene in Britain dull.

At that time the European Tour was on the drawing board and tournaments were played for by the humble golf professionals. Humility was not Jacklin's bag. 'There was a dour crowd in Britain. If you wore bright clothes they thought you were distinctly odd. If there was a pair of gold lamé trousers I would be the man for them. I was far more American in outlook and I felt comfortable there. In Jacksonville I beat Gardner Dickinson, which was great. I hated him.'

Jacklin relished the challenge, and the hostility he received from some US Tour members simply made him more determined. 'The softest thing about me had to be my teeth,' he said. Apart from exploiting America to perfect his technique, which involved far more use of the legs than had ever been taught in Britain and without which he said he would not have stood a chance of winning the Open, he took great pleasure in beating Americans at their own game and in their own back yard.

'There was an element on the tour that was jealous of foreign players,' Jacklin said. 'Their attitude was that every time a foreigner did well, the Americans were another place down the money list. No one who thought like that ever did any good because they live in a small, small world. I remember a players' meeting when Dave Hill said we shouldn't be allowed on the tour. And he was sitting next to me.'

At the end of the 1970 US Open at Hazeltine, Hill was again sitting next to Jacklin – at the prize-giving ceremony as a distant runner-up, seven strokes behind. Hill had described the course as a cow pasture. 'Hazeltine was the single most satisfying win I had,' Jacklin said. 'Hill was a fairly volatile character. Still is. He sticks his foot in his mouth but he took a lot of heat off me. He was waffling away and I was simply enjoying the golf.'

Jacklin ran away with it. In the first round there was a gale-force wind and heavy rain and the Lincolnshire lad was in his element. While people like Palmer, Player and Nicklaus were blown away, Jacklin was the only player to beat par on the opening day. 'I increased my lead every day,' he recalls. 'I was three ahead after the second round, four after the third and seven after the fourth. It was two fingers up to the small-minded lot. They were an inspiration to me because they got right up my nose. That feeling stayed with me a long time. Nick Faldo and Severiano Ballesteros have experienced a similar thing.'

Jacklin, of course, did not regard everyone on the American Tour as though they were Machine Gun Kelly. There were others, notably Tom Weiskopf and Bert Yancey, who befriended the young Englishman. On the morning of the final round at Hazeltine, Weiskopf and Yancey taped a piece of paper to Jacklin's locker. On it was written one word in capital letters: TEMPO.

Jacklin's caddie was a teenager, Tom Murphy. 'We got along very well right from the start,' said Murphy, now a businessman. 'I was scared to death most of the time. On the last day I still remember him saying, "Just keep me calm." I can still see his face on the penultimate hole. It took a couple of seconds but then he smiled and that's when we both knew it was his.'

Jacklin won $30,000. On Sunday night he sent his trousers to the cleaners and the winner's cheque was still in the back pocket. When the garment was returned the ink on the cheque had faded. After his novel attempt at laundering money, Jacklin had to ask the USGA to write him a new cheque. 'I wanted,' Jacklin said, 'to be the best player in the world. Maybe I was for a short time.' He had certainly become one of only three players to break par in four rounds of a US Open, the others being Casper in San Francisco in 1966 and Lee Trevino in Rochester in 1968. Jacklin was also one of only four to have led after every round, joining Walter Hagen in 1914, Jim Barnes in 1921 and Ben Hogan in 1953.

When Hazeltine hosted the US Open again in 1991, the club was determined to rid itself of Hill's legacy. The course underwent major surgery, with nine of the holes virtually unrecognisable from 1970. The sharp dog-legs and blind landing areas were more or less obliterated. The players formed a chorus to sing Hazeltine's praises.

Nonetheless, Hazeltine was destined once again to be remembered for the wrong reasons. When a violent thunderstorm struck the course, six spectators who were sheltering beneath a tree by the 11th green were floored by lightning. One of them, William Fadell, 27, from Minnesota, died shortly afterwards.

The show, of course, went on, but not with the enthusiasm with which it had started. Over the first two days there were 56 sub-par rounds; on Saturday there were two. A strong wind was the explanation, and at the end of the third round Scott Simpson and Payne Stewart led on 210, six under par.

The two were still leading and were still at six under after the fourth round. Simpson, who had finished brilliantly to deny Tom Watson four years earlier, left his art in San Francisco. Leading Stewart by two strokes with three holes to play, he had a bogey five at the 16th and another at the 18th. If Simpson's driving off the tee was erratic, though, Stewart's putting was vulnerable over the closing holes and he missed shortish putts for birdies at the 15th, 16th and 17th. They both finished with par rounds of 72 for aggregates of 282.

Stewart, wearing a brace to support his back and his plus twos to support the NFL, was plus three in the 18-hole play-off the following day and he still managed to beat Simpson in the all-American final. He had a solitary birdie on the fifth day, his first in 31 holes, which helped to improve his score to 75, and that was two strokes too good for Simpson. Over a course which became more difficult as the championship ground on and on, Stewart, who had been inactive for ten weeks, won the second major title of his career.

His first was the US PGA at Kemper Lakes near Chicago in 1989 when he scored spectacularly in the last round and then watched the leaders throw away their advantage. 'Winning this gives me much greater satisfaction,' Stewart blubbered on the Monday evening. 'It was the way it was earned.'

He was bedecked in stripes in the red, white and blue of the NFL's Superbowl. Appropriately, there were no stars. Earlier in the week he had appeared as a Minnesota Viking, a Buffalo Bill and a Miami Dolphin, a cross-section of natural history covering looting, shooting and talking to Flipper.

Stewart embraced his wife, embraced Simpson's wife and embraced the American tradition of shedding tears on the 18th green, or, in this case, the 90th. He was choked. Not half as choked as Simpson, though, who for the second day running relinquished a two-stroke lead with three holes to play. To do so once may be unfortunate but to do so twice suggests that the man who lives in Hawaii may have been a coconut shy of the full bounty. Stewart led from the front from day one but, in the absence of any serious challenger but Simpson, still needed to rely on the frailty of his opponent over the closing holes.

Going into the 14th in the play-off, Stewart led by one stroke. He found the rough on the left, took a bogey five to a birdie, Simpson holing from 25 feet, and found himself one behind. Stewart was in even deeper rough at the long 15th and when he three-putted for a bogey six to a par, Simpson, enjoying a three-shot swing in two holes, was two ahead. But what he gained on the swing he lost on the roundabout. Simpson took three putts at the 16th, Stewart one, from 20 feet: a five to a three. Thus they were back to all square, but once again Simpson had lost control. There are 10,000 lakes in Minnesota and at the 182-yard 17th Simpson found one of the smallest. He hooked his tee-shot into the water and emerged with a bogey four.

He had his third bogey in succession at the 18th, coming home in 40 in a round of 77 to Stewart's 75. Twice Simpson had managed to turn the wine into water. A crowd estimated at 20,000, understandably less than half the previous day's figure, took a Monday off to watch the third play-off in four years.

The USGA, in what is probably a misguided conception of tradition, adheres to the format of an 18-hole play-off. It is strange that in a country which invented razzmatazz, it favours a formula which invites tedium. Even when the field was reduced to two players, the round took four and a half hours. The scoring, whilst close, was high, just as it had been in the play-off the previous year. In terms of excitement, in recent years the US Open has not compared with the Masters, which, in the event of a tie, is decided by sudden death, or the Open Championship, which has a diluted play-off on the fourth day.

'Every golfer in the world understands that the best test of golf is 18 holes,' said Grant Spaeth, then the president of the USGA. 'It's like taking a full examination. Tell me what a game of golf is? It's 18 holes. That's our tradition. There's no compelling reason to alter something that's been part and parcel of the USGA from the beginning.' In fact the USGA used to have a 36-hole play-off, and another 36 if it was still tied. They changed that in the 1930s and adopted an 18-hole compromise. 'I'd be very surprised if any player didn't want to tee it up for another 18,' said Spaeth.

Well, at Hazeltine, Stewart, for one, was not in favour of an extra day. 'The fans came to see a champion crowned,' he said. Half of them did. The trouble with another 18 holes involving two players is that the nature of the championship is dramatically changed. An element of match play is introduced and safety first is the order of the day, hence disappointing scores. Nobody has to look over their shoulder or even look at the scoreboard. Another day, another guaranteed dollar. And if 90 holes isn't enough, the USGA swallows its tradition and bites the capsule of sudden death.

The Boston Stranger

Curtis Strange had a reputation for being the nearly man of American golf. Highly respected by his peers; a pin-up to the women in the gallery. He had it all. Nearly. What Curtis Northrup Strange did not have, and what any self-respecting golfer who wishes to leave his mark on the game must have, was a major championship to his name.

Strange, before his hair had the chance to turn any greyer, made the quantum leap in the 1988 US Open at the Country Club at Brookline, on the outskirts of Boston. To emphasise that he was no one-hit wonder, he did it again 12 months later.

The Country Club is one of the ancestral homes of golf in America and its members were among the founding fathers of the USGA. The modern-day protagonists have little in common with Francis Ouimet, a store clerk whose portrait is plastered, and rightly so, all over the primrose clapboard clubhouse. Ouimet's exploits are among the most outstanding and inspired in the rich history of the game. Seventy-five years before Strange was to leave his mark in Boston, Ouimet, a native of Brookline, won the US Open.

The scale of the upset defied belief. Ouimet was 20 years old and an amateur to boot. After four rounds he tied with the Englishmen Harry Vardon and Ted Ray, figures so dominant in the game that the USGA moved its Open from its June date to September to accommodate them. In a play-off over 18 holes, Ouimet, who was accompanied by a 13-year-old caddie, Eddie Lowery, shot a one-over-par 72. Vardon had a 77 and Ray 78. According to Bernard Darwin, a grandson of the naturalist Charles and the then golf correspondent of *The Times*, Ouimet's round on a wet, muddy day was by far the most enthralling game he had ever seen. 'Mr Ouimet gave an exhibition of skill, nerve and courage that, considering the circumstances, has never been equalled,' he said.

Ouimet's achievement was the origin of the species. The realisation of an American dream catapulted golf into the public imagination, helped to relax the image of exclusivity and changed the course of the game. That was in 1913. Fifty years later the US Open returned to the Country Club and, to an extent, history repeated itself in that there was a three-way play-off and the championship was again won by a New Englander. Julius Boros returned a one-under-par 70, three strokes better than Jacky Cupit, whom you would have heard of had he won, and six better than Arnold Palmer.

The 88th championship in 1988 saw Jack Nicklaus appearing in his 32nd US Open, a fact announced while Nicklaus was playing in a practice round with Greg Norman. Norman was aged one when Nicklaus played in his first US Open.

'So many players have trouble with their temperament that you can rule out more than half the field,' said Nicklaus. 'Temperament is something you have to cultivate.' So who was cultivated enough to occupy the Country seat? Sandy Lyle's incentive was to become the first man since Nicklaus in 1972 to win the Masters and the US Open in the same year; Nick Faldo's was to emulate Tony Jacklin by taking the Open and the US Open; Curtis Strange's was to win a major, and this one would do nicely.

The small greens, fast and contoured, held the key. The temperature, for the most part, was in the nineties, salt tablets were more popular than hot dogs and the Environment Department said that the quality of the air was unhealthy. Mr Ouimet would not have believed it. 'To me,' he once remarked, 'the property around here is hallowed. The grass grows greener, the trees bloom better, there is even a warmth in the rocks. And I don't know, gentlemen, but somehow or other the sun seems to shine brighter on the Country Club than on any other place I have seen.'

Mac O'Grady also waxed lyrical, although in 1988 he put it somewhat differently. O'Grady is an eccentric American golfer, an oddball, as they say Stateside. He played the game right- and left-handed, sometimes during the same round. His views on life and sport and other minor matters were so frequently chronicled, he was almost quoted on Wall Street. 'The mementoes in the Country Club locker room,' observed O'Grady, 'represent relics of times when Spartacus's warriors went to battle. Those relics used to be the bones and skulls of the fallen; today it's pictures. We modern-day gladiators must pay special tribute to follow their majestic yellow brick road.'

There were other gladiators out there spoiling for a fight and the championship was placed in doubt over an incident that threatened to make the Boston Tea Party look like a storm in a teacup. The Irish-Americans were up in arms over a tongue-in-cheek article in the magazine *Golf Digest*. It referred to the early Irish settlers as 'Boggies' and it said that when the course at Brookline was being built, the English construction manager had to tell the Irish labourers 'green side up' when they were laying the turf.

The late Peter Dobereiner, the highly respected correspondent of *The Observer* and the author of the article, was denounced on television by a cardinal. That was the opening shot. *Golf Digest* had distributed the article as an advertisement in the *Boston Sunday Globe* and copies of the paper were subsequently thrown into Boston Harbour. Mayor Ray Flynn demanded apologies from *Golf Digest* and the *Globe*. In the land of the free press and the home of the brave, he got them. In their apology, *Golf Digest* called the story 'tasteless' and 'unnecessary'. In addition, the New York Times Company, the parent company of *Golf Digest*, sent Mayor Flynn a written apology.

Although 250,000 copies of the *Globe* were supposed to contain the article, delivery drivers removed many of the offending pages after a plea was made to their union from the Irish-American Labor Council. The USGA were made aware that the union had the power and the will to pull the plug on the tournament itself. Dobereiner, who had a torrid time at Customs when he set foot in Boston, had pressure (in some cases extremely sinister pressure) applied from all sides to retract and apologise. After a meeting with the mayor's office, he issued a statement: 'I am sorry it was so thoroughly misinterpreted. It was intended to make fun of the snooty, stuffy founders of the club. That was the whole point of the article. I don't think any true Irishman would take issue at what I wrote. I am not apologising for the article, because it wasn't intended to be racist.' The *Globe* carried a picture of Dobereiner across six columns underneath the headline 'Dobereiner Regretful'. It had a sub-head: 'But Not For What I Wrote.' The 88th US Open was saved.

In the first round Strange shot 70, one under par, with the help of an eagle three at the 527-yard 14th, where he chipped in from 90 yards. Faldo – 'I hit only one bad shot all day' – scored 72. His errant shot came at the 12th, the only bastardised hole on the course. For club members it is a 450-yard par five. For the purposes of the US Open it was made a par four and Faldo played it like a member, taking a bogey five.

On the second day, while Faldo was buoyant, Greg Norman, the Great White Shark, hit rock bottom. Norman withdrew after injuring his left wrist while playing the ninth hole. He hit a rock with his seven-iron and damaged a ligament. Faldo and Strange both shot 67; in the third round it was Faldo 68, Strange 69. Faldo was six under, Strange seven. In the final round the status quo was maintained until the Virginian squandered the lead with a three-putt bogey at the 17th, the 71st hole. At the final hole he hit his approach shot into a bunker at the front of the green.

Hale Irwin had called Strange the best golfer in the world, but despite amassing a mountain of money in 12 years on tour, until now he was remembered for his demise in the 1985 Masters. Now, in front of thousands of people packed around the 18th green, he had the chance to let the sands of time blow over the memory of Augusta National. 'You don't go into a bunker saying, "This is for the US Open." If you do you don't have a chance in hell,' Strange said. 'You just have to go in there and believe in yourself. I'd done it a million times in practice.' He blasted the ball to about a foot from the flag.

Strange made par for 72, Faldo par for 71 and they were tied on 278, two strokes clear of anybody else. They had been paired together in what amounted to a private duel, a preliminary skirmish before the play-off the following day. They had ringside support from their wives, Sarah Strange and Gill Faldo. 'He's very much a body-language person,' said Mrs Strange. 'When things are going well he carries himself differently. When they're not, his shoulders are slumped, his head is down.'

In the play-off she liked what she saw. The occasion dictated the mood of a tense, long fifth day and the scoring was no better than moderate. Although there were only two players on the course, the gallery was huge. Strange had said earlier in the week that the time had come for an American to redress the balance in world golf which had swung towards Europe. The crowd was in agreement.

The round took more than four hours – because of the intransigence of USGA officials it was impossible to report the play-off out on the course – and it was in the closing holes that Strange drew clear. At the 13th, a par four of 433 yards, Strange, who was leading by one stroke, proceeded to sink an extraordinary 29-foot putt for a birdie. It went from right to left and then straightened to drop into the middle of the hole. Strange dropped to his knees in sympathy.

Faldo, who had driven into the rough on the right, hit his approach 35 feet past the hole and his birdie putt ran seven feet beyond the flag. He missed the return to take a bogey five, his third bogey of the round. Suddenly Strange held a three-stroke lead. It wasn't the American who was on his knees.

Faldo finished bogey, par, bogey, bogey for a round of 75 to Strange's 71. Faldo had refused to accept that his Boston marathon had run its course until he hit his second shot on the 17th hole on the fifth day. He hit what he thought was a perfect seven-iron but made a gesture of surrender when he saw the ball pitch on top of the slope instead of below. 'Everything I tried just didn't come off,' Faldo said. 'At least when you tie you leave your mark. You get your picture in the clubhouse.'

Strange, when he paid tribute to his father, who died at the age of 39, was in tears. 'I have to thank my dad. This was for him. This is the greatest thing I've ever done.' Faldo had a word with him: 'You'll love the feeling. Cherish the moment.' Strange did not have to wait long for the moment to be recaptured.

The Oak Hill Cluster

At first there were intrepid settlers who built their log cabins and staked their claims. Then there was Colonel Nathanial Rochester. He bought the land in 1811 and the city was named after him, but he would not recognise it now. Rochester became famous for flour and flowers – and innovation. A young bank clerk named George Eastman spent his evenings experimenting with dry plates and film in his mother's kitchen. Eastman's first camera, introduced in 1888, launched a new industry. A century later Eastman Kodak were employing about 45,000 Rochesterians. In 1906 the Haloid company – renamed Xerox in 1961 – had its start in a loft above a shoe factory and went on to develop the world's first automatic paper copier. Rochester is upstate and upmarket.

You need good connections to become a member of the Oak Hill Country Club and the membership fee of $25,000 is almost incidental. Oak Hill hosted the US Open in 1956, Cary Middlecoff's year; 1968, when Lee Trevino, with a four-leafed clover in his back pocket, became the first player in the history of the championship to break 70 in all four rounds; and 1989, when Curtis Strange would not let go of the cup.

Middlecoff, who won the 1949 US Open, was staking a claim as Ben Hogan and Sam Snead began to make an exit from the major stage as leading players. Middlecoff, the son of a dentist, graduated from the University of Mississippi and the University of Tennessee Dental College. He won the Tennessee Amateur four years running and when he turned professional in 1947 he gave himself two years to make it or return to staring into people's mouths. He was good enough at driving – some say the longest and straightest in the game – to forget about drilling.

In his book *The US Open*, Robert Sommers said, 'Middlecoff was a mass of nerves. He was at once the fastest walker and slowest player on the tour. He moved along with quick, impatient strides, but once he reached the ball, he studied the shot for long and aggravating periods. He'd pick one club, then go back and pick another. He'd address the ball, then step away. Once over the ball, he'd set the club, then peek down the fairway, set the club, peek again. Endlessly. He chain-smoked. He fidgeted restlessly. He drove the gallery and other players mad.'

In the US Open at Oakmont in 1953, Middlecoff was so furious about his starting time, he deliberately hit his ball into the Pennsylvania Turnpike and walked off the course. At Oak Hill in the summer of 1956 he was in the driving seat. After rounds of 71 and 70 he trailed Peter Thomson by two strokes and Hogan by one but then he pulled ahead. In the third round Thomson lost four strokes over the last three holes and shot 75, Hogan 72 and Middlecoff 70. Middlecoff consolidated his lead in the fourth round until wavering over the last three holes, all long, demanding par fours. He bogeyed the 16th and 17th and drove into the rough at the 18th. He was short of the green in two but pitched to two feet to save par for another round of 70, and an aggregate of 281.

Three players were breathing down the dentist's neck. Hogan needed three pars to tie. His approach shot at the 17th jumped across the green and settled in heavy rough, his chip rolled three feet past the flag and he missed the putt. He also missed a birdie putt from 30 feet at the last, and Hogan, who had won four US Opens, was a stroke adrift on 282.

With four holes to play, Julius Boros needed a birdie to tie. It was like drawing teeth. At the 15th his putt died on the lip of the cup, at the 16th he grazed the edge of the hole and at the 18th his putt for a birdie from 17 feet caught the right edge of the hole and spun out. Boros's total was 282.

The New Yorker Ted Kroll had the best chance to overtake Middlecoff. Kroll needed to par the last four holes to win but he missed the green at the 15th, an innocuous par three of 133 yards. Needing three pars to tie, Kroll's dream turned into a nightmare on the 16th, where he hooked into a spruce tree *en route* to taking a seven. Middlecoff was the champion – by the skin of his teeth.

When the US Open returned to Oak Hill in 1968 it was treated to a Mexican wave that would leave the world in its wake. Lee Trevino was tidal. Later they would call him Super Mex and his new-found supporters Lee's Fleas. They got up the back of Arnie's Army. A star was born and the game got a shot of tequila.

Trevino, a novice on the tour, surmounted Oak Hill with rounds of 69, 68, 69. The last round began with Bert Yancey leading at 205 with Trevino second, a stroke behind, and Jack Nicklaus a distant third. Yancey had led for the first three rounds. In the fourth he had to go out with Trevino, and he saw red.

The Mexican was wearing a red shirt – he later went on to say that such a colour was necessary in the fourth round of a US Open in order to disguise the bleeding – a red glove and startlingly red socks. In between the black shoes and the bottom of his black trousers there were at least three inches of visible red cotton. For some reason, in those days Americans tended to wear trousers that never stood a chance of shaking hands with the foot.

Trevino's performance produced a miracle – the Flea with a voice.

'Whip the Gringo,' they yelled. In unison. Trevino is short, barely pin high to a flagstick, and podgy, and has jet-black hair to go with the trousers and reddened cheeks to go with the shirt. Beaming in between is a smile or a laugh and a flash of white that Dr Cary Middlecoff could not have improved. It wasn't so long ago that Trevino had been an all-purpose attendant at a club in El Paso, cleaning clubs, polishing shoes and picking up balls on the practice ground.

Trevino, despite his unorthodox swing and unorthodox background, was 'sponsored' by the cousins Jess Whittenton and Don Whittington. The target of their largesse was a Dick Whittington, for Trevino would find that many of his roads, from San Francisco to St Andrews, were paved in greenbacks.

At one point in the third round Yancey led by five strokes and at the end of the day he had set a record for 54 holes, 205 strokes. Nobody expected Trevino to last the pace. 'You know Yancey can play and you know how badly he wants to win a big one. You just don't know anything about the jumping bean,' said Dave Marr.

When Trevino bogeyed the first hole people were convinced they were watching the jumping has-been. The wheels did indeed fall off, but not from Trevino's wagon. Yancey played more wild shots over the first five holes than he had in three rounds. He lost the lead for the first time and Trevino effectively applied the *coup de grâce* when he got down from 30 feet for a birdie at the 11th and from 18 feet for another at the 12th. Trevino finished with a 69, Yancey with a 76.

'I guess I must have just choked,' Yancey said. According to Trevino, 'I was trying to get so far ahead that I could choke and still win.' Yancey didn't even finish second, Nicklaus overtaking him with a 67.

Apart from making him the first man to shoot four rounds in the sixties, Trevino's 275 tied the record set by Nicklaus at Baltusrol the year before. And he finished in some style. He hit his tee-shot at the last into rough and asked his caddie for the sand iron, the intention being to hack it onto the fairway. His caddie, a local boy, asked Trevino if he wanted to be remembered as the US Open champion who laid up on the last hole. Trevino took a six-iron and left the ball in the rough. He reverted to the sand iron and knocked it to two feet from the hole.

'I haven't got no shirts and shoes and cap contracts like the big-timers do,' Trevino said. This was music to the ears of Bucky Woy, an agent from Akron, Ohio. He threw a margarita party in honour of the new champion and although Trevino did not know it at the time he would become Woy's boy. It was Bucky who named Trevino Super Mex and it was Bucky who marketed the sombrero symbol that became Trevino's trademark. When Trevino was asked what he was going to do with the $30,000 prize money, he replied, 'Buy the Alamo and give it back to the Mexicans.'

He left Oak Hill with a flea in its ear. Nobody had treated the course with such disdain and the gringos at the club decided that nobody would do so again. They completely remade the fifth, sixth and 15th holes and made changes to eight others. The US PGA once had to ask the club to widen some fairways, so severely was the course set up. When Nicklaus won the US PGA Championship at Oak Hill in 1980, he was the only player under par.

Nicklaus returned to Rochester for the 1989 US Open and found that the Hill was as harrowing as ever. The course measured 6,902 yards and par was a mean 70. 'With only two par fives, neither reachable in two, and half a dozen long par fours, it's a very intimidating course,' Nicklaus said. 'I would be looking for the guys with the steel-plated nervous systems to shine through at the end.' Nicklaus shone through at the beginning.

A few months short of his 50th birthday, Nicklaus flew into Rochester in a new $20 million private jet, blew the cobwebs off an old putter which he had bought in Phoenix in 1962, reverted to a wooden driver and shot 67, four strokes better than Curtis Strange.

The greens were punch drunk from heavy and persistent downpours that had the ground staff mopping up from 5 a.m. 'The weather is having a very adverse effect on the golf course,' said the splendidly named P.J. Boatwright Jnr, an executive director of the USGA. 'We aren't getting the green speed we want for a US Open.'

A record 21 players broke the par of 70 on the first day, followed by 17 on the second day, but one of them didn't just break par, he shattered it. Strange equalled Hogan's course record of 64 and passed 49 players to take the lead. That put him at 135, five under par, one stroke in front of Tom Kite and two ahead of Scott Simpson and Jay Don Blake. Nicklaus slipped to a 74 and eventually finished tied 43rd with Severiano Ballesteros.

In proof of the power of negative thinking, Ballesteros, after playing a practice round, remarked to Sandy Lyle that it was the toughest course he had ever played. Lyle replied, 'Every course to me these days is tough.' Lyle missed the cut for the ninth time in 11 tournaments.

Bernhard Langer opened with a 66 and followed it with a 78, while Nick Faldo, who two months earlier had won the Masters, could not get close to matching the 68 he had scored in the first round. It was Ian Woosnam, the shortest European in the field, who managed to keep his head above water. Woosnam, short on the tee and extremely long off it, played one of the better rounds of his career on American soil. After a level-par 70 in the first round he came in with a 68, and that after missing a string of putts. Woosnam, a vision in bright purple, was striking the ball in that almost effortless, languid style that two years earlier had enabled him to turn almost everything he touched into sterling.

He found dollars harder to come by. Europe was his playing ground, America, when he infrequently visited it, his playground, and he seemed to be at his happiest during the happy hour, the American way of making up for prohibition. In all he had played in 12 tournaments in America and had not done himself justice in any of them. This, however, was his first US Open. 'If you can keep hold of your nerve and keep the ball on the fairway, there are birdie chances. I have never doubted that I can win a major. I am just praying my putting gets better.' Woosnam kept the ball on the fairway all right and consistently and accurately attacked the flag but he had 33 putts. When he missed a short putt on the 17th he admonished his putter, giving it a violent slap.

At least when he missed a chance on the fifth hole he had an excuse. Ahead on the sixth the crowd were losing their voices and the noise caused the Welshman to back away from his putt. Nick Price had just holed in one, which prompted the USGA to consult the *Guinness Book of Records*. Price was the fourth player during the morning of the second round to ace the sixth, a par three of 167 yards. Doug Weaver, Mark Wiebe and Jerry Pate had beaten him to it. All four aces were dealt with a seven-iron.

Strange and stranger. Curtis cut four strokes off par on the first four holes with two birdies and an eagle of his own when he holed a wedge shot from 115 yards on the fourth. Strange did not need reminding that when he won at Brookline he had an eagle courtesy of a chip in from 90 yards. When, at the end of four days, there is no room for error, these can be put down as strokes of outrageous fortune. As for the aces, somebody calculated that the odds against four players achieving it on the same hole on the same day (in fact the span was two hours) was eight million to one. A really lucky gambler could have cleaned out the US Treasury with a wager of a dime by stipulating the names of the four players (not necessarily in order) and that they would use the same-numbered club.

Scott Simpson, in an example of the power of positive thinking – on somebody else's behalf – commented, 'I think Curtis can do it. The pressure is not going to bother him because he's so tough. I think we have to beat him. I can't see him beating himself.'

If this was Simpson's divine prophecy, the USGA were looking to the skies for divine intervention. A storm closed in after the second round and by Saturday morning it looked as if Oak Hill was merging with the mouth of the Genesee River and the south shore of Lake Ontario. Boatwright Jnr was launched again; 'I've never seen a course as damaged as this one,' he said.

After a five-hour delay, the third round began with the players in threes instead of twos and off the first and tenth tees. For the USGA this was a radical departure from the script. Strange also got his lines wrong with a 73. 'I played bad, putted bad and hit some dumb shots,' he said. 'Nothing felt good.' Kite, with a 69, his third consecutive round in the sixties, held a one-stroke lead over Simpson and was three clear of Strange.

Woosnam, like Strange, scored 73, after which he rang home. 'My wife told me that on television they were saying I couldn't handle the pressure. That pissed me off.' In the final round nobody handled it better than Woosnam – and nobody handled it worse than Kite. Kite had a string of noughts to his bank balance (he would become the first six million dollar man) but he had led only one major after three rounds, the 1984 Masters, and been found wanting.

By Sunday morning the Fire Department had pumped thousands of gallons of water from Oak Hill but it was not enough for Tom Kite. Although saturated, the course was playable, at least in parts. Kite was on high until he crash-landed into water on the fifth hole, and behind the visor and the spectacles the colour almost drained from his face.

Perversely, Kite had benefited from the rain at the first hole. He had hit his drive into rough and also his second shot but, under the rule of casual water, was allowed a free drop, and the nearest point of relief was the fairway. He exploited the situation by getting to within ten feet of the hole and making the putt for a regulation four, and when he holed a 20-footer at the short third he was six under par for the tournament and had a three-stroke cushion.

The fifth, a par four of 406 yards, marked the beginning of the end for Kite. He blocked his drive into a creek guarding the right side of the fairway and, after taking a penalty drop into rough, laid up short of the green. His chip ran nine feet past the flag and his initial putt was no more than 18 inches too long. He missed that as well and limped to the sixth, his mind in turmoil from a triple-bogey seven. 'I will be nervous,' Kite had said. 'Anybody who has a chance to win will be nervous. A lot of people enter a tournament and do not have an opportunity to be scared to death.'

Kite continued to free-fall when he dropped a stroke at the eighth, where he hit his approach through the back of the green, and another at the tenth, where he missed a three-foot putt. Simpson, lemming-like, was following him over the cliff. He too suffered at the eighth, where he three-putted, missing the second from two feet to take a double-bogey six. When Strange, wearing a red shirt, looked at the scoreboard, he must have thought he was walking on water. 'My first reaction was surprise that Tom would do that. My second was that I had a chance. I knew they were playing into my hands. I didn't have to force things.'

By now Kite's decline was terminal, his loss of control absolute. The Hill was burying him alive. He etched another seven into his card when he took a double bogey on the 13th that included a topped four-wood shot that never got airborne. At the short 15th he dumped his tee-shot into the water and emerged with a double-bogey five. He finished, or was finished, with a 78. In 11 holes he had collapsed from a three-shot lead to a tie for ninth place, five shots behind Strange. If Kite had shot a two-over-par 72 he would have won. 'My play stunk,' said Kite, which was a fair summary.

Strange settled into cruise control in the slow lane and recorded par after par. When he knocked in a 15-foot putt for a birdie at the 16th it was his first in 35 holes. An affordable bogey at the last gave him a level-par 70 for 278, two under for the championship. He became the first player since Hogan in 1950–51 to win the US Open back to back. 'Move over, Ben,' said Strange. What mattered was that he had consistently kept the ball in play, and when it mattered. 'I like to think of it as fortitude and guts. I think it's something you're born with. You can only teach somebody so much. You can't teach him to be meaner than he is or tougher down the stretch than he is.'

Oak Hill's reputation, as well as the champion's, was enhanced. So too was Ian Woosnam's. He had a 68 in the final round which included a double-bogey six on the ninth and he finished in joint second place, one stroke behind Strange. Nobody had been more accurate from tee to green than Woosnam, but in the first round he had taken 33 putts, in the second 32, the third 35 and in the fourth 30. 'If I could average 30 putts a round I would win everything I entered. I was swinging so easy you wouldn't believe it. I am good enough to be the best in the world but sometimes I wonder whether I'm dedicated enough. When I go home I may not practise for two weeks. I like to have a drink with my friends. I don't want to drink Perrier water until I'm 45. I'm lucky enough to be able to play well after I've had a few beers.'

Woosnam, who won $67,823, had to rely on his caddie's gold card to pay a $2,090 bill for a seat on a private jet from Rochester to New York to catch Concorde. 'A major title will come before long,' he predicted. When it did he bought his own jet.

Irwin Crosses the Divide

Hale Irwin faced a ludicrously long putt on the 72nd hole. The journey confronting the ball was so long and so tortuous it could only travel not in expectation but in hope. The putt measured about 45 feet, had a break of six feet and had to cross a hump. Most players would have been pleased to get it close enough to avoid three-putting.

When the ball disappeared into the hole, Irwin gave a reasonable impression of a shoeless man crossing a bed of red-hot coals. He shed ten years and ran a lap of honour around the green, blowing kisses and throwing a series of high fives for good measure. He travelled farther and faster than the ball had done. Irwin, surely, could not have expected to have holed that putt? Having done so, he could not have expected to win the US Open Championship at Medinah. Could he? His putt at the 18th on the final day gave him a closing round of 67 and an aggregate of 280, eight under par for the championship. He played the back nine in 31.

Irwin knew what it took to win a US Open. He had won it in 1974 at Winged Foot with a score of seven over par and he had won it again at Inverness in 1979. But when he came to the Medinah Country Club on the outskirts of Chicago in 1990, Irwin, at the age of 45, was there to make up the numbers. He only played at Medinah by virtue of a special exemption. He had been a grinder, he had been in the money, but there were signs that the Seniors Tour could not come quickly enough. In the mid- to late-'70s he had made 86 halfway cuts, a record bettered only by Jack Nicklaus and Byron Nelson. He enjoyed 13 successive seasons of winning $100,000 or more, but that had ended in 1986 and for the next four years he was anonymous, a member of the faceless supporting cast. If he had lost face, though, he had not lost faith. 'I approached the game methodically. I didn't have Weiskopf's temper and beautiful swing, I didn't have Jack's booming drive – but I consider myself an equal of Jack's.'

Running his golf services business in St Louis meant that he did not play and practise as much as he would have wanted or, perhaps, as much as his age demanded. When he accepted a dispensation to play at Medinah (the name of the site of Muhammad's tomb), which was founded by members of Chicago's Medinah Temple, the Shriners would not have given a prayer for his chances.

In any case, all eyes were on two champions who had all to play for. Curtis Strange was bidding to win the US Open for the third time in a row, a feat achieved by only one man, Willie Anderson, from 1903 to 1905. 'For two years I have had this fictional person beside me,' Strange said. 'If I don't win I will lose my best buddy.' And Nick Faldo, having won the Masters two months previously, was being fêted as the player to achieve the improbable if not the impossible: the grandest of Grand Slams by winning all four majors in the same year.

Medinah, which was given the alias of 'The Monster', was expected to conform to the needs of a US Open. At 7,195 yards, it was longer than any other venue for the championship; the fairways were narrow, some no more than 28 yards wide; the rough was rough, the grounds boasted 18,000 trees and the greens were fast, notably the 13th and 17th, which were dominated by severe slopes. It is not unusual for golfers to complain about the harshness of a US Open course but even the USGA was in agreement. 'It is almost to the point where it isn't fair,' a spokesman said.

So they watered the greens. Talk about pouring oil on troubled waters. On the eve of the tournament a storm broke, one and a half inches of rain fell and the course was awash. Medinah's fire was extinguished. Where 39 players had broken par in the first round, 47 bettered a score of 72 in the second and the cut fell at 145, the most generous ever. Tim Simpson led at nine under par after two rounds, which was another record score for a US Open. Hale Irwin was five under on 139. 'The more I play well, the more I remember what it takes,' Irwin said.

After the third round Strange was very much in the picture. Hitting fairways and greens monotonously, he shot 68, and as Medinah, with a little help from the wind, began to defend its reputation, the history man was only two strokes off the lead shared by Mike Donald and Billy Ray Brown.

Faldo also moved into a challenging position with a 68, while Irwin lost ground with a 74. Once again Strange and Faldo were the centre of attention. At the first hole Strange hit what appeared to be a perfect tee-shot. When he got to it, he found it sitting in a divot. 'I'm thinking to myself, is it going to be one of those days?' It was. His best buddy, the US Open title, with whom he had shared two memorable years, was now looking for a fresh partner. By the time he reached the tenth tee he was six strokes adrift and the championship was exacting alimony. He was a stranger to a course he had dominated in the third round. Sometimes he mishit shots, sometimes he chose the wrong clubs. He shot 75. It was not the Strange of old. 'Maybe I've lost some weight because of the pressure,' he said. 'I still think I've got another Open in me.'

Ahead of him, just as the wind was getting fresher, Irwin was shooting the breeze. With eight holes to play he was only three under par and he shot four consecutive birdies from the 11th. 'When I started my little binge the leader was nine under and when I came off the 14th the board still showed nine under,' Irwin recalls. 'I thought if I can just make one more birdie and get to eight under that would be on the leaderboard for about two hours. The fellows in the last two groups had to play some pretty difficult holes and being last out has additional pressure. Put it on the board and let 'em shoot at it.'

The 18th was one of Medinah's most difficult holes. Its stroke average was 4.22 from 296 pars, 118 bogeys or worse and just 32 birdies, the lowest number conceded of the 18 holes. Irwin got one of them, the one that mattered. It wasn't just the length of the putt – the ball's journey took seven seconds – that prompted him to behave like Hiawatha on the 18th green. In scoring 67 he had rediscovered that he still had the game to compete at the highest level. He was back on the leaderboard.

In the event only three players, Faldo, Donald and Brown, had a shot at Irwin's target. Faldo began the day at four under par and when he came to the 16th, another of Medinah's meanest holes, he was eight under. After hitting a one-iron he had about 220 yards to the green. With the wind blowing from left to right he aimed a three-iron left of the flag, hoping it would drift towards the hole. The ball stayed on line, leaving him 45 feet from the flag. His first putt came up six feet short and he missed the next, the ball shaving the cup on the right.

Faldo had only one wood in his bag and he used it only twice on the last day. He left himself with long irons into long par fours but his iron fortification kept him on the fairways and kept him on the greens. He was invariably putting for birdie. When he walked to the 18th he knew he would have to birdie the hole. Again he hit an iron off the tee and then he hit an approach from 212 yards which nearly struck the pin. The ball pitched just short of the flag and rolled 12 feet past. The putt for a three and a round of 68 looked destined to drop but the ball hit the lip and slid by. The Grand Slam dream was over. At the site of Irwin's celebrations, Faldo was in tears. He had, he maintained, hit the right putt. He left Chicago with the promise that he would win the Open Championship at St Andrews. A month later he kept the promise.

And then there were two. At nine under par Donald, a 13-year journeyman with one tour victory to his credit, led the championship by one shot but, like Faldo, he bogeyed the 16th. Unlike Irwin, Donald could not hole a huge putt on 18 that would have restored his one-stroke lead.

Brown, a qualifier who was playing in his first US Open, birdied the 17th and missed a 15-foot putt for another birdie at the last which would have put him in a play-off. Irwin and Donald finished on 280, Faldo and Brown on 281. 'I don't think Faldo should have been questioned as to why he hit an iron off the 18th tee,' reflected Irwin. 'An iron for Nick is not an unreasonable play. He's strong and very long. For me it was certainly a driver. I hit a driver and a seven-iron, and Nick a one-iron and a three-iron. I'd rather play a driver and seven-iron than a one- and a three-iron. I had a better score but he played a better second shot.'

Nobody, however, could have played a better third. 'In my 22 years of pro golf I had never made a putt like that to win or come close to winning a tournament,' Irwin said, 'particularly one of that magnitude. It was easily four times longer than any putt I had made all week.

'I had lined it against a spot just the other side of the crown. I wanted to get it over the top at the right speed as if the hole were there and the ball went right over that spot. I never thought it was in until it was three or four feet away. Looking at the hole from straight on, it was probably coming in at a 45-degree angle from the right. When you have a putt doing that, you're not really sure. It was only in the last couple of feet that it really had a chance. Then it was right on track.

'That's what started the body language. My reaction was a spontaneous eruption of joy. It was the single most exciting moment in my career. I had to birdie it. I didn't think the others would play poorly enough to finish on seven under but I felt they might not do better than eight under. After my putt went in, Faldo, Donald and Brown all played one over par.'

In the 18-hole play-off the next day, Irwin was two behind with three holes to play when he gained the rarest of birdies at 16. He was still one stroke behind at the 18th but Donald drove left into the trees, punched it into a bunker near the green and took a bogey five. Irwin had escaped at the 72nd hole and he escaped again at the 90th in the 90th US Open Championship.

Sudden death, anathema to the USGA, was the last resort and Irwin won it with a birdie three at the first extra hole, making a putt from nine feet. He began punching the air but it did not compare to his animated performance at the 18th hole 24 hours earlier. 'I guarantee you that what happened there won Irwin the US Open,' Greg Norman said. 'That putt had eyes.'

When Irwin won in 1974 and 1979 he wore glasses. In 1990, when he became the oldest champion in the history of the US Open, he was wearing rose-coloured contact lenses. He earned a ten-year exemption and no longer would he have to rely on the benevolence of the governing body who granted him a privilege at Medinah on the grounds that he was still genuinely competitive. It was an inspired decision. Irwin won again a few days later, taking the Buick Classic, and the high fives were given an encore. So was his career.

Billy Ray Brown, incidentally, nearly lost his cheque for $56,879 on the toss of a coin. On the seventh green in the final round, Brown charged a putt 15 feet past the hole and while his ball was still in motion he threw a dime at it out of frustration. His aim was stunningly accurate. The coin, which he was using as a marker, hit the ball. Had the ball been deflected it would have cost him a two-stroke penalty. Officials studied a video tape of the incident and decided not to penalise him on the grounds that the film was 'inconclusive'.

For Arnie Read Ernie

Ernie Els described the 94th US Open at Oakmont, Pittsburgh, as the 'survival of the fittest'. He was right. Oakmont staged its seventh US Open in the middle of a heatwave and many had thrown in the towel long before the denouement.

Before lunchtime on the final practice day, four people had been carried from the course on stretchers, the first succumbing as early as 9.30 a.m. Not for the first time, nor the last, the players complained about the heat, the speed of the greens and the height of the rough.

If Oakmont were a woman, Tom Watson said, it would never say 'I do'. What with Watson, Jack Nicklaus and Hale Irwin appearing on the leaderboard, it might have been assumed that Miss Oakmont favoured the older man, but the younger generation also beat a path to her door, led by Els and Colin Montgomerie.

Nicklaus had been here before. In 1962 he had defeated Arnold Palmer in a play-off at Oakmont and it was the beginning of the most successful career in the game's history. Aged 22, Nicklaus had defied the crowd by defeating the local hero.

Oakmont revisited in 1994 saw Nicklaus and Palmer playing together in practice rounds. At the sixth, a par three of 195 yards, Palmer wondered whether to hit a four-iron or a five-wood. 'Can I hit it, Jack?' Palmer asked. 'You can hit it,' Nicklaus replied. 'You won't get there but you can hit it.' Palmer elected to hit the four-iron and his ball veered left towards a greenside bunker. 'Get in the hole,' a spectator yelled. 'It's in the hole . . . the big hole,' Palmer said.

In 1962 Nicklaus had three-putted on only one occasion. Now he couldn't buy a two-putt. Palmer had a solution. He would drive the ball, Jack could knock it onto the green and they would get somebody else to do the putting. Jack did not find this particularly amusing. He saw himself as a contender, almost Jack the Lad. For Palmer it was different. At the age of 64 he had been given a special exemption to compete in his last US Open. 'It's a little icing on the cake,' Arnie said. You could hardly see the icing for the number of candles. Palmer, a local boy, had first played at Oakmont when he was 12. He shot 82. 'The Pennsylvania Turnpike wasn't there then,' Palmer recalled. Nicklaus leant over and whispered something into Palmer's good ear. 'Jack wanted to know if they had cars back then,' Palmer revealed.

In the first round, Nicklaus, and Els, shot 69. 'I really didn't think I had the game to score well on this golf course,' the Golden Bear said. 'My wife Barbara put a spell on me. She kept telling me I was 22 again.'

In the heat of the battle, Montgomerie and Patton went their separate ways. While Big Monty hit the leaderboard with a 71, Chris Patton headed for a cool, darkened room and a bottle of smelling salts. Monty and Patton are two of the largest players to swing a club and both were affected by the extreme heat and humidity. 'When you stand over a putt, the blood rushes to your head,' Montgomerie said. As for Patton, the former US amateur champion, he withdrew after eight holes, suffering from heat exhaustion.

Montgomerie, however, refused to allow the conditions to affect his concentration. He shot a stunning 65 in the second round, a score that Watson felt was within his own compass but for the fact he had 36 putts. 'I'm going to work on the Catholic method,' Watson said. 'Rhythm. Is that politically correct?'

Meanwhile, Arnie bowed out with an 81, but nobody was counting. He was given a standing ovation around the 18th green and afterwards gave one of his briefest press conferences. Using a towel to soak up the sweat and the tears, he could hardly utter a word. He had brought an era to an end and Arnie's Army was demobbed.

The stage was left to the younger generation of Els and Montgomerie and a 39-year-old from Memphis, Loren Roberts. Following a 76 in the first round, Roberts had come through the field with 69, 64 and 70. Montgomerie, who also had a 70 in the final round, was the leader in the clubhouse at five under par. First Roberts then Els squandered chances to post a winning score. Nobody ever improved on seven under for the championship and only three reached that mark, Els, Montgomerie and Roberts.

After reaching the turn in 33, Monty had three bogeys in a row but a birdie on the 17th proved to be crucial. Roberts got to seven under with birdies at the 11th and 13th but dropped a shot at the 15th. He and Els needed pars at the last to finish a stroke in front of Montgomerie. Roberts missed a four-footer and took five. Meanwhile, Els's driving had gone haywire. When he stood on the 17th tee at six under, he assumed Roberts would finish at six under. Els attempted to drive the 17th green (the hole was 315 yards) and lashed it way left of a stand. It was classed as a temporary immovable obstruction and from a dropping zone he pitched to seven feet and missed the putt for a birdie.

He still led by a stroke but his drive at the 18th again flew left and when he chipped onto the fairway his luck had run out. His ball came to rest in a divot and his third shot came up short. Finally Els holed from four feet for a bogey five in a round of 73, but he lived to fight another day. Els admitted he had not looked at the leaderboard when he arrived on the 18th tee and thought he needed to birdie the last. 'I didn't know what I was doing,' he said. 'I was stupid.'

The South African, the American and the Scotsman, tied on 279, had to return the following day for an 18-hole play-off. As the agony was prolonged, they threw bogeys and double bogeys at each other, and, in the Three Rivers City, it was a bridge too far. In terms of winning major championships all three were rookies, and the title eventually went to Els. He defeated Roberts in a sudden-death play-off after they had finished 18 holes at three over par. Montgomerie dropped out after going round in 78, seven over par.

They kept their worst until last. For the most part the golf over the front nine holes enabled spectators to identify with the game. It looked like a Saturday morning three ball with a fiver at stake rather than the blue riband of American golf with a purse of $1.5 million. By the turn, Montgomerie was out of it. He went out in 42, six over, compared to the 38 of Els and Roberts. Whether they liked it or not, the USGA were confronted with a sudden-death play-off after Els and Roberts had both gone round in 74. In the middle of a heatwave, they had all gone off the boil.

At this point television coverage of the championship in America was interrupted by the appearance of O.J. Simpson in a criminal court in Los Angeles.

Both survivors parred the tenth, the first extra hole (that was the sixth time they had played it), but the timeless US Open was finally, and mercifully, resolved at the 11th. Roberts's drive found the rough on the right, from where he put his approach shot into a bunker. Els found the heart of the green in two. Roberts was about 35 feet from the flag after coming out of the sand and his putt to save par hit the hole but lipped out. His opponent, from 15 feet, had two putts for the title and he made no mistake.

Els became only the fourth non-American since the Second World War to win the US Open, following another South African, Gary Player, in 1965, Tony Jacklin in 1970 and the Australian David Graham in 1981. At 24 he was the second youngest winner since Nicklaus, who had won at the same course in 1962 at the age of 22.

For Arnie read Ernie? On the practice putting green before the start of the championship, Els had spoken to Palmer and the message from the Pennsylvanian to the player from Johannesburg 40 years his junior had been inspirational. Palmer's view was that Els had the game to win at Oakmont. It was not the only support he received. He found a note in his locker from Player and had faxes from the South African cricket team and F.W. de Klerk. Later in his career, Els would receive congratulations, via mobile phone, from President Nelson Mandela.

There was a lot of money riding on Els at Oakmont. After the second hole in the 18-hole play-off, the betting slips were heading for the wastepaper basket. He began bogey, triple bogey. 'I just wanted to get out of there,' he recalled. 'I said to my caddie, why the hell did I make that putt on 18 on Sunday to get into this thing? Man, what are you doing here? It was a horrific start and I never really felt comfortable.'

His caddie, Richard Roberts, who was born in Halifax, Yorkshire, and who emigrated to South Africa as a child, played his part when the going got tough. The Americans were rooting for Roberts – Loren, that is. 'Miss the green!' and 'Get into that bunker!' were remarks that could be heard directed against Els. His caddie spurred him on: '"The whole of Europe is behind you, the whole of Africa is behind you." I got him fired up.' Els and his caddie subsequently parted company.

Montgomerie, who had been third in the US Open at Pebble Beach two years earlier, said Oakmont was by far the most difficult course he had ever played. 'I really earned every cent. Some weeks we don't. With the heat and the pressure, I was physically sick when I came off the course.'

As for Roberts, he was left to reflect on a ruling error made by the USGA. On the first hole in the fourth round, when Els drove left into deep rough, they gave him a free drop on the grounds that a television tower was on his line of sight. Officials later admitted they had made a mistake. The mobile obstruction should have been moved and Els should have played the ball where it lay.

Janzen Takes a Bough

When Lee Janzen walked into the media centre after winning the 98th US Open, the first question he was asked was, 'Does your mantel have room for a second trophy?' Janzen replied, 'My mantel has plenty of room. There's always room for something like this.'

Never mind the mantelpiece. Janzen, who had won his first US Open in 1993, should have placed the trophy in an arboretum, for his remarkable victory stemmed, to a significant degree, from a cypress tree. 'I don't know what it was but it was beautiful to look at,' Janzen said later.

Payne Stewart was the man dreaming the Olympic dream in 1998 until history repeated itself. Stewart led from day one, keeping the formidable Olympic Club in San Francisco, with its par of 70, at bay with a 66. Janzen, in contrast, shot 73 in the first round.

After three holes of the final round, Janzen was still seven strokes behind Stewart, bogeys at the second and third holes dropping him down the leaderboard. Although he had a birdie at the fourth, an errant drive at the fifth meant he was looking at a double bogey, if he was lucky. He was much luckier than that.

'I hit a four-wood off the tee to my right. The wind was right to left all week but I overplayed it and it hit the trees. The marshals were looking around and then someone yelled that my ball had stayed in a tree. They had spotted it with their binoculars. I grabbed a ball from my caddie and was ready to hit another drive. Before I got back to the tee, the ball fell out of the tree.'

Instead of playing three off the tee, Janzen faced a chip out of the rough onto the fairway. From there he played a six-iron which flew over the green. He had a 20-foot chip to save par and his ball, which minutes earlier had been given up for dead, rolled into the hole. 'You can imagine how much better I felt,' Janzen said.

It is one thing to get a stroke of luck, quite another to fully capitalise on it. Out in 35, Janzen still trailed by three, but birdies at the 11th and 13th had a dramatic effect on the leaderboard. At the 11th he made an eight-footer and at the 13th, a par three of 199 yards, he hit a five-iron to within five feet.

After the third round, Stewart, who followed his 66 with 71, 70, was on 207, three under for the championship, and he led by four strokes from Tom Lehman and Bob Tway and by five from Janzen and Nick Price. Tway and Price both shot 73 in the final round; Lehman had a 75. Only Janzen, the Olympic Club and a controversial divot stood between Stewart and a second US Open triumph. If Janzen had the rub of the green, Stewart had sand kicked in his face.

To Janzen it felt like Baltusrol revisited. That was the scene of his first US Open victory in 1993, when he had another story to tell about trees and when, of course, Stewart finished runner-up. At the tenth hole at Baltusrol on the final day, Janzen had driven right, into the rough. 'I decided I'd hit a five-iron over a tree and onto the green. Well, I didn't catch the ball quite solidly enough and hit it a little low. It went straight between a couple of big branches and landed on the front of the green and I two-putted for par.'

Back at the Olympic Club, it became clear that Lady Luck was not only smiling at Janzen, she'd also given him her telephone number. She never even looked at Stewart. At the 12th hole, the leader, already hurt with bogeys at the fourth and seventh, where he missed from six feet, found the fairway with his drive and the ball came to rest bang in the middle of a divot. Nor was it an ordinary divot. By Sod's Law, this one had sand in it. 'If you put sand in divots in an effort to repair the turf then that should be ground under repair,' Stewart protested afterwards. 'I'd like to see divots unfilled. When you put sand in them you don't know what's underneath the ball or how deep the sand is.' Stewart believes a free drop should be allowed.

To make matters worse, Stewart, who wasn't sure what to play out of the divot, finally hit his approach right of the green and into a bunker. At that point a USGA official, Tom Meeks, approached Stewart and warned him about slow play. 'You got a bad time,' Meeks said. It was an understatement. 'That didn't sit real well with me,' Stewart said, 'because I was trying to figure out what to do and what kind of shot to play. I've always been a slow player.' After playing into the bunker, Stewart asked Meeks, 'What happens if I get another warning?' Meeks replied, 'You get a one-stroke penalty.' Stewart said, 'Thank you very much.'

When he got to the bunker he failed to get it up and down, missing a 12-foot putt. He dropped another shot at the 13th, hitting a five-iron through the green before recording his only birdie of the round at the 14th, where he holed from 15 feet. It did not arrest his decline and fall. Despite using a three-wood on the 16th tee, he ran out of fairway. A five-iron put him back on course but, with 173 yards to the flag, he got a little quick with a seven-iron, found a bunker and again failed to get it up and down. The result was a bogey six and for the first time Stewart was behind.

Up ahead, Janzen was sitting pretty, closing with a 68 for an aggregate of 280, level par. 'After 11 holes I realised I had a chance to win but at the 13th I made a point of not looking at the scoreboard for the rest of the round. I didn't want to play safe. I just wanted to continue to hit good shots.'

By the time Stewart got to the 18th, he needed a birdie to tie. 'I finally hit it on the fairway and I had 105 yards up the hill, into the wind. I couldn't get there with a sand wedge so I choked down on a pitching wedge and I thought I played a pretty good shot.' He was left with a 20-footer for a birdie. 'I thought I chose the right line at the right pace but it was just a little bit off.'

The man with plus fours finished with a 74 (plus four on the day) for a total of 281, one shot behind Janzen. It was the biggest final-round comeback to win the US Open since Johnny Miller in 1973. 'I know I can play tough courses well and it just gets better as time goes by,' Janzen said. Janzen, only the 18th player to win the US Open more than once, also paid tribute to his English caddie, Dave Musgrove. 'The first time he caddied for me I didn't understand a word he said but I knew he could do nothing but help me.'

As for Stewart, he took a pragmatic approach. 'I hit six fairways in regulation, Lee hit 12. I hit nine greens in regulation, Lee hit 14. Bingo. That's why I didn't win the golf tournament. Nobody in contention shot under par except Lee and he was the only person to finish even par for the tournament.'

If the Olympic Club once again proved its pedigree, that's more than can be said for some of the spectators who made Colin Montgomerie's week a misery. The Scotsman, who had secured the winning point for Europe over the US in the Ryder Cup at Valderrama in 1997, was baited and heckled. 'I seemed to be blamed for Europe winning,' Montgomerie said. He finished tied 18th on 290, ten strokes behind Janzen and one in front of Casey Martin.

Martin, who provided the championship with a historic footnote, had no problems with the gallery. Whenever his name was announced on the first tee it was to thunderous applause. Afflicted with a rare blood disorder, Martin split the golfing world down the middle by becoming the first man to play in a major championship whilst riding in a golf cart. Martin, who plays with a limp, earns a living on the Nike Tour but got into America's biggest event in a sudden-death play-off during the qualifying tournament.

And that presented the ruling bodies of golf with a unique dilemma: should Casey negotiate Olympic on foot, like the other 155 competitors, or should he be allowed a buggy? Some traditionalists like Jack Nicklaus and Tom Watson saw it as a precedent that would damage the nature of the professional game. In their view it would literally drive a cart through the ethos of golf. Payne Stewart and, judging by the reaction of the crowd, half the population of San Francisco saw it differently. 'This gentleman is handicapped,' Stewart said. 'But he has got the ability to play golf. Let him play. I don't think he has an advantage over me because he uses a cart in between shots.'

Casey shot 74, 71, 74 and 72. He won $34,043, finishing a stroke behind Tiger Woods and four in front of Nicklaus.

The US PGA

The only stats I care about are pay cheques and victories

– Greg Norman

Tway to Go

During the mid-'80s Gary Player and Lee Trevino independently predicted that the next superstar of golf would be a tall, fresh-faced youngster from Oklahoma called Bob Tway. By the turn of the decade the former college star had failed to match those expectations but had still earned his place in immortality. He did it with one shot. One bunker shot. A bunker shot which went straight into the hole – and straight into history – to win him his first major championship.

There has rarely been a more dramatic shot on the 72nd hole of a major than Tway's effort at the Inverness Club, Toledo, Ohio, on Monday, 11 August 1986. The fact that it took place on a Monday was rare enough. The tournament had been delayed by a day because of a downpour on the Sunday afternoon. The fact that it was Tway's only bunker shot of the entire tournament was another statistical quirk. But it remained in the minds of golf followers around the world because the shot won Tway the 68th US PGA Championship, which Greg Norman had dominated from the first round.

That dramatic moment completed the four majors of a remarkable year in which Norman had been the key figure as he threatened to take over at the peak of the sport. This was the Year of the Shark, a time when the blond Australian was never out of the headlines, whether for winning tournaments, having them snatched away or allowing them to slip from his grasp.

He really was on the brink of becoming a great superstar. But, although he came a lot closer than Tway to achieving such an exalted position, Norman, too, was to fall short of the highest expectations. The following years were to feature repeated inquests into the near misses and unexpected failures of the man from Queensland. Somehow it all went wrong – and the rot set in on that fateful Monday in Ohio.

During the summer of 1986 Norman had emerged as a player of awesome talent. He won nine tournaments and topped the US Tour Order of Merit. But, above all, he proved that the Grand Slam – victory in the four major championships in the same year – was possible by leading all four at the end of the third round. His achievement was labelled the 'Saturday Slam', yet it was the manner in which he contrived to lose three of the four rather than the outstanding form he displayed in reaching that position which left the bigger impression and led to doubts being expressed over Norman's credentials as a truly great champion.

In the Masters, a third-round 68 took him a shot clear of the field. On the last day Norman double-bogeyed the tenth to drop out of contention but then scored four successive birdies from the 14th to finish with a 70 and lose by a shot to Jack Nicklaus, who, with a last-round 65, won at the age of 46. Even then Norman had a chance on the 18th to force a play-off if he could simply par the hole. But from the middle of the fairway he pushed a four-iron approach into the gallery on the right, ended up taking a bogey five and had to be content with a tie for second place.

Nine weeks later Norman was again a shot ahead after three rounds of the US Open at Shinnecock Hills on Long Island, New York. But, having clashed with a spectator who had accused him of 'choking' on the Saturday, Norman slumped to a last-round 75 and slipped to 12th.

The Open at Turnberry brought the long-awaited Norman conquest. A brilliant second-round 63, equalling the major-championship record, gave him the lead and although he was still only a shot ahead at the start of Sunday's play, the long-hitting Antipodean was not to falter this time. A final round of 69 gave him victory by five shots over Yorkshireman Gordon Brand – and his first major title. At the age of 31 Norman had made the breakthrough and was ready to go on to greater triumphs.

When he opened with a blistering round of 65 in his next major, the US PGA Championship, it seemed that the weight had been lifted from his shoulders, allowing him to reap the rewards of his exceptional talent. Who could stop this golfing colossus? As it turned out, the man who brought him tumbling down was the other Greg Norman, the one who stumbles within sight of the finishing line when it seems that all he has to do is stand up to win.

As the giant fell, along came Tway to deliver the *coup de grâce* in sensational style. At the time, there was no more appropriate character for such a task. For what is generally forgotten in the recollections of 1986 is what an excellent year Tway was enjoying.

Back in 1981, the Oklahoma State student was voted college player of the year and tipped for stardom. At first it didn't happen. Tway failed three times to win his US Tour card and had to play in Europe, Asia and Africa to gain experience. Once into the big league, however, he soon made up for lost time, finishing 45th in his first year, 1985, with winnings of $164,023. Now, in his second year, he was causing a sensation, winning four events on the US Tour, the most since Jack Nicklaus had claimed five, 23 years earlier. Superstar material indeed. He had performed well in the majors, too, leading the US Open after one round before finishing eighth (also his final position in the Masters).

If anyone was to catch Norman, then, Tway was the man. Yet nobody would have bet on such an eventuality as the Australian led by two strokes after day one, had increased his lead to four shots at halfway and was still four ahead going into the deciding 18 holes. The two men set out in the last group on Sunday with American Peter Jacobsen, who trailed Norman by six shots, Tway by two. Torrential rain around 2.30 p.m. caused a suspension with the leaders only on the second fairway and, after a two-hour delay, play was called off for the day.

When they returned on Monday, there was little in the early holes to indicate anything but Norman completing the formality of victory. Although he bogeyed the third hole (where Tway birdied) to see his lead cut to two, his four-stroke advantage had been restored by the time they turned for home. 'I felt comfortable with my lead,' said Norman. 'Nine times out of ten you're going to hold it.' This must have been the tenth.

If the leader was to be caught, either Norman would have to collapse or Tway would have to be inspired. Over the next eight holes Tway was a little bit inspired but his rival collapsed quite a lot. A significant turning point came at the 11th, where the new Open champion took a double-bogey six after unluckily driving into a divot mark on the fairway. When Tway birdied the 13th and Norman bogeyed the 14th, they were level with four holes to play.

Both men scrambled for pars at the 15th and gained routine pars at 16. On the penultimate hole Tway played a brilliant shot to stay on terms. When his approach dropped into deep rough, the six-foot-four professional faced a difficult task of making his recovery shot stay on the green. Yet he stopped it three feet from the pin and holed out for his par. 'That shot was harder than the one at 18,' he was to say later. 'It's a shot I practise, a lob shot. But you never know how it's going to come out. Fortunately it came out soft and gave me a chance.'

And so they came to the last with everything resting on the outcome. The 18th at Inverness is deceptive. It measures only 354 yards, which, in view of the distances the professionals can comfortably achieve, makes it little more than 'a drive and a flick'. But Nicklaus called it 'the hardest easy hole I ever played'. From an elevated tee, great accuracy is needed to find a fairway that dog-legs to the right towards a small plateau green. A wayward tee-shot to the right invariably leaves a difficult downhill lie from the rough. Any drive struck too hard or pulled will present a similarly difficult shot from the left.

Faced with this puzzle, Tway and Norman both took one-irons from the tee. The Australian's ball landed in the right rough at the corner of the dog-leg but bounced through into the fairway. Tway was not so lucky. He found the deep grass on the right – and stayed there. He took a nine-iron in an attempt to force the ball from the rough on to the 'dance floor'. But from 130 yards he was short, the shot landing in the bunker guarding the front right of the putting surface. 'I was just trying to get it on the green,' said Tway. 'When it came down, my first thought was that it might be buried, but it was much better in the bunker than the rough.'

The initiative was with Norman but, in his own words, he 'hit a good shot with a bad result'. Using a pitching wedge, he aimed for the flag, only to see the ball 'bite' hard and spin back off the green into a small collar of rough. Of the two players, however, Norman still seemed to have the better chance of saving par. The problem for Tway was to put the right pace on his shot out of the bunker. From five feet below the green he had to play the ball high enough to clear the front lip of the trap and, on a green sloping away from him, stop the ball near the flag.

That was his intention as he settled his feet firmly in the sand. 'I wasn't trying to make it,' he admitted later. 'I was just trying to get it close.' Whether he judged the speed correctly is open to debate. But his aim was immaculate. As the ball splashed out of the sand, it came down on a perfect line and ran 20 feet towards the hole before rolling in. Tway's joy was unconfined as, putter clasped in his left hand, he repeatedly leapt up and down in the bunker. 'I was so excited,' said the tearful Tway later. 'If I could have jumped that high in school I probably would have made the basketball team.'

Although Norman still had to play, Tway's shot of a lifetime had effectively won the championship. Realising that his chances of victory were disappearing, the long-time leader had no choice but to gamble. He had been planning to chip a sand wedge below the hole, leaving him an uphill putt for par. Now he had to try to hole the chip and could not be short. So he switched to a pitching wedge, sent the ball eight feet past and missed the meaningless return. Norman had bogeyed the last hole and lost by two shots.

What had scuttled his chances, though, was his form throughout the day. His last-round score of 76 cost him a second successive major title as much as Tway's miracle shot did. He had failed to hit seven fairways and 11 greens in regulation. 'I obviously didn't play very well,' he said. 'But you can't control what other people are doing. You have to take what happens. I had a chance to win the tournament but I didn't.'

Playing partner Jacobsen was impressed with Tway's relaxed attitude over the closing holes. 'I thought he showed a lot of poise,' he said. 'At 15, and especially 17, where he got it up and down, I thought he was going to win the tournament. And I'll never forget that shot at 18.'

But was the shot inspired or merely fortunate? Norman claimed that if the ball hadn't dropped in the hole it would have run 20 feet past, leaving Tway to face the real possibility of a bogey five.

By such small margins are mighty matters decided. Tway, though, should be given due credit. He played the ball at the right height on the right line and at the right speed to produce a rare last-hole winning birdie and take the US PGA Championship.

It was a great lucky shot.

★ ★ ★

Thanks to the wonder of TV, Tway's shot made him famous around the world and became the most memorable moment in the event's history. But from the outset the US PGA Championship has provided examples of last-hole drama.

The inaugural tournament at Siwanoy Country Club in Bronxville, New York, in 1916 featured a final between two British-born players: Jim Barnes, a lanky 30-year-old native of Lelant, Cornwall, and Jock Hutchison, a 32-year-old Scot from St Andrews.

In those days the PGA was a match-play event, which produced the inevitable excitement of a head-to-head contest. Barnes, a tall, quiet man who had emigrated to San Francisco 12 years earlier, was never in front until the 25th hole, lost the lead and regained it on the 33rd. Hutchison gamely took the match to the last, where Barnes, whose habit was to silently walk the course with a sprig of grass or clover clamped between his teeth, held on to win.

The Scot, whose finest moment came when he returned home to win the 1921 Open at St Andrews, was to triumph in the PGA Championship too. In 1920 he reached the final again, where he met the unknown J. Douglas Edgar. Again the match went to the last after Edgar, four down with seven to play, won three holes out of five. But this time Hutchison held off the challenger for his first major championship.

The 1923 final at Pelham Golf Club, New York, featured an epic battle between two of golf's all-time greats, Gene Sarazen and Walter Hagen. Sarazen, only 21 and the holder of the title, was dormy two when Hagen staged a typical fightback. The flamboyant New Yorker won the 35th and then got up and down from a sand-trap at the last to take the contest into extra holes. The reprieve was temporary, however, for at the second extra hole Sarazen successfully played out of a cluster of crayfish mounds to clinch his second straight title.

Hagen's defeat was the last he was to suffer in the event for four years. Recognised as the greatest match-play golfer of his era (and one of the best ever), 'The Haig' regained the title in 1924. The final was a repeat of his first victory in 1921, when the opponent was Long Jim Barnes. The former Cornish assistant professional made him fight all the way, taking the match to the 36th before Hagen won, two up.

In the next two years Hagen was untouchable but he claimed his fourth consecutive title in the tightest of finishes against Joe Turnesa at

Cedar Crest Country Club, Dallas, in 1927. The final produced one of the many colourful stories of Hagen's remarkable life. His disregard for convention was displayed by his arrival on the tee 30 minutes late. The champion promptly conceded three long putts to his surprised opponent and then said, 'That makes up for me being late. Now we'll play!'

Turnesa, the third of seven sons born to an Italian immigrant greenkeeper, played in two Ryder Cup teams but this was the closest he came to winning a major championship. He led nearly all the way until Hagen drew level at the 29th and went ahead at the 31st. On the final hole Turnesa had the chance to force a play-off but his putt hung on the lip of the hole – and stayed out.

This was the last of Hagen's five record-breaking PGA Championships, for he lost in the quarter-finals the following year to end a run of 22 consecutive match victories. He did not reach the final again, but his long-time rival Sarazen did, in 1930, only to be beaten by Tommy Armour on the last green in what the referee, Leo Diegel (the champion of 1928 and 1929), called 'the greatest golf match I ever saw'.

Armour had already shown how he could win under the ultimate pressure when in the 1927 US Open at Oakmont he needed to birdie the demanding 460-yard final hole to force a tie with Harry Cooper. The Silver Scot promptly sent his second shot to ten feet, holed the putt and went on to win the play-off.

Against Sarazen he triumphed with some superb clutch putting. Sarazen was one up after nine, Armour was one up after 18, and they were all square at the 27th. Amid growing excitement, Armour proved to be the man of the hour as he holed a 14-footer on the last, while the little American, though nearer the hole, missed. Thirty-five years later Sarazen was presented with that same putter with which Armour had holed the winning shot, by a rich amateur golfing friend of the Scot. Sarazen's initial reaction was one of disappointment because he had predicted to his wife that the rich man was going to give him a million dollars. 'When he handed me an old putter I wanted to throw it in the river,' said Sarazen. However, he christened it 'The Million Dollar Putter' and grew to like it so much that he used it regularly in tournament play, including his final public appearance in the 1991 Masters.

Putting was the key to the 1934 PGA Championship in which Paul Runyan, nicknamed 'Little Poison' because of his skill on the greens, beat his former instructor Craig Wood on the 38th green. It was a classic contest between the power-hitter, Wood, and the man with the magical short game.

Wood's length off the tee was legendary. In the 1933 Open he hit a drive which stopped in a bunker 430 yards away. The man from Lake

Placid was one of the unluckiest golfers in major championships. He was the victim of Sarazen's famous double eagle at Augusta's 15th in 1935. The shot that rang round the world enabled Sarazen to reach the play-off and beat the luckless Wood, who also lost play-offs for the 1933 British Open and the 1939 US Open. He lost this one, too, when Runyan exploded from a bunker to within eight feet of the cup and holed out for victory. The champion, who was the US Tour's leading money-winner in 1933 and 1934, later became renowned as a teacher specialising in putting problems.

Wood was to achieve a remarkable feat during the '30s when he finished tied first for all four majors at the end of the final round. But instead of following Sarazen by completing the Grand Slam (later to be achieved only by Ben Hogan, Gary Player and Jack Nicklaus), he lost all four in play-offs. Such a talent deserved its reward, which duly arrived in 1941 when Wood won the Masters and the US Open, becoming one of only four players to accomplish this 'double' in the same year.

When historians recall the greatest sporting misses of all time, the name of Harold 'Jug' McSpaden is not high on the list. But perhaps it should be. For the asthma-sufferer from Kansas is in the same league as Doug Sanders. In the 1937 US PGA Championship at the Pittsburgh Field Club, Aspinwall, Pennsylvania, McSpaden had a four-foot birdie putt to win the final against Densmore Shute – but missed. Although he won 17 US PGA Tour events, his miss – like that of Sanders at the 1970 Open – meant he was destined never to win a major championship. Shute must have known just how he felt for he, too, had erred from a similar range at Southport and Ainsdale in 1933 to lose the Ryder Cup.

From 1939 to 1941 the US PGA Championship featured three successive last-hole dramas, all of them involving Byron Nelson. In 1944 the Texan won 11 successive tournaments on the US Tour and 18 for the entire season, at an average of 68.33 shots per round. Bobby Jones said of Nelson, 'At my best I never came close to the golf that Nelson shoots.' As a haemophiliac he was exempt from military service and achieved much of his success while other players were away in the war, a reason for some critics to question Nelson's record. Yet his scoring suggests it would have been impressive against any opposition.

He had won the 1937 Masters pre-war and the 1939 US Open when he was pipped in the PGA final of the same year by Henry Picard, the 1938 Masters champion. Picard, who had modelled his swing in the style of Bobby Jones, was recognised for his fluent action. He proved his mettle against Nelson, when he stood on the final tee one down and promptly birdied both the next two holes to take the title. Some finish.

Nelson claimed his first PGA Championship a year later at the Hershey Country Club, Pennsylvania, by beating Sarazen in the semi-final and Sam Snead in the final. He trailed by one with only four holes left but played immaculate pitch shots at the 34th and 35th holes to take the lead – and edged out Snead, then aged 28, at the last.

When Nelson reached the final for the third year running in 1941 at Cherry Hills, Denver, he was strong favourite to triumph against Vic Ghezzi, a 28-year-old professional from New Jersey. But his unfancied opponent staged a remarkable rescue act on the last nine, recovering from three down to finish all square on the 36th green. So it went to extra holes, with Ghezzi completing a famous fightback by holing a 30-inch putt for victory at the 38th.

The shocks weren't over for Byron Nelson, however. In 1944 he reached the PGA Championship final again, where he met Bob Hamilton, a professional from Indiana rated no better than a 10–1 long shot to win. Hamilton triumphed in another dramatic finish. Trailing by one at the last at the Manito Golf and Country Club, Spokane, Washington, Nelson knew he needed a birdie to draw level. And that's what he scored. But so did Hamilton, for the greatest moment of a modest career which included only three other tournament victories.

The Nelson Years finished on a high note as the legendary golfer won the 1945 PGA Championship with a four and three victory over Sam Byrd to be ranked among the best the game had ever seen. He had reached five of the previous six PGA finals, four of them going to the last green. But he had won only twice.

Some one-sided victories by Ben Hogan and Sam Snead dominated the subsequent finals before the next dramatic climax in 1952. Victory came to the Turnesa family thanks to Jim, the sixth of the seven brothers, who beat Chick Harbert at the last – 25 years after his brother, Joe, lost to Walter Hagen at the last. Although three down at one stage to the long-hitting professional from Dayton, Ohio, Turnesa had pulled back to be level on the final tee at the Big Spring Country Club, Louisville. Harbert's accuracy then failed him when it mattered most. He sent his drive under an evergreen, leaving Turnesa to claim his only major championship.

The PGA switched to a stroke-play event in 1958 but although it lost the excitement of head-to-head combat the drama continued unabated. The 1961 tournament at Olympia Fields, Illinois, produced one of the most thrilling finishes ever witnessed in a major championship. Certainly there has been no more remarkable display of putting in the closing holes. Going into the final round, Jerry Barber, a 45-year-old professional from nearby Woodson, trailed the leader Don January by two shots – and had slipped to four behind with only three holes to play. Barber, one of the smallest players to hit the big time at five foot five, promptly rolled in putts of 20 feet for birdie, 40 feet for par and 60 feet for birdie to force a play-off, in which he beat January (67–68) the following day.

The champion was a rare character. He had poor vision and carried different spectacles for different times of the day. He had a cranky, unreliable swing but was so devastating at chipping and putting that he became the favourite partner in money matches of Sam Snead, who nicknamed him Rock. Barber's habit was to practise long putts for confidence and when faced with his famous 60-footer thought only of holing it. 'When I hit it I thought, "Holy smoke, it's got a chance," ' he recalled. And he was right.

Dave Marr's victory at Laurel Valley, Pennsylvania, in 1965 had his supporters quaking on the 72nd hole. The Texan, leading the tournament, hooked his drive into a trap and then played out short of a lake in front of the green. If ever there was a moment for Marr to produce a great shot, this was it. The player later to be known for his commentary for ABC and BBC TV hit an eight-iron to three feet and holed the putt for par and a two-stroke victory over Billy Casper and Jack Nicklaus. Not exactly the mother and father of all championship wins. More a case of Marr and par.

As an example of fortitude under pressure, the win by Julius Boros – at the age of 48 – in 1968 takes some beating. When he came to the treacherous 18th at the Pecan Valley Country Club, San Antonio, the Moose, as he was known, was in danger of wilting under the blistering, midsummer Texas sun. Arnold Palmer had, minutes earlier, boldly parred the hole to finish with a closing 70 and set the target of two-over-par 282. Boros had to make par for victory and was in trouble when he missed the green in two. But he then played an immaculate pitch shot to two feet and holed out to win the 50th PGA Championship, thus becoming the oldest man ever to win a major and denying Palmer the one Grand Slam title he was destined never to hold.

In 1976 Dave Stockton, the US captain who won back the Ryder Cup in 1991, enjoyed his finest moment as a player. When he came to the last at the Congressional Country Club in Maryland, Stockton needed a par to beat Ray Floyd and Don January. Having suffered a broken back at the age of 14, the Californian had a restricted swing but believed that successful golf was defined by mental attitude under pressure. Stockton proved the point admirably when, faced with a ten-foot putt to win, he rolled the ball unerringly into the cup.

The following year's championship involved a disastrous collapse, within sight of victory, by Gene Littler. The former US Open champion was poised for a memorable victory at the age of 47 when he led from the first round and was still five ahead of Lanny Wadkins, the eventual winner, with nine holes to play. But Littler, whose swing was described by Sarazen as 'perfect, like Sam Snead's . . . only better', then bogeyed five of the next six holes and Wadkins, sensing his chance, swooped for his only birdie of the day at Pebble Beach's testing 18th hole to force the first sudden-death play-off in major-championship stroke-play history. A six-foot putt for par at the third extra hole brought Wadkins his first major.

The trend was continued 12 months later at Oakmont, where John Mahaffey, Jerry Pate and Tom Watson finished level at the last. Mahaffey, after a final-round 66 to make up seven shots on Watson, then holed a 12-foot putt for a birdie at the second extra hole, to become a major champion for the first time. How Watson was to rue that final-round 73. The winner of eight majors, he is still waiting to add his first US PGA Championship and join the four all-time greats who have completed a career Grand Slam.

For sheer drama, David Graham's triumph at Oakland Hills in 1979 was something special. This was the third year in succession a sudden-death play-off was needed – but this one was different, as Graham put an old theory to flight. In the final round the Australian played brilliant golf and, as he stood on the tee at the 459-yard 72nd hole, he needed a par four to equal Bruce Crampton's 1975 record of 63. But he pushed his tee-shot and hit his next over the back of the green. His first chip pulled up short and the next went five feet past the pin. He missed the uphill putt coming back and was faced with a tricky downhiller for a double-bogey six to tie Ben Crenshaw. He holed out to take the championship to extra holes.

At this stage Graham should have been so shattered at throwing away the title that he would be incapable of making a serious challenge. But not a bit of it. The 33-year-old from New South Wales holed putts of 18 feet for par and ten feet for a birdie to keep the match alive – and then birdied the third extra hole to win. It was an outstanding display of strong nerve.

In 1987 Lanny Wadkins, the beneficiary of Gene Littler's collapse ten years earlier, was the victim of a last-green miss. The man who folded on this occasion was Mark McCumber, the joint leader at the end of the third round, who would have won his first major championship with a 74 at the par-72 PGA National in Florida. He came to the last still in contention but saw his hopes sink when he dunked his second at the 578-yard hole into the lake. He finished with a 77 to lose the tournament by two shots. Larry Nelson was already in the clubhouse, having taken a safe par five at the last for a round of 72, which set a target of 287.

Wadkins had happy memories of the 18th. He had been America's saviour there in 1983 when he put a 78-yard pitch stone dead to clinch the Ryder Cup. This time, though, he could not repeat the heroics. His third shot stopped only eight feet from the pin but on a bumpy green he missed the birdie putt. Unlike Graham, Wadkins did not redeem himself in the play-off. He bogeyed the first extra hole and Nelson parred to win his second PGA Championship.

The 1989 event at Kemper Lakes, near Chicago, belonged to Mike Reid for all but the final three holes. The thin, bespectacled professional from Utah, nicknamed 'Radar', led for the first three rounds and was three ahead going into the final day. When he stood on the 16th tee he was still two ahead of Payne Stewart, who had birdied the 18th from ten feet for an inward half of 31 and a last round of 67. Reid then pushed his drive into the lake on the right and had to bravely hole a curling five-footer for a bogey. He was still a shot ahead but struck more disaster at the par-three 17th, where he missed the green and then three-putted from 15 feet for a double-bogey five.

So it all came down to the last hole, where Reid, from being favourite to win, had to score a birdie to force a play-off with Stewart. He made a worthy effort, leaving himself a seven-footer to tie. But the putt stayed out and Reid was later to break down in tears in front of the world's press. 'I've never felt so bad for anyone in my life,' Jack Nicklaus told him. 'You played too well not to win.'

As in life, not always in golf is justice seen to be done. You need that little bit of fortune, especially on the last hole. Greg Norman has good reason to know that. And so, perhaps more than anyone, does Bob Tway.

Zinger and the Flashing Eyeballs

The Inverness Club in Toledo, Ohio, will never be remembered as Greg Norman's favourite golf course. The Australian played well there, figured prominently in two major championships on its testing layout, but came away with a set of memories to trouble his sleep.

It was bad enough that he should lose the 1986 US PGA Championship to Bob Tway's stunning holed bunker shot, but when the same championship returned to Inverness seven years later, Norman was denied at the very last again, beaten in a play-off by Paul Azinger.

What really rubbed salt into the wound were the unwanted statistics that Norman accumulated in completing those near misses. In 1986, the year of the 'Saturday Slam', the Great White Shark led all four major championships at the end of the third round but went on to win only one, the Open Championship at Turnberry. He pulled off another Grand Slam in 1993, becoming only the second player to lose a play-off in all four major championships, having been beaten by Fuzzy Zoeller (in the 1984 US Open), Larry Mize (the 1987 US Masters), Mark Calcavecchia (the 1989 Open) and finally Azinger.

The record shows how close Norman was to true greatness. By the time he entered his forties with only two major championships to his credit, he could easily have been challenging Tom Watson or Gary Player in the all-time pecking order of majors won and even joined the august company of Gene Sarazen, Ben Hogan, Jack Nicklaus and Player as the only men to complete the Grand Slam during their careers.

Yet whenever this supremely talented golfer was within reach of the big prizes, so often something went wrong. Murphy's Law could have been retitled Norman's Fate, as time after time circumstances would conspire against him to produce another sickening setback. Perhaps it would be the unexpected brilliance of an opponent. Maybe an unfortunate bounce at the wrong moment. Or, frustratingly, Norman being unable to produce his best when he desperately wanted to. Often it was a combination of all three.

When Tway blasted his way out of the sand and into the history books in a moment of unimaginable excitement, he had only been allowed into a challenging position by Norman's 76 in the final round, which he had started four shots clear of the field. His frailty under pressure was to be exposed again in Inverness revisited, as a three-putt bogey on the second play-off hole handed the Rodman Wanamaker Trophy to his American rival.

Yet if there was sympathy for Norman, few people doubted that Azinger deserved to join the ranks of major-championship winners at the age of 33. The God-fearing fisherman from Florida had served his apprenticeship, proved his pedigree and, at last, enjoyed the good fortune that always seemed to elude Norman. At the time Azinger was one of the leading players on the US Tour and therefore in the world. Three times he had finished in the top four on the tour's money list, he had played in two Ryder Cup matches and he held the longest active winning streak on the tour by claiming a victory in seven successive seasons.

Two previous major championships had slipped from his grasp. In the 1987 Open he was in the lead after the second and third rounds and was still in a position to get his hands on the old claret jug with two holes left to play. But he dropped a shot at the 71st and then drove into a bunker on the final hole, missed a 30-footer for par and lost by a shot to Nick Faldo's relentless 18 successive pars.

As a 27-year-old experiencing his first taste of golf's most choking pressure, he could be excused those lapses. But if he did blame himself on this occasion, he had less reason for self-admonishment a year later when a second opportunity came along. Just as he had at Muirfield, Azinger led the field after the second and third rounds of the 1988 US PGA Championship at Oak Tree Golf Club, in Edmond, Oklahoma. This time he would lose, not to an opponent's grinding efficiency but, instead, finding himself blown away by Jeff Sluman's outstanding last round of 65 which swept him to a three-shot victory.

Having found two different ways to miss out, Azinger could still take lessons in the art from the unfortunate Norman. When they came head to head in the certain knowledge that one of them would experience a significant turn in his career, the contest produced tension and drama in the best traditions of the sport.

Another coincidence of Norman's chance to bury his Inverness hoodoo was that he arrived at the event on the back of an Open Championship victory, just as he had in 1986. At last, he seemed ready to confirm his immense potential. Having waited so long for a second major, he produced a display at Royal St George's of sheer wonder.

While Norman somewhat immodestly said in victory that he had been 'in awe of myself', others were equally fulsome in their praise. Sarazen, at the age of 91, having witnessed the development of the game since his first major victory in the 1922 US Open, described Norman's win as 'the greatest championship I have known. I have never seen such golf.'

For once nothing went wrong. Certainly nothing that mattered, as Norman had every aspect of his game in perfect working order. He left a gathering of the leading players of the time, including runner-up Nick Faldo, Bernhard Langer, Corey Pavin, Nick Price and Fred Couples, floundering in his wake as he set a crop of records. His closing 64 was the lowest Open-winning final round ever. His 287 total beat Watson's mark set at Turnberry in 1977, and he became the first champion to break 70 in all four rounds.

Only two years previously the disappointments, frustrations and repeated mental batterings the charismatic Aussie had been forced to withstand had pushed him to the brink of giving up the game and concentrating on his expanding business empire. Yet here he was proving his critics wrong. He had the nerve, the style, the ability to walk with the golfing giants. At 38 there seemed no end to what he might achieve. And as he set out on his next challenge, bursting with enhanced confidence, Gregory John Norman appeared to be embarking on a new, triumphant chapter in his life.

The Great Scriptwriter had other ideas. Nobody could take away the excellence of his Open Championship victory but it was not to be the harbinger of a dramatic change in Norman's fortunes. Instead, it was a beacon in a sea of lost opportunities. Immediately he would suffer another shattering defeat of the kind that had littered his career. And he remained marooned on two major championships alongside the likes of Andy North, Hubert Green and David Graham, scant reward for a man who had held the No. 1 ranking for longer than any other player and who had won more than 70 tournaments world-wide.

For three days in Toledo he was on course to change that. After two respectable opening rounds of 66 had left him five shots behind the halfway leader Vijay Singh of Fiji – whose second-round 63 equalled the tournament record – Norman moved into the lead with a third-round 67 as Singh dropped back with a 73.

Azinger was handily placed a shot behind Norman going into the last day as a high-quality line-up of challengers promised to make this one of the most thrilling final days since the US PGA Championship switched to stroke play in 1958. The cast included multi-major winners Faldo, Watson, Lanny Wadkins and Hale Irwin, plus surprise contenders such as Singh and American journeyman Bob Estes. Just to add poignancy to the occasion, Richard Zokol, a Canadian, completed the tournament by holing out from the same bunker where Tway had struck his historic shot. In Zokol's case it only earned him a share of 14th place. But the moment provided an uncomfortable reminder for Norman's followers of the strange things that happen in golf. Was it, perhaps, an omen?

Azinger, the eventual champion, had himself 'done a Tway' earlier in the season when he holed his bunker shot from beside the 18th green in the final round of the Memorial Tournament to beat Corey Pavin by a stroke. He would need no such heroics this time.

Norman made a solid start on Sunday, maintaining his lead for the first five holes, only to fall back into the pack when he dropped three shots in two holes. A double-bogey five at the short sixth, where he took two shots to extricate himself from a bunker, was followed by a thinned chip at the seventh. It seemed as if the old disasters were coming back to haunt him. But he regrouped and kept himself in close order with the new leader Estes, a 27-year-old from Austin, Texas. The comparative unknown headed the field at 11 under par with nine holes to play before reality dawned and he slipped back to finish joint sixth.

He was a shot behind Watson, who was once again thwarted in the tournament he wanted to win more than any other. The five-times Open champion needed the US PGA to complete his collection of majors but, not having won on the US Tour for six years and dogged by putting woes, the prospect was looking increasingly less likely. A second-round 65 had offered hope and he went into the final day only a shot off the lead. But 72 was not good enough and left him four strokes back at the end, frustrated again.

Wadkins, the 1977 champion, threatened to become a serious threat when he moved to within two of the lead but he faded badly, playing the last six holes in three over par to be alongside bunker man Zokol in 14th place. Singh, eventually to win the title handsomely in 1998, also had his chance this time. He shared the lead with four holes left but suffered a costly three-putt bogey at the 16th and had to settle for a very creditable fourth place.

While all these contenders had their opportunities – and, in their different ways, would have proved surprise winners – the man who wore the air of a champion for much of the day was Faldo. Like Watson, the Englishman was desperate to claim this title to go with his US Masters and Open victories and had the proven class to pull it off. But history was against him. No British-born player had won the event since Tommy Armour beat Sarazen in the 1930 match-play final, and no one at all from Britain had won under stroke-play rules.

When Faldo birdied the 13th to take a one-shot lead, he was a good bet to become the first. Not a man to buckle under the strain of the closing holes, he was playing with an ominous assurance. But, for once, the 36-year-old Brit's killer instinct failed him. The key moment came at the 16th, where Faldo struck an immaculate seven-iron to four feet for the chance of a birdie that would have given him a two-stroke lead – and made him very difficult to catch. But Faldo pushed the putt, which trickled past on the right-hand side. Still needing a birdie at the last to set a testing target, he pulled a comparatively simple wedge from

110 yards 30 feet left of the pin and could do no better than make par. He was to finish one shot back, no doubt reflecting on the three shots he dropped at one hole in the second round.

So two men emerged to duel for the prize. When Azinger reached the turn he was in joint sixth place, three strokes off the lead. But, as champions do, he came good at the right time. Playing what TV commentator Peter Alliss described on the air as 'wonderful iron shots', he put the ball close on the 10th, 12th and 14th greens and converted the birdie opening each time. He had taken advice from legendary former PGA champion Byron Nelson to play for the centre of the small greens rather than risk trouble by attacking too strongly. He still picked his moments to shoot for the pin, though. Another superb shot to four feet at the 17th also got its reward to enable 'Zinger' to complete a 68 and finish on 12-under-par 272, ensuring that Faldo was beaten.

Norman, meanwhile, was still very much alive. After his troubles on the front nine he staged a storming comeback. Even though he missed a sitter from three feet for a birdie at the tenth, the Australian showed his mettle as he rolled in birdie putts at the 11th and 13th to join Singh, Faldo and Azinger in joint first place. When he struck a majestic iron shot to three feet at the 16th, Norman was in the lead again on his own. The sole possession of first place was to last only seconds, though, as Azinger, up ahead, holed his birdie putt at the 17th and the battle lines were drawn.

Norman came to the last hole needing a par to force a play-off and a birdie for victory. As he knew from painful experience, the 354-yard dog-legged 18th is an inviting birdie opportunity. Any drive in the fairway usually sets up the chance to put a pitching wedge close to the pin on a tight, sloping green. Norman duly found the fairway to leave himself a 110-yard approach, which he placed 15 feet above the hole.

As Azinger watched from the scorer's tent, the Shark's putt was close enough to keep him interested. A few feet from the hole it had a chance of dropping but was marginally too quick and stayed up on the high side. As Norman tossed his putter into the air in anguish, he knew that his first opportunity to clinch the win had gone.

But it was not the last. The two men went back to the 18th tee and prepared to play this hole made for drama yet again. In the tension of the occasion, either could have been excused for mishitting his tee-shot. But no. Both kept the ball ideally in play down the left side of the fairway. Azinger put his second 15 feet from the flag. Norman was 20 feet away. Now the strain was getting unbearable. This was becoming the classic shoot-out.

Norman putted first and sent the ball dead on line. For a moment or so the championship looked his. But, again, the pace of the putt was slightly too fast and the ball hit the back rim of the cup and spun out.

As the gallery gasped in unison, those who cared deeply showed their dismay. Norman let his putter fall to the green and looked to the heavens. His seven-year-old son Gregory banged the ground with both fists and his wife Laura hung her head so that her face disappeared under a large straw hat. Their worst fears, however, were not realised. Azinger's slow left-to-right putt trickled past on the right side and the drama moved on.

The action switched to the 361-yard, par-four tenth, another hole with real birdie possibilities. Norman, in fact, had made a birdie there in three of the four rounds. However, the one that got away – when he missed from three feet in the final round – was to prove the most significant.

Both men drove in the fairway and Norman then sent his second shot to 20 feet, a reasonable effort but lacking the accuracy he had previously displayed there. Perhaps the pressure was telling. Azinger promptly turned the screw with an immaculate approach to six feet. The odds had switched decisively towards the American and were to become even more in his favour as Norman, needing to hole a long putt, tentatively left the ball five feet short.

Ideally, Azinger would have holed out to claim victory in style. Instead both men missed their putts and he won anyway. After all the previous excitement, there was a sense of anti-climax about the way the play-off ended. Azinger's putt hit the right lip of the hole and stayed out. Norman, facing a putt on the same line and direction as the one he had missed in the final round, only longer, saw his ball spin out on the left lip.

It was all over. Poor Greg had three-putted to add to his catalogue of major-championship disasters. He had been unlucky, too. During the play-off two putts had lipped out, compared with one by Azinger. By such small margins are reputations decided.

As his daughters Sarah, seven, and Josie, four, and wife Toni ran out onto the green to embrace him, Azinger was visibly overcome with emotion. 'I was so nervous,' he said. 'Looking at putts my heart was beating so hard I could see my eyeballs flashing. I just feel very fortunate on that last putt.

'I thought about the Lord all day today and I had an inner peace. But I was still nervous. Some things are more important than golf. I gave it my best and I just feel very fortunate the way it worked out.'

Azinger's conviction that some things are more important than golf was to prove chillingly accurate later that year. He had been suffering from pain in his right shoulder for such a long time that in 1991 he had undergone surgery in an attempt to correct the problem. In December 1993 he was diagnosed as suffering from lymphoma, a form of cancer, in the shoulder. An intensive programme of chemotherapy and radiation treatment stopped him competing for seven months and ended his run of seven successive years with a victory on the US Tour. But he beat the disease and dedicated his life to becoming an inspiration to others.

'I have the chance to reach out to thousands of people,' said Azinger, who hosted the Zinger Stinger Pro-Am every year to raise money for lymphoma research. His courage was recognised in 1995 when he was awarded the Ben Hogan Trophy, given to the person who continued to be active in sport despite physical handicap.

Eventually fit enough to play a full schedule again, Azinger was unable to reach the standards of 1993, his most successful year. He had been cut off in his prime, leaving people to wonder what a player he might have become. But in his performance that Sunday in Ohio, and in the example he provided in subsequent years, Paul Azinger proved himself to be a champion in every sense of the word.

Exposed: The Full Monty

As Steve Elkington stood on the tee of the first play-off hole in the 1995 US PGA Championship, one particular thought kept popping into his head. Reflecting on the fate awaiting him and his opponent Colin Montgomerie, the Australian decided, 'One of us is going to go down in history. And one of us isn't.'

In a sense he was right. But he was wrong, too. For although the smooth-swinging Aussie claimed his first major title in exciting style by holing a 25-foot birdie putt at the first extra hole, he was not alone in adding a new entry into the record books. The defeated Scot and South African Ernie Els both put in scoring performances never before achieved to emphasise the merit of Elkington's triumph and also under-line their own contributions to an extraordinary event.

Els recorded the lowest 54-hole total in major championship history before a final-round 72 blew his chances of adding to his US Open win the previous year. Montgomerie kept up the pressure right to the end, returning a score of 17-under-par 267 which tied Elkington for first place and left the pair of them alongside Nick Faldo on the lowest total ever returned in a four-round Grand Slam event.

Critics of Europe's long-term Order of Merit winner might well have pondered that fact before repeating the harsh opinion that Montgomerie, for all his talent, lacked the extra quality needed to win a major. In the 130 years or so since major championships began, no one – not Hogan, Snead, Nicklaus or Watson – had beaten his score in a four-round championship event. It may not have been the statistic that Montgomerie wanted to own more than any other. But it spoke volumes, nonetheless.

Even though friendly conditions during that August weekend in California were an invitation to take the course apart, the finest players of the modern era – who were all there – could not do so with the same skill and consistency as Elkington and Montgomerie. For that reason, rather than being derided for another narrow miss in his quest for a Grand Slam breakthrough, the 32-year-old golf club secretary's son should have been applauded. If his performance was not the best ever not to have won a major, it would certainly be a contender for that honourable title.

What Montgomerie unquestionably did achieve was to set up the ultimate tense finish which exemplified golf at its finest. The venue for the occasion had much to do with its theatrical climax. The Riviera Country Club in Pacific Palisades, just off Sunset Boulevard, Los Angeles, is pure Hollywood. Shown in a different light recently by its association with the infamous O.J. Simpson, who was a member there, Riviera has been revered for more than half a century through the staging of memorable championships and its links with the legends of the past.

Built in 1926 by George Thomas, one of the pioneers of American golf-course architecture, it acquired a tradition rivalling that of Pebble Beach, among outstanding Californian courses. Originally a site for the Los Angeles Open, Riviera's majestic layout, featuring eucalyptus and oak trees bordering its fairways and small greens, was to earn selection for the US Open and US PGA Championships. Its list of winners included Sam Snead, Byron Nelson, Tommy Bolt, Lloyd Mangrum, Tom Watson and Johnny Miller. Yet its connection with one man led to Riviera being known as Hogan's Alley.

Ben Hogan had such a mastery of Riviera that in his third victory there in 1948 he set a US Open record of 276, which was to last for 19 years until Jack Nicklaus lowered the figure by one at Baltusrol in 1967. Hogan made an emotional return to Riviera in the 1950 Los Angeles Open a year after he was nearly killed in a car accident. He failed to win only because Snead birdied the last two holes and then beat him in a play-off.

In 1988 the Marukin Shoji Co. of Japan bought Riviera from the Los Angeles Athletic Club for a reported $108 million. It was the intention of the new owners to restore the course to championship status, and after it was awarded the 1995 US PGA, they launched a $1.5 million scheme to upgrade the greens.

Putting expert Ben Crenshaw was called in as a consultant with a brief of returning the greens, which had sunk over the years, to their original standard. The decision was made to replace the *poa annua* with bent grass. It was Crenshaw's opinion that the best solution was to reseed the greens. But the management decided to resod – with unfortunate consequences. The grass did not bed in sufficiently well, so that as the championship approached, the greenkeeping staff knew they were in trouble. Ideally, the surfaces should have been smooth and fast to place a premium on accurate iron play and a sure putting touch. Yet the ground staff were unable to cut and roll them because the poor-quality grass could not cope. 'The bent grass can't take the stress of the rolling,' head superintendent Bill Baker lamented.

So, in the words of one observer, Riviera's greens looked 'purple from the air and lumpy from the ground'. Heavy watering made them defenceless against attacking play, as the players soon discovered that even from 190 yards out they could fire at the flag and stop the ball quickly. With the greens having a tendency to 'spike up', the main concern was whether the players could keep their putts sufficiently on line to fully capitalise.

Even though the soft surfaces were roundly condemned as the worst greens in use for an important championship since the 1963 US Open at the Country Club in Brookline, where sheets of ice had killed the grass, they could not prevent the subsequent glut of birdies. There were two rounds of 63 (Michael Bradley in the first and Brad Faxon in the fourth) and three 64s (from Mark O'Meara, Jay Haas and Jim Gallagher) and altogether 12 men shot 65 or better.

The emergence of Bradley, a comparatively unknown 29-year-old from Florida, in a windless first round played under clear blue skies completely overshadowed the 66 of Els and the 68s of both Elkington and Montgomerie. Yet, with the weather expected to remain just as favourable for the rest of the week, it was clear from the first day that consistently low scoring would be needed to win. After his seven-under-par 64 O'Meara remained suitably cautious. 'I'm thrilled to shoot 64 but it's still early,' he said. 'You could see a lot of low scores this week. The way the greens are holding, there's a good chance someone will break a record.'

Within another two rounds Els had. The 25-year-old from Johannesburg, already confirmed as one of the best in the game, had a 65 in the second round for a total of 131 to be one shot outside the previous major-championship best set by Faldo in the Open at Muirfield in 1992. Another 66 put him on 197 to beat the previous 54-hole total of Tom Lehman at the 1996 Open at Royal Lytham by a stroke. The elegant South African was in such command of his game that when he started the final day three shots clear of the field, there appeared to be only one winner.

However, the PGA had a reputation of providing talented players with their breakthrough into the élite group of major winners. Four of the previous five champions savoured this experience. Els, who had won the US Open in a play-off at Oakmount 14 months earlier, was to suffer only bitter disappointment this time. Maybe it was the weight of expectancy. Or perhaps he had used up his allotted supply of good fortune in the first three days. But, to the amazement of all, Els lost his form.

After stretching his lead to four with a birdie on the opening hole, he bogeyed the fourth and sixth holes and missed short birdie putts at the seventh and eighth. He was still clinging precariously to a one-shot lead when he turned for home, only to be overtaken by the charging Elkington soon afterwards.

Although he could see the title slipping away, Els was still in with a chance as he came to the final three holes. But at the par-three 16th a 12-foot birdie putt hit the back of the hole and spun 360 degrees back in the direction it had come from. In a state of shock, Els then pulled his tee-shot at the par-five 17th and ended up making his only six of the week after missing a five-foot putt for par. The loss hit the amiable giant hard. 'I didn't play well today,' he confessed after his unexpected one-over-par 72. 'I really tried my best on the back nine but the putt on 16 took everything out of me. I couldn't believe it. I played so well all week and to come so close really hurts.'

As the Els challenge crumbled, the focus of attention switched to Elkington and Montgomerie, playing in the two groups ahead of him. The Australian, six off the pace at the start of the day, made a flying start with birdies at four of the first eight holes to put himself right on to Big Ernie's shoulder. He then announced himself as the man to beat with three successive birdies from the tenth to leap into a two-shot lead. If Elkington maintained this rate of progress for the rest of the round, he would not only win comfortably but also smash every conceivable record out of sight. The single-round lowest of 63 and the aggregate lowest were both within his reach.

But the fire died. Over the final six holes his putter went cold, he claimed not a single birdie and he parred in for a 64. His magnificent effort had deserved to win but he had left the slimmest of chances for someone with the courage to step forward. Montgomerie proved himself to be that man. Recognised as a straight driver, the powerfully built Briton had been playing the best tee-to-green golf of anyone in the championship. In the first three rounds he hit 37 of 42 fairways plus 45 of 54 greens in regulation, putting from the fringe on five more.

Four birdies in the first 11 holes on Sunday kept him in touch with Elkington's rampage through the field but a costly mistake at the 13th would have finished off lesser players. Monty put his wedged approach into thick rough around the green and dropped a shot. He failed to make up any leeway on the 14th or 15th and came to the last three holes needing three birdies to force a play-off. Not impossible (and the previous year Nick Price had played the last three at the Open in three under to squeeze past Jesper Parnevik). But extremely difficult.

Showing great heart, Montgomerie hit his tee-shot at the 165-yard, par-three 16th to four feet and holed out for a birdie. At the 576-yard, par-five 17th an immaculate wedge also stopped four feet from the hole. And that disappeared for another birdie. The 447-yard, par-four 18th, a dog-leg right with a blind tee-shot, was described by Jack Nicklaus as his favourite at Riviera. 'It is a strong finishing hole where you have to hit two excellent shots,' he said. Montgomerie did precisely that to find the green and leave himself with a 20-foot putt. Unfortunately a dreaded spike-mark, inconveniently obstructing his line, posed another problem. He struck the putt boldly and watched as it hopped over the protruding obstacle and held its line to drop into the cup.

Elkington looked on with some concern. 'It's a terrible feeling when someone makes a long putt to tie you, especially when there's so much at stake,' he would admit later. 'You always have to be prepared for them to make it even though there's a little voice in the back of your mind saying, "If he misses, it's all over." '

He may have had misgivings about being forced into a play-off but would soon be pleased that he had watched Montgomerie's putt drop. In the play-off both men met Nicklaus's demands for accuracy. There was little between them as they returned to the green facing potential winning birdie putts. After a perfect drive and an eight-iron from 175 yards, Elkington was adjudged to be slightly further from the hole. He took aim and rolled the ball unerringly home. Montgomerie could not match his opponent, unaware at the time that his tieing putt on the 72nd hole had been the key to Elkington's moment of triumph. 'I had a similar putt to Colin's,' he said. 'I recalled what I'd seen on TV and visualised it running in there.'

Elkington, ranked No. 17 in the world, had been an enigmatic figure during a career beset by health problems. An allergy to grass, of all things, frequently affected his sinuses. He went into hospital in January 1994 because of a virus infection and while there also had a malignant tumour removed from his shoulder. In May of the same year he returned for another operation in his sinuses.

Even his preparation for Riviera was affected by his sinus problem. 'I came into the week feeling terrible and having almost no practice,' he said. 'But I played the round of my life at the end. I was so confident I felt I could attack when I should have been defensive. All the things that you're supposed to do – go for the centre of the green, hit three-woods off the tee – I didn't want to do. I felt aggressive and felt my swing was perfect for hitting shots. I felt like I was shooting at pins, which is a rare feeling in a major.'

The tall former University of Houston student, who made his home in Texas, had a swing rated among the best. Simple, powerful and easy on the eye. His closing 64 was the best by a champion in the history of the US PGA, while his feat in surging from six shots back at the start of the day was surpassed only by John Mahaffey, who was seven behind Tom Watson in 1978, caught him with a final-round 66 and then completed the victory in a three-man play-off.

Montgomerie was understandably shaken by the outcome. 'I did nothing wrong,' said the Scot, who hit 50 out of 56 fairways and 61 out of 72 greens. 'I knew I had to get three birdies in the last three holes and I managed that. Then I parred the first extra hole so I still did nothing wrong. Steve won the tournament and I didn't lose, so I can take something positive from that.'

Months later he would admit that he was still shattered by the result. People have played far worse and won. When you shoot 65 in the last round, equal the all-time record and lose by a single putt, you are entitled to consider that fate can be cruel.

But sport surely mirrors life. And who said either of them were supposed to be fair?

Perry Falls on his Sward

In the Bluegrass state of Kentucky, he who lives by the sward dies by the sward. Kenny Perry, the pride of Western Kentucky University, appeared to have the 78th US PGA Championship at Valhalla Golf Club, on the outskirts of Louisville, in his pocket. Perry, a 36-year-old journeyman from Franklin, Kentucky, played the greatest golf of his life – until he came to the 18th in the final round. Up to that point, more than 30,000 homestate fans had become wildly excited at the prospect of hailing a local hero.

Perry, who had taken the first-round lead with a 66, followed with rounds of 72, 71 and began the final day four strokes off the lead which had been established by another Kentuckian, Russ Cochran. On the Saturday, when Ernie Els shot a 79, Cochran, a left-hander, set a course record of 65 which gave him a two-stroke lead over his closest challengers, Mark Brooks and Vijay Singh. Also on the leaderboard were Greg Norman, Nick Price, Steve Elkington . . . and Perry.

'When things are going well, I think you can feed off the crowd,' Cochran said, referring to the local support, a mass version of the Louisville Lip. In the final round Cochran did not feed off the support, he choked, closing with a 77. In Norse mythology Valhalla is the palace in which souls of dead heroes feasted. Cochran and Perry were to discover that the menu consisted of Kentucky fried chicken.

Perry shot 68 in an extraordinary final round. His card included three twos but he failed to birdie any of the par fives. Nevertheless, when he walked to the final tee, doing high fives with his fans along the way, he held a two-stroke lead. The 18th is a par five of 540 yards. High fives? All Perry needed was par, but twice he hit his ball into the bluegrass and when his putt for par shaved the hole he dropped back from 12 under par for the championship to 11 under. That six at the 72nd was the only blot on his card. It was not, however, his only mistake of the day. Instead of composing himself for a possible play-off, Perry sat in the CBS television tower near the 18th green and commentated on the closing stages.

Perry's bogey provided a glimmer of hope for the final pairings but Elkington, after finding a bunker, failed to birdie the 18th and a 70 gave him an aggregate of 278, a stroke outside the total posted by Perry.

Singh, who had shot three 69s, also made a mess of the last, a six giving him a level-par 72 for 279. And then there was one. Brooks, last out with Cochran, had birdied the sixth, the seventh and the eighth to go to the turn in 33, at which point he was 12 under. By the time he had bogeyed the 11th, 12th and 14th, he was three behind Perry. However, a birdie three at the 15th stopped the rot and when he reached the 17th tee his caddie informed him that Perry had slipped back to 11 under.

The previous month Brooks, a 35-year-old from Fort Worth, Texas, had finished joint fifth in the Open Championship at Royal Lytham and the experience was to prove invaluable. Brooks, of course, was not the sentimental choice of the gallery. 'It wasn't a factor,' he said. 'The crowds were very courteous. There are very few places in the world where you're going to get spectators who become rude.'

Even so, when he stood on the 18th, he would have had to have been deaf, dumb and blind not to appreciate that virtually everybody at Valhalla was gunning for the Lone Star Texan. Brooks needed a birdie four to tie Perry, who was still sitting in the television tower, and he got it despite hitting a four-wood approach shot into the same bunker that had trapped Elkington.

Brooks came home in 37 and his round of 70 was good enough to match Perry's aggregate of 277. By now the awful truth had dawned on the Kentuckian. When he descended from the TV tower, he wanted to hit some balls on the practice range before the sudden-death play-off but officials told him there wasn't time. The news got worse. The play-off hole was Perry's nemesis, the 18th. During the week, the 18th had been the second easiest hole on the course. Not on Sunday, and certainly not for Perry.

Once again he semi-hooked his drive into the rough, whereas Brooks found the centre of the fairway. Perry could not extricate himself from the bluegrass. He hit his second shot left of the fairway . . . and his third, and he still wasn't on the green. Brooks, meanwhile, had hit a magnificent approach shot to the heart of the green. By the time Perry got within putting distance of the flag, its colour had changed to white and he was waving it at the opposition. He had played five and he picked up his ball to signify submission. The blue, blue grass of home had done him no favours.

'The 18th hole is a wide driving hole and it's really not that hard off the tee,' Perry said later. 'I just swung too hard, I guess, or got too excited and came over the top of it. I told my wife that if I could shoot the round of my life I would probably win the tournament. I was sitting in the rocking chair. The thing is I'd never been in that situation before. I hate it for all the fans in Kentucky who were rooting for me so hard. But this is going to be good for me. I'll be remembered for this.'

Maybe, but not as much as Valhalla. The US PGA liked the course so much they bought it. Not only that but they announced that their championship would return to Louisville in the year 2000. Nor has Valhalla been ruled out as a Ryder Cup venue.

Not that everybody enjoyed it. 'I'd blow up at least four of the greens,' said Paul Azinger, who finished 31st with a three-under-par 285. 'I thought the course was too easy.' Nick Faldo, who tied for 65th, disagreed. 'It played tough all week. It beat me. The bluegrass is the toughest rough in the world.' There was no argument on that score from Kenny Perry.

Perry, of course, is not the first player, nor will he be the last, to choke when the big game goes for the jugular.

Bibliography

Golf World
Golf Weekly
Sports Illustrated
The Book of Golf Quotations (Stanley Paul, 1987)
Tony Jacklin: The First Forty Years (Queen Anne Press, 1985)
The Masters of Golf (Stanley Paul, 1975, 1988)
The Open Championship, 1989 (Transworld Publishers, 1989)
Getting to the Dance Floor (Heinemann Kingswood, 1988)
Ian Woosnam's Golf Masterpieces (Sidgwick and Jackson, 1988)
The Four Majors (Heinemann Kingswood, 1988)
How We Won the Open (Anaya Publishers, 1990)
The Bobby Jones Story (Foulsham, 1990)
Strokes of Genius (Simon and Schuster, 1987)
Great Shots (Anaya Publishers, 1989)
The Sackville Illustrated History of Golf (Sackville Books, 1987)
The Guinness Book of Golf (Guinness Superlatives, 1987)
Jack Nicklaus: My Most Memorable Shots in the Majors (Stanley Paul, 1988)
The St Andrews Opens (John Donald Publishers, 1990)
The Who's Who of Golf (Orbis Publishing, 1983)
The Encylopedia of Golf (Dorling Kindersley, 1991)
Mark H. McCormack's The World of Professional Golf 1985, 1986 (Springwood Books), *1987, 1988, 1989* (Collins Willow), *1990* (Sackville Books), *1991, 1992, 1993, 1994, 1995, 1996, 1997, 1998* (IMG Publishing)
PGA Media Guide
The Official PGA European Tour Guide
The Official US PGA Tour Book

$4 \overline{)174}$ 348

43.5

2 1 8

21 7.5
3.48

220 98